Stillwater Dry Fly Fishing

Stillwater Dry Fly Fishing

by

Roger Fogg

A & C Black · London

Published by A & C Black (Publishers) Ltd
35 Bedford Row, London WC1R 4JH

© A & C Black (Publishers) Ltd., 1985

First published 1985

Fogg, Roger
 Stillwater dry-fly fishing.
 1. Trout fishing   2. Fly fishing
 I. Title
 799.1'755   SH687

ISBN 0-7136-5521-6

Printed and bound in Great Britain at
The Camelot Press Ltd, Southampton

For Catherine and Christopher

Acknowledgements

I would like to thank members of the Oldham Game Fishing and Fly-Tying Club who inspired the completion of this book and would like to thank them for their companionship by the waterside. Thanks are also due to Christine, who spent many hours typing the manuscript, and to my publishers for all their hard work.

All the illustrations are by the author.

Contents   Page

Introduction

Although its popularity is on the increase, it is still a rare thing to see an angler employing a dry-fly on still waters. Nevertheless, that is not reason enough to conclude that the stillwater dry-fly is fruitless. The fact that more people are killed driving cars down the M1 than are killed riding elephants says little about the relative safety of elephants as a means of transport on the highways and byways of Britain. Equally, the fact that few people fish the dry-fly on lakes and reservoirs, cannot be hailed as a pointer to the lack of success of the stillwater dry-fly when fished *correctly* and *at the right time*.

Many books have been written on the subject of dry-fly fishing on rivers and some of them do mention stillwater dry-fly fishing in passing. There are now plenty of good books on stillwater fly-fishing, though few of them say much about the use of dry-flies. However, as far as I am aware, there are no books written specifically on the subject of stillwater dry-fly fishing, so that the present book seeks to breach that gap. And thus I hope the reader will forgive me if the present book appears somewhat raw, as is often the case when attempting to make inroads into new areas. Undoubtedly, future books will approach the subject differently and will add new experiences and further knowledge. If I can at least achieve a more balanced regard for the use of dry-flies on lakes and reservoirs, then I will have achieved something.

Although I trust that the beginner to the sport of fly-fishing will gain a little food for thought, it is not really with the beginner in mind that this book has been written. I have assumed a certain degree of knowledge on the behalf of the reader and hope that I have not left too many gaps. It would be best for the beginner to read a few general books on stillwater fly-fishing and fly-dressing before giving the present book and its philosophy a fair appraisal.

Dry-fly fishing is often thought to be the simplest of techniques: you see a fish rise, cast a floating fly to it, the trout takes and you tighten. Perhaps it is sometimes like this, yet on seventy-five per cent of the occasions when the dry-fly might be successful, the situation is quite different. If the initial view of stillwater dry-fly fishing were correct, the present book would neither have been necessary, *nor possible.*

Perhaps it is because of this misconceived notion that no books have previously appeared on the subject, and that as a result, few anglers regularly practise the technique. There is nothing really difficult about stillwater dry-fly fishing although the traditional view of dry-fly fishing on rivers must be drastically revised if success is to be achieved.

If I can encourage a few more anglers to try the dry-fly, and gain pleasure and success from its use, then my book will have been well worth writing. Dry-fly fishing is certainly a pleasurable and exciting pursuit and must not be considered a form of élitism or one-upmanship. It has perhaps been neglected because in the minds of many men, it smacks of snobbishness. There is no élitism in the following pages, I hope; indeed I might even be accused of offending propriety. There are many techniques described which would make the likes of Halford and Marryat turn in their graves, but they fished on chalk streams, whilst our fisheries are of quite a different nature. It is necessary to tailor your techniques according to the demands of the fishery (and its rules) and clearly our ultimate aim must be to catch fish.

It is necessary to add one final note of warning. In no way am I intending to promote the exclusive use of the dry-fly on stillwaters. Personally, I use the dry-fly only when it is either necessary, or when either the wet-fly or dry-fly are likely to succeed and I am able to choose as a simple matter of preference. It would be silly to persist in the use of the dry-fly at a time when trout are unlikely to take it. On the other hand, actual visual rises are not a prerequisite for the use of the dry-fly, for trout will accept floating artificials at times when they are not actually feeding on natural insects at the surface.

Whilst I enjoy using the dry-fly, nymphs and wet-flies are also used extensively in my typical fly-fishing season. Thus, although the book concentrates on the dry-fly, I have attempted to point out, from time to time, those occasions when the floating fly will come a poor second to the nymph or wet-fly. A fly-fisherman must enjoy a balanced diet of techniques if he is to enjoy his sport to the full.

1

An approach and a philosophy

Some catch fish and some tell lies
Weaving stories round their flies.
Some fish lures with furious retrieve,
Hoping large rainbows to deceive;
Yet some there are, I know not why
Forsake the wet, and fish the dry.

Dry-fly fishing on stillwaters is often very effective and exciting; so
why has it been ignored for so long? In effect the answer lies in the
history of stillwater fly-fishing and since the subject has been so
delightfully elucidated by Conrad Voss Bark (*Fishing for Lake Trout*)
a most complete answer *must* involve a reading of his book. For our
present purpose I will restrict my comments to a few brief thoughts.
After all, unless something is said, the reader may well be inclined to
reject the stillwater dry-fly as a worthless technique simply because
it has so few devotees. It is easy to accept that the wet-fly works
because so many people have successfully practised it and just as easy
to conclude that the dry-fly doesn't because few anglers have
committed themselves to print in its favour.

Stillwater trout fishing is a growth industry which effectively began
no more than a hundred years ago; it is still expanding. In a sense,
it is still in its infancy and still searching for a standard approach, a
matter which is partly reflected in the hundreds of new patterns which
have been introduced during the last decade. It all really began at the
turn of the century; industrial growth, a rise in population and a new
social enlightenment increased the demand for water supply and this
was met by a number of new reservoir schemes. Trout were stocked
as indicators of water purity and also to reduce the number of aquatic
insects present in the water (or at least to keep them under control).
A natural result was to allow anglers to catch the trout to bring in
additional revenue. Bristol Waterworks really led the way and soon
other water boards followed suit.

Reservoirs offered a brand new kind of fishing and initially mixed
methods were allowed (fly, bait and spinning) in order to cater for
the anglers who were to fish for trout. Trout fishing had at last shaken

1

off its élitism and become available to all. Gradually, bait fishing and spinning became outlawed on many waters although their influence remained. At first, anglers did not know how to tackle the vast new waters and large fish, some used scaled down salmon fishing techniques, or lures which were substitutes for spinners (from which modern lure fishing derives), others used traditional loch tactics and flies, and some, perhaps only a few, tried to copy the kind of insects prevalent on the waters. The last category of anglers were as likely to fish dry as wet (men such as Bell and Sheringham) and approached stillwater fishing much as they had been used to fishing on rivers.

This original confusion of tactics has largely remained, for it has spawned the varied approaches of today — imitative dry-flies and nymphs, lures, flashers, loch flies and nondescript 'nymphs'. The dry-fly was only practised by a few anglers and it wasn't likely to catch on generally since many coarse fishermen (for whom the supposed snobbery of the dry-fly was anathema) turned to stillwater fly fishing and essentially looked for ready returns from the wet-fly. I am certainly not implying that this is true of all coarse fishermen but it certainly includes those for whom the match fishing motive is almost inbred. The wet-fly, in its many guises and disguises, became dominant and although some anglers did use dry-flies on reservoirs they rarely went into print and thus their influence was strictly limited.

Because very little had appeared on stillwater fly-fishing, when T. C. Ivens produced *Stillwater Fly Fishing* in 1952 it had the effect of a bombshell. At last someone had written a book on this type of angling and it confirmed most people's opinions, the dry-fly was useless. Evoking the god of science, Ivens proclaimed that trout in stillwaters spent most of their time feeding subaqueously and concluded that the dry-fly would be inevitably beaten by the wet-fly. At a later date, Ivens did modify his position; but the damage had already been done. It must be said that the influence of *Stillwater Fly Fishing* was in no little part attributable to its excellence, but it is still blind to the possible value of the dry-fly and, even when I consult the enlarged third edition of 1970, I can only discover a single, brief chapter on the dry-fly. Ivens had yielded a little ground, yet we may detect something in the tone of his writing which reveals that he had yielded grudgingly.

There *are* anglers who spend most of their time on stillwaters casting floating patterns. I wonder how Ivens would explain the remarkable success of some of these anglers, who not only catch a very creditable total of fish each season, but also account for larger than average individual trout. Particularly on small lakes, it is notable how many of the largest fish actually fall to the dry-fly, and at last other anglers are beginning to take notice. Perhaps the renaissance of the dry-fly is imminent.

Ivens had never been keen on the entomological approach and I have a feeling that present interest in fly fishing entomology will renew an interest in the stillwater dry-fly. Bell and Sheringham may have copied the natural insects of Chew Valley Lake way back at the beginning of the century, but the naturalistic approach only really began to catch on a decade or so ago (perhaps at a time when the influence of Ivens had waned a little). It began with J. R. Harris's *Anglers' Entomology* (1952), developed through C. F. Walker's brilliant book *Lake Flies and their imitations* (1960) and reached its most complete expression in John Goddard's *Trout Flies of Stillwater* (1969). Add to these books many fine articles by such great anglers as Richard Walker, Geoff Bucknall, Conrad Voss Bark and Taff Price and the perfect antedote to Ivens's non-entomological approach begins to take shape. Yes, you can copy the insects of lakes just as you can copy those of rivers, and the imitative approach does recognise the need for dry-flies when conditions dictate.

The time was ripe for a new stillwater fly fishing bible and it appeared a couple of decades after the original publication of Ivens's book. In 1975, A. & C. Black published Brian Clarke's *Pursuit of Stillwater Trout* and it soon became a best seller and extremely influential. Take a sharp wit, a pen dipped in poetry and a dash of entomology and mix them together – then you have Clarke's delightful book. What is most important about this book is that although Brian Clarke may spend most of his time discussing the importance of the nymph, he also recognises the needful role of the dry-fly, even if he only sees it as an occasional tactic.

Clarke calls the dry-fly 'a minor tactic' (though remember the good results obtained by those who concentrate on the dry-fly) yet, paradoxically, it becomes a major tactic when it is really needed. What is 'a minor tactic' anyway? Didn't Skues himself begin by referring to nymph fishing as a minor tactic!

How effective is the stillwater dry-fly? Let us begin to assess its effectiveness by ignoring the possibility of using dry-flies extensively and concentrate on the 'minor tactic' approach. Consider for a moment an artificial dry-fly which may only succeed for a couple of days out of an entire season of six or seven months. Certainly that fly would constitute a minor tactical approach, but is that a real reason for us to ignore it? What happens if we happen to fish on the particular day when the pattern is likely to fish well, and when no other fly will take fish? Are we still likely to think of that fly then as of minor importance?

At the moment we have offered merely an abstract hypothesis, yet it has a solid foundation and this will become clear if we regard a specific example, the ant perhaps, for it offers the classic case.

Ants are terrestrial creatures and if they fall on to the surface of the lake, they float (unless conditions are very rough, in which case they may be swamped). They do not have an aquatic stage and trout are therefore accustomed to taking them only from the surface and not beneath it. It is simple to deduce that a dry-fly will catch far more fish than a wet-fly in this instance.

Ants may only be of significance to the angler for a day or two during any season, indeed, there are some seasons when you will never encounter them at all (simply because you were not fishing at the time of their appearance). However, when they do fall on to the water in vast numbers, trout go crazy and demand nothing but a diet of ants. When fish are preoccupied with a single food item in this manner you must offer an appropriate pattern or else resign yourself to a fishless day. The reason why ants are not common on the surface of the lake is easy to explain — they only become airborne for very short periods each year. At any time from July to September, when the weather is hot, the great mating ritual of ants may occur. They develop wings for their nuptial flight, which results in the coupling of males and females. Male ants die after intercourse (often falling on to lakes and rivers) whilst females rub off their wings and search for a nest in which to lay their eggs. In breezy conditions it is usual to find many females as well as males deposited on the surface of the water and, as a result, trout may indulge in a feeding orgy.

Terrestrials such as ants may thus be extremely important when they occur and dry-fly tactics will become essential, which is rather strange since we tend to associate dry-fly fishing with upwinged flies, sedges and so forth. However, ants, hawthorn flies, heather flies, terrestial beetles and crane flies are extremely important at times on stillwaters and essential fishing tactics must include the use of the dry-fly. It takes a great number of surface flies to induce a good stillwater 'rise' yet terrestrials do often fall in very large numbers and therefore fit the bill. On the other hand, the position may not be quite the same in the case of flies which possess aquatic life-cycle stages since trout will often prefer nymphs and pupae to adult flies. It will take a considerable hatch of aquatic flies to produce an extensive surface rise and although this does occur, aquatic hatches are often rather sparse, during the daytime at least.

Clearly, though we will need to discuss the relative importance of the dry-fly when considering aquatic flies, much of our time will be devoted to the terrestrials or semi-aquatic insects which are often ignored. Incidentally, since ephemerid hatches are dwindling on rivers, due to water abstraction and pollution, terrestrial insects are becoming increasingly important items in the trout's diet. Still, that is another story, and if the present reader already fishes for trout on streams, he would do well to read Vincent Marinaro's book *A Modern Dry-Fly Code* in which terrestrials on rivers are discussed in considerable detail.

By now, it is to be hoped that some kind of perspective on the stillwater dry-fly has begun to emerge, but I think that a review of the situation must face up to the kind of forceful arguments which have been offered against the use of the dry-fly.

The first argument involves the statistics game, which offers little more than a scientific 'proof'. Because mathematics are involved, readers are lulled into complete belief like innocents led to the slaughter. Don't trust statistics whenever fly-fishing is involved; after all, look how easily they are perverted by politicians and advertising agencies. When we apply logic to the facades of statistical evidence they begin to crumble and sometimes reveal a completely different picture beneath.

And now to the anti-dry-fly argument itself which runs something like this: 'It takes a considerable hatch of flies to induce surface feeding. Trout prefer subaquatic food forms and spend at least 90 per cent of their lives feeding beneath the surface of the lake.'

There may be some truth in the opening sentence, although it is characteristic to find the word 'hatch' used and no reference made to terrestrial insects. Nevertheless, my main concern is with the suggestion that 90 per cent of a stillwater trout's time is spent feeding beneath the surface.

First of all, it is wrong to generalise about stillwaters because there is a considerable difference between the lush Southern and Midland reservoirs, and the rocky lakes of the North. In the latter waters trout will often spend a much greater amount of time surface feeding because the subsurface food is in limited supply.

Second, we may all have the impression that trout feed more beneath, than at the surface (from observation at the water-side) but just how do you quantify the accurate statistic? The 'scientific' school of anglers usually offer the evidence of autopsies taken by a variety of anglers in perhaps a number of circumstances, yet often there are too many variables. Once again we will construct a typical argument: 'Of the 1,000 fish examined only fifty trout actually had adult flies in their stomach contents and of those only twenty contained more than one adult fly.'

A convincing argument – or is it? What you are not told is that the majority of those 1,000 fish were caught by anglers using wet-flies or lures so that the fish were most likely to have been feeding on subsurface food forms anyway. Since the whole purpose of the exercise is to disprove the value of the dry-fly, and since those anglers wanted to *catch* fish and probably didn't believe in the dry-fly, they were not likely to have used it. Had all those anglers used dry-flies and all the fish been caught in that manner, what would the autopsies have shown then? Perhaps they would still have shown a dominance of nymphs and pupae but that doesn't prove very much; if they had been caught on dry-flies, at least we would know that they were prepared to accept them.

Remember also that fifty fish did have adult flies in their stomachs even though they were probably caught on wet-flies which suggests that they might just as well have fallen to dry-flies. The truth is that there are fewer floating naturals around than there are subsurface food forms, yet there are many who would argue that trout prefer floating flies when they can get them. In support of this idea I can recall a number of trout caught on dry-flies which didn't even have a single adult fly in their stomach contents simply because there were none around to speak of. I had merely speculated with the dry-fly at a time when most people would have considered that technique quite pointless. Autopsies carried out on these trout would ostensibly have supported the arguments of those who decry the dry-fly — but not, I think, when you consider that these fish had actually been caught on dry-flies!

Often, when there are few natural adult flies around, trout will still fall to the dry-fly and this serves to explain the frequency with which some anglers catch trout by concentrating on the dry-fly rather than by neglecting it. However, these anglers are in a minority (reason enough perhaps for the shades of élitism to persist) and the reason why the dry-fly only gains minor acclaim in the log books of fishing lodges up and down the country is simply that so few people use it.

If the dry-fly were to be given a fairer trial I am sure that the scope of the technique would be enlarged in the minds of most anglers. There are undoubtedly times when only nymphs and pupae will take fish, there are times when the dry-fly remains supreme, *and* there are occasions when either technique will catch fish (at such times an angler may tailor his methods according to preference rather than necessity). I recall last season watching three anglers fishing close together and each succeeded in catching a limit bag of fish. The interesting fact was that two were using nymphs and one was using a dry-fly; it didn't really seem to matter. However, if they had been watched by a beginner, and all three had been using wet-flies, he would reasonably

6

have concluded that wet-flies were the order of the day simply because no alternative proof had been offered. Since dry-fly fishermen are a rare sight on lakes and reservoirs, dry-fly fishing doesn't really possess an adequate advertising campaign.

Let us now turn to the important matter of the trout's window of vision, for to do so will undoubtedly help us to assess the enigma of the dry-fly. For instance, it will resolve the dilemma of fishermen who become frustrated when their floating artificial fails to catch fish during a substantial rise (a fact which often seems to discredit dry-fly fishing on stillwaters) and help to explain why the dry-fly will catch fish when no fish are seen to be rising.

It is often true that trout are simply on the lookout for food and when anything juicy enough enters their window of vision, they will eat it, be it on the surface or beneath it. If subsurface food is very plentiful, then perhaps they will concentrate upon it and largely ignore surface food (unless perhaps they see an item such as a large sedge or daddy-longlegs). Trout see greater distances underwater than they do at the surface, which may also explain subsurface feeding, yet they will still rise to floating flies if there is enough incentive. This may be governed by the size of the food item or, perhaps more mysteriously, by a preference for adult flies. I say 'mysteriously' because even in waters that are rich in underwater life, large trout will rise to the surface on occasions to engulf moderately sized or even minute insects.

In waters possessing a rather more restricted source of underwater food (that is, in terms of either number or variety) trout are more likely to rise to floating flies even though the trout may be lying quite deep in the water. The deeper a trout lies, the more it sees of the surface. At least this is true unless the water is murky, in which case rays of light will not penetrate very deeply into the water. If the trout does have an extensive view of the surface, it is likely to see surface insects even during the most moderate of hatches. Thus, the speculative dry-fly often succeeds when no fish are seen to be feeding at the surface and when they are lying deep.

If the surface of the lake is barren of natural fly life, or if the insects are very small, fish may not have the incentive to rise, but if the angler's cast presents them with what appears to be a *large* natural fly, the picture changes. Up they come, the fly disappears and a good fish is hooked. You offered them something they were willing to take, but was not naturally in evidence at the time. This fact makes nonsense of one of Ivens's complaints against the dry-fly approach that 'for most of the season the only flies present can be classified as small, very small and completely inimitable'.

So why try to imitate them? I agree in part with Ivens here, it is not often worth it, but it *is* worth imitating the kind of flies which trout enjoy eating when they can get them, sedges for instance. A palmer-dressed fly offers an excellent imitation of sedge flies and is often therefore a killing dry-fly when fish are not actually rising to naturals.

However, there are no absolutes in fly fishing. I have known times when trout were feeding beneath the surface and no sunken artificial would tempt them. In desperation I have tied on a small grey duster and they have risen to take it quite confidently. Thus, although a large dry-fly seems logical when trout are lying deep, even a small fly is by no means useless.

We have now reached a position whereby we can accept the success of dry-flies when there are no surface rises, but we may also go further by suggesting that the dry-fly will sometimes succeed *better* under such circumstances than it will when there is a genuine rise in progress! This may seem not only paradoxical but also contradictory, yet there is sound logic behind it.

First of all, when trout are surface feeding in numbers they are doing so either because there is a considerable aquatic hatch in progress or terrestrials have appeared in quantity. As a result they may often be feeding in a preoccupied manner so that your dry-fly will fail unless it is a good imitation of the natural insect. Then again, because of the number of natural insects around, your artificial will have a great deal of competition. Just consider the number of natural flies that any trout will see in proportion to your lonely artificial fly. If the artificial is cast out and left to drift, then it may eventually be seen by a cruising fish and therefore taken, but it will take time and this requires considerable patience. Too often, anglers will persist in casting and retrieving so that the fly will only rest on the surface for a very short time during each cast. It will not, therefore, be taken simply because no fish has had chance to see it and in such circumstances the statement that 'the longer your fly is on the water the more chance there is of catching a fish' is true. The dry-fly *does* often fail when a hatch is under way but only because it has been fished incorrectly.

You will recall that we said that a fish sees a greater surface area when it is lying deeper in the water (Figure 1 should help to explain this). If the water is clear enough, a fish which is lying at a depth of 10 feet will see a fly within an area of approximately 401 square feet; at a depth of 4 feet, he will see a fly within an area of 64 square feet; at a depth of 2 feet, this will be reduced to 16 square feet and at a depth of 1 foot, to only 4 square feet. Consequently, since fish will lie at a depth of 1 or 2 feet during a surface rise, their window of vision will be very restricted and if your fly does not fall within this small surface area they will not take it, simply because they will not see it.

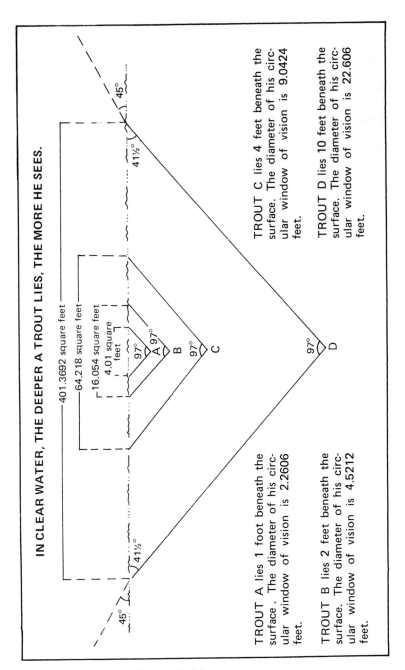

Figure 1: The trout's window of vision

9

If trout are taking fairly static positions during a hatch, an artificial fly will catch them if it lands within the rings of the rise and here there is the great advantage that they probably won't be scared since the thickest part of the leader, and the fly line itself, won't be seen, they will be outside the trout's window of vision. Since trout tend to hold static positions on rivers, this may well explain why dry-fly fishing is often thought to be more successful. On stillwaters trout tend to move around more. Under such circumstances the angler who can achieve accurate and delicate casts (often at quite a distance) will catch fish on the dry-fly. The dry-fly will fail if the cast is clumsy and lands heavily on the water, or if the fly falls short of the trout's position. Often, the fly will fall short either because a clumsy approach has been made along the bank or indiscriminate wading has scared the fish and driven them further out, thus making necessary a longer cast. During a rise, dry-fly fishing demands a great deal of stealth and, for me, this is one of its major attractions, you really do get the impression that you are stalking your prey. It is the atavistic pleasure of the hunt.

So far, we have considered rising fish which keep to one position, or perhaps explore a small surface area of water. However, during a rise, fish will often keep on the move and this will produce further problems. Trout will only be able to hold a position when either a hatch is of incredible proportions or a breeze maintains a constant supply of food over them. In relatively calm conditions, or when the hatch is a little sparse, trout are more likely to cruise around in search of food and at times they will swim quite quickly from position to position.

A rapid sequence of rises at some distance apart may suggest a number of feeding fish, whereas, in fact, there is only one. At times like these the dry-fly often fails, not because the fish don't want it, but because it has always landed as the rings of the rise are spreading outwards and the fish has already moved elsewhere. Repeated casts to rises produce only frustration unless the casts are made very quickly. Since most anglers pursue rises with increasing anger they become not only clumsy but disillusioned with stillwater dry-fly fishing.

Unless your casting is of expert standard or you are able to fish a shortish line (to facilitate quick switches from position to position) the best policy is either to cast in the general feeding area and wait patiently, or to plot the feeding path of individual fish. In either case it takes an amount of time to catch a fish, much of the time being spent not in casting, but in observation. A single fish may describe a great ellipse as it rises from point to point and its feeding path may take fifteen minutes. You observe its first voyage and then cast to the nearest point on the ellipse as it completes its second journey, which means that you may only have made one cast during the best part of half an hour.

Dry-fly fishing to stillwater rises may be simple enough to execute, yet it still makes a great number of demands on the angler. However, once the theory behind it is fully understood, there is no reason why it should not succeed.

My final consideration in this chapter is to stress the need to avoid generalisation, particularly when our concern is the stillwater dry-fly. Stillwaters are as varied as the people who fish them, while the trout they contain, though their biological functions may be similar, possess greatly varied habits. Trout react differently according to size, environment and type. Type differences are perhaps on the increase at the moment in Britain, for not only has the brook trout now become established in a number of waters but also various cross-bred strains of trout. I must readily admit that I know little of brookies (although recent experience with brook trout suggests that they take most kinds of flies quite readily and are more than willing to rise to floating flies), tiger trout and the like, and it will take a few years' experience to assess their value to the dry-fly fisherman. However, the majority of trout which we will be fishing for will be brown and rainbow trout so I will restrict my remarks to them.

Brown trout (*salmo trutta*) and rainbow trout (*salmo gairdneri*) do not react to the dry-fly in the exact same manner, partly because they are 'in season' at different times and are basically different in habit.

Writing of American streams in 1935 (*A Book of Trout Flies*) Preston J. Jennings discussed the readiness of indigenous brook and rainbow trout to accept gaudy deep sunk wet-flies, whilst the imported European brown trout required 'sober hued flies, more nearly of the coloring of the natural flies found in the stream'. He, like many other American anglers, had discovered that the brownie was much more selective in its feeding habits and required an imitative dry-fly approach. Thus, imitative fly fishing grew in the States, while conversely, with the introduction of the less discriminating rainbow trout into British stillwaters, lure fishing has grown in popularity in the United Kingdom.

It would be quite wrong to say that lures will never catch brown trout and that rainbows will never rise to dry-flies, but it is true to say that at certain times of the year the dry-fly is more likely to catch brown trout, whilst fisheries which are predominantly stocked with rainbows will show a flourishing trade in lure fishing.

Lure fishing is unfortunately so popular because smallish rainbow trout take them so readily and because the high growth rate of rainbows make them more economical to stock. In fisheries where the owners stock brown trout for preference (and would there were more of them), the dry-fly is often one of the most popular methods by which trout are caught. Even this is something of a generalisation since very large brown trout are often caught on deep sunk lures in lochs and large reservoirs, whilst large rainbows often fall to the dry-fly in small lake fisheries.

In spring it is particularly useful to use the dry-fly if you prefer catching brown trout rather than rainbows. Rainbows do not breed naturally in English stillwater fisheries and often are in very poor condition in early spring, being black and gravid. Indeed, I have caught rainbows in June which have fought hard and looked in good condition only to find them shedding milt or eggs all over the place when landed. There can be little fun in catching spawny fish (even if you are not depleting future fish stocks since the eggs will never develop) and there is certainly no sense in killing them since their flesh is not worth eating. Recent stockings with 'Triploids' may indicate a change in this situation. Such rainbows, being barren, do not lose condition in this manner.

If you find that the wet-fly or lure is only attracting small stock rainbows, or rainbows which have wintered badly, then give the dry-fly a chance and see what happens. You may well contact a decent brown trout which is in much better condition. At the beginning of the 1978 season I fished a local reservoir with a companion and whilst the hordes crammed together at one end, pulling out poorly conditioned rainbows with monotonous regularity, we caught our limits of well-conditioned brown trout and only encountered one black rainbow. Try something different, it is often well worth the trouble.

Even at the end of the season, in late August and September, brown trout seem more ready to take dry-flies than rainbow trout even though the latter are in peak condition since they spawn later in the year. I have often done well with the dry-fly in September, as far as brown trout are concerned, and have been amazed at the readiness with which they have taken the fly. Perhaps the confident rising of brownies reflects their need to store up food, and thus energy, in preparation for the winter and the rigours of spawning.

If it is wrong to generalise about species of trout when discussing the dry-fly, it is even worse to generalise about stillwaters as if they were all one and the same. If there is a difference between browns and rainbows, then there is often a greater difference within each species, dependent upon variation of habitat.

It is not possible to expect the same response to a dry-fly from, let us say, brown trout living in high lakeland tarns and brown trout living in rich lowland reservoirs. The dry-fly will succeed in most environments but the difference in environment and food structure will necessitate a difference in tactical approach. Disregarding large hatches of flies and huge falls of terrestrials, which may evoke similar responses in various environments, a trout in a lakeland tarn may accept any small fly whilst a trout on a lush lowland reservoir will be much more choosy. Because he has a richer store of underwater food you may well have to offer him a large dry-fly in order to make him think that a rise will be worth his while.

The dry-fly is often very successful in small lake fisheries simply because if you keep on the move (or use a boat) you can guarantee that you will cover a good number of trout with your fly and by the law of averages one or two are bound to go for it. In fact, the dry-fly will often tempt the very best fish in small lake fisheries since it differs so much from the usual wet-flies and nymphs which other anglers use from day to day. These patterns will have passed the noses of trout so many times that they will have become educated and hook shy. The dry-fly, being quite unlike the usual bombardment, will in contrast be taken without scrutiny and with innocent abandonment. Often, when large fish in small lakes are described as uncatchable, the dry-fly will paradoxically render them relatively easy.

Large upland reservoirs, such as Ladybower and the reservoirs in the Elan Valley in Wales, will offer the stillwater dry-fly fisherman some of his most lucrative fishing. Items such as snails, mussels, shrimps and worms (the latter being evident in newly flooded lowland waters) are in short supply, or are entirely absent, and although subsurface food is by no means as barren as some writers imply, it differs in structure. These foods (apart from snails) remain underwater and trout are seduced into deep feeding as a consequence. Snails, on occasion, do migrate to the surface and trout will follow them. However, the underwater food forms in upland reservoirs are often more likely to represent the aquatic stages of fly life. When I explored such a lake it became quite clear that the most dominant underwater creatures were (apart from tiny corixidae), stonefly creepers, caddis larvae and pupae, various larvae and pupae of the Diptera order and Ephemerid nymphs such as the nymphs of the Claret and Sepia duns. Accordingly, with the absence of creatures which remain entirely underwater, adult flies produce a higher proportion of the total available food supply than they do on rich lowland reservoirs. For this reason even moderate hatches of fly will produce quite satisfactory rises.

2

Tackle for stillwater dry-fly fishing

TACKLE

> There is always one moment in childhood when the door opens and
> lets the future in. (Graham Greene)

During much of my youthful apprenticeship with a fly rod I fished
with traditional soft-hackled wet-flies. However, on balmy evenings
in May and June the trout of my Pennine reservoir were free-rising
and it eventually occurred to me that I really ought to try the dry-fly.
Having purchased half-a-dozen beautifully tied Greenwell's Glories
(the like of which I am sure I shall never see again) and a tin of
'Alcock's Linefloat', I was ready to try the stillwater dry-fly.

It was a beautifully calm evening in late May and apart from a lone
angler on the far bank, I had the reservoir to myself. As I tackled up,
the weird and distant sound of yapping dogs echoed down the valley
from a hillside farm. Trout were rising in numbers, mainly at a
distance of twenty or so yards from the bank, although several fish
were working much nearer to the bank a hundred yards to my right.
My only rod was a 7ft 6in built cane rod matched to a single-tapered
silk line stored on a tiny Condex reel: unthinkably light tackle for the
modern reservoir fisherman, but, as it turned out, quite adequate for
the distances required on that occasion. There was something almost
animate about the tackle: the cane rod had a natural life of its own
whilst the smell of the oil dressed silk line was not only pleasant but
also a far cry from the clinical smell of modern synthetic lines. The
most intoxicating smell of all was the spiked-lavender smell of the line
grease which I smoothed along the whole length of the cast and line
before reeling it back again, ready for action. Finally, I annointed the
fly with oil and prepared myself for the quest.

The greased silk line cast beautifully although it was difficult to
shoot through the rings, which meant aerialising a fair amount of line.
However, with effort I could reach the fish and my tackle presented
the fly with such delicacy that few fish seemed to be scared. They
continued to feed at the same distance from the bank and were not
driven further out − which is often the result when casts are made

14

with more powerful modern tackle. With hindsight, it is also significant to note that I did not wade, simply because I did not possess waders, so that the water was not disturbed. Sadly, recent trends have been towards indiscriminate wading which has resulted in driving the fish further out with the subsequent need for the development of tackle which will cast further in order to reach them. Additionally, wading destroys the insect life of the shallows which, if left to flourish, would encourage trout to feed near to the bank during the evening.

My first three casts all produced rises of such lightning speed that I missed them. I had only read two fishing books at this time: one, on chalkstream fishing, was by far the most influential yet it stressed the need for a leisurely strike. No doubt that was appropriate for the heavy fish of the chalkstream but it didn't work here. These lithe little fish could engulf a fly and eject it again in a split second and the tightening of the line had to be incredibly fast. Eventually, I hit the fifth (or was it the sixth?) rise and a fighting fit brownie of half a pound was in the net. Another small brown trout soon followed and I began to glow with success. What a pleasant way to fish, and how exciting to see a trout rise to my floating fly even when I missed it! As I pondered upon the past events and dried my bedraggled Greenwell on a piece of amadou (whatever happened to supplies of

Difficult conditions. A fish rises in a glassy calm. Time to use a light line, a fine leader, and a tiny fly.

15

that fascinating fungus?) my attention was attracted to a resounding rise about fifty yards to my right. It could only be a very big fish and it was rising no more than four or five yards from the bank.

When you don't possess much tackle, you have no temptation to clutter yourself up with unnecessary items of tackle. Thus it was that I was as mobile as any angler may be, and, unburdened with bulky gear I set off quietly in pursuit of my huge trout. I have already mentioned that I had read a book on chalkstream fishing (and I just cannot remember who it was written by) and it conditioned even my approach to fishing a fairly acidic upland reservoir. As it turned out, this was not such a bad thing as it taught me the importance of stalking fish. It was as natural for me to creep through the bracken as it is for many modern reservoir fishermen to stake their claims with long-handled landing nets (or even green umbrellas!) and plough uncompromisingly into the water. We may both catch trout, but the indiscriminate wader will find his fish feeding far out from the bank and he will exhaust himself with long casting.

I am digressing . . . I crawled slowly through the rustling bracken and brambles, scared stiff that my fish would disappear before I reached it or would bolt away each time I knelt on the crackling undergrowth. My progress was painfully slow and line tangles were a frequent menace, but eventually I reached a position no more than ten yards from the fish which rose again obligingly so that I could mark its location. When the ripples subsided the fish eventually came into view − and what a fish! I literally shuddered in fear and awe at this huge brown trout swimming lazily in tight circles, its huge jaws looking fearsome and almost evil. Some struggling insect or other buzzed and fizzed into his feeding territory and he rose. The white of his mouth and the snap of his jaw symbolised his predatory nature and yet he was actually rising to a *floating fly*!

Legend had it that there were huge trout in this water yet they were always believed to be cannibals restricted to a diet of other fish. He certainly didn't look like a cannibal for he was beautifully pro-portioned and by no means thin and lanky. What did he weigh? I had never seen a fish so big before and my imagination placed his weight at six pounds or beyond even that magical figure. Through the mists of time I still possess a very clear image of that leviathan, yet it is perhaps likely that his weight was nearer to four pounds. Nevertheless, it was a fine fish and in the pre-Grafham, pre-Avington days of huge trout, it was a trophy fish. My thoughts spanned the pages of *Angling Times* and my local newspaper where I could already see my complacent grin, the fish cradled lovingly in my arms. The world of romance was shattered by reality as he rose again with gusto and conviction: I had to catch him before I could become a piscatorial celebrity.

Gently, I pulled line from the reel, checked the fly and tried to estimate the distance of the cast. I had to get it right because it didn't seem likely that I would be allowed a second cast. The trout hovered in a fixed position. The false cast was made well behind the fish, then the line was switched into the full cast landing the fly delicately a couple of feet in front of the mighty fish. The trout vibrated gently, moved a few inches forwards and then stopped.

Would he take it? Would he ignore it? My heart pumped vigorously and I could actually feel a throbbing at the back of my neck. Then, ever so gently, the fish moved forwards again and then swept upwards taking the fly with a splash. He bore away and I had no need to strike. I just held on tight and got rapped on the knuckles as the reel drum screamed round. Line sped from my reel, nearly down to the backing — then it happened. The trout swirled on the surface, dived again and the line went slack. . . . I couldn't believe it. Had I offended the deity? No. It was the simple stupidity of innocence: I had been using a cast point of no more than one-and-a-half pounds! Vaguely conscious, I watched the surface subdue into a flat mirrored calm and began to reel in slowly. I didn't mention that fish to anybody because nobody would ever have believed me and although I searched for him again and again he never appeared. Perhaps I began to learn the importance of stoical acceptance, perhaps not. What I did discover was how exciting dry-fly fishing on stillwaters could be.

Later that evening I caught another trout and then headed home again, kicking my heels along the dusty road which led back to the town. A man passed by with a dog:

'Had any luck, son?'

'Yes, three,' I replied.

'Not bad. Not bad at all.'

I grinned enigmatically and shuffled on. Luck! What an irony! I began to hate the non-fisherman's jokes about 'the one that got away' and I kicked a pebble at the dry stone wall. It seemed but characteristic when the pebble bounced right back again and hit me on the knee. Still, it really was my fault. Fancy using such a fine point, and yet, would I have caught those three other fish with a cast point like a hawser?

For me, this little episode, which occurred over twenty years ago, has a great deal to do with the tackle I use today and there are a number of important conclusions that may be drawn.

Stillwater dry-fly fishing is not all that different from river fishing and stalking fish can be just as important on lakes and reservoirs. For this reason the angler should travel light.

Long-casting may be necessary in an area frequented by many wading anglers, yet trout do move close inshore and light rods are a viable proposition since they land a fly delicately. Incidentally, the distance achieved by short rods and lighter lines is often under-estimated by British anglers whereas American anglers often cast good distances with their preferred short rods.

A very fine point will provide delicate presentation and result in the capture of small and average trout but it will be found inadequate when larger specimens are encountered. As a rule, a cast point between three-and-a-half and four-and-a-half pounds breaking strain will suffice on most occasions.

When you only possess one fly pattern, it will often catch fish no matter what the trout are feeding on if it is presented accurately. Nevertheless, at times trout do rise more selectively yet delicate presentation is still a necessary requirement. Heavy tackle is generally useless in true stillwater dry-fly fishing.

Having introduced the subject of tackle I hope that I have made it clear that this is a personal approach. You will not find a detailed discussion of the techniques of fishing with long and powerful rods nor a praise of double-hauling with shooting head lines.

Although I intend to consider each item of tackle separately, let me emphasise that the key factor is really the sum total of all tackle — lightness and mobility. The successful stillwater dry-fly fisherman must move around a great deal in search of his prey and must not be encumbered by a clumsy array of heavy gear. We are stalking fish and not flogging a single area of water to a foam.

RODS

Anything I may say about rods must be accepted in the spirit in which it is intended. All I intend to do is to comment on the rods which I have found personally pleasant and effective to use for this branch of stillwater fly-fishing. Undoubtedly, there are many other rods which are equally effective and I do not wish to imply disparagement by omission.

Traditionally, dry-fly rods have been described as 'stiffish' and wet-fly or nymph rods as possessing a 'soft action'. However, particularly since the beginner will wish to use the same rod for different styles of fishing, what might be described as a 'medium action' will suffice. Today, with the efficiency of modern floatants, it is not necessary (nor advisable even) to continually false cast in order to dry the fly, and since that was one of the principal functions of the 'stiff' rod, it is no longer essential to purchase that kind of weapon. However, rods which possess a very 'soft' action, though admirable when fishing wet-flies, will not deliver a dry-fly with adequate accuracy and delicacy and may even drown the fly on its impact with the water. In many ways, even rod action seems to be a subjective matter, for no two people will agree completely about a description of a rod's action. The most suitable rod is one which most suits the individual angler − given the methods by which he intends to fish.

The first consideration when choosing a rod for stillwater dry-fly fishing is the matter of line selection. Considering distance and delicacy, the lightest which I use is an AFTM 5 double-tapered floater. This line is perfectly suitable when conditions are very calm and even small flies can be presented with delicacy and with a minimal amount of surface disturbance. For general fishing, I use a size 6 double-tapered line and move up to a double tapered 7 or even a weight-forward 7 when conditions are rougher. Although an experienced fisherman may well be able to use a line as light as AFTM 4, size 7 must form the upper limit since I consider that a size 8 line (weight-forward or double-taper) is far too heavy for stillwater dry-fly fishing.

Having used greenheart, cane and glass rods, I have now settled for carbon rods for most of my stillwater fly-fishing. As yet, I have not tried out the new rods made of boron. The principal advantage of carbon (apart from its light weight) is that it will accept a variety of line sizes so that a single rod will cope with all the lines we need (from AFTM 5 to 7). My personal choice is a 9ft graphite rod which, though rated 6 − 7, will cast a size 5 line quite beautifully. This rod suits me perfectly: its action is crisp and precise, it will land a fly delicately at long range and picks up line quickly when a fish takes. I also use a 9ft 3in graphite rod (rated 7 − 8) occasionally although this rod is mainly employed when adopting techniques other than the stillwater dry-fly. Since I still possess a number of glass rods, they still get an occasional airing and particularly when fishing rougher locations (dam walls for instance) which might easily result in the damage of expensive carbon rods. In particular, I use an 8ft glass rod which will cast size 5 or 6 lines (for calm conditions) and a 9ft glass rod which will cast size 6 and 7 lines (when conditions are rougher). Perhaps it is illusory, but I do get the impression that the carbon rods kill fish more quickly without any loss of sensitivity or pleasure during the playing of a fish.

Although carbon makes it possible to use longer rods without adding a great deal of weight, I do not feel that the angler needs to go much beyond a nine footer when choosing a rod for the dry-fly. If you are careful and stealthy, trout will often rise quite close to the bank and, at such times, a longer rod is counter-productive as it will not facilitate a delicate short cast. Equally, long rods often produce difficulties when netting fish and, although they may cast a long distance, pick up lines easily and avoid obstacles on the back-cast, they do not provide the same control over the delicate delivery of a dry-fly – particularly when conditions are very calm. There is another point worthy of consideration. Although a longer rod (10ft – 11¼ft) may be relatively light in weight, its extra length will add a greater force to the angler's wrist and may eventually induce tiredness and clumsy casting. To the dry-fly, the clumsy cast is anathema.

WHEN LONG RODS ARE NECESSARY

Where the longer rod comes into its own, is with the specialised techniques of dapping and bob-fly fishing; techniques which are generally adopted from boats. Long rods made of glass fibre are not a good proposition. On the one hand, they are generally too heavy and tiring (on average, from 5¼ to 7 ounces in weight) whilst they are invariably rather 'floppy' in action. The result is that they lack 'backbone' in the cast, strike slowly (resulting in many missed rises) and play fish rather badly (often resulting in broken leader tippets). Nevertheless, if you decide to try these techniques on a budget, you will have to settle for the vagaries of glass fibre since the cost of similar carbon rods may well be prohibitive for a rod which is only to be used occasionally. Ideally, however, carbon rods are best suited to these specialised forms of fishing.

Bob-fly, or drift-fishing, is perhaps more reasonably considered a branch of wet-fly fishing, although it does utilise a bushy fly at the surface towards the end of the cast's retrieval. Short casts are flicked out in front of a drifting boat and then retrieved near the surface. When the cast approaches the boat, the long rod is raised high so that the bushy fly, positioned on the top dropper, trips and splashes. This is a deadly technique and induces dramatic and positive rises. For this style of fishing, a carbon rod of 10ft to 10ft 6in, taking line sizes 5 and 6, is suitable. There are many such rods on the market either in completed form, part-built (having the handle already fitted) or kit form.

Dapping (discussed in more detail at a later stage) is most definitely a branch of dry-fly fishing and necessitates an even longer rod. Traditional rods (still in evidence on Irish loughs and especially at mayfly time) were often as long as eighteen feet and were reasonably manageable since no casting, as such, was necessary. In dapping, a long rod and light floss line enables the angler to pay out line with the wind (windy conditions are essential) so that the large and buoyant artificial fly trips along the waves and is occasionally lifted right off the water by the breeze, and then allowed to alight again. Rapid splash takes are both common and dramatic: no doubt the fish are driven to attack quickly in the instinctive belief that their prey may escape from them. Although this technique is little used on English reservoirs, it might gain a good number of converts if the right tackle were to become readily available.

At the moment, as far as I am aware, there are no commercially made dapping rods. At a pinch, a light coarse fishing rod might suffice, although a carbon fly-rod of at least eleven feet in length would be a reasonable alternative. At the time of writing, there are only four suitable rods available. As an example of what is possible in carbon fibre, one rod only weighs 4½ ounces which is remarkable considering its length.

Coupled with a long rod, it is necessary to obtain some floss dapping line which is attached to a great amount of nylon backing (10lbs breaking strain being amply strong). For this rig, an ordinary centre-pin reel or the 4in Carbon 'Line-shooter' is preferable to a conventional fly reel.

A FURTHER NOTE ON GLASS RODS

At the time of writing, it becomes obvious that a lot of famous glass fibre rods are being phased out. Carbon has taken over the market completely and it is now possible to buy carbon rods more cheaply than the better classes of glass rods. Cheap carbon rods are often billed as being 'ideal for the beginner' or useful as a 'second rod'. Beware! A really top quality glass rod will perform much better than a cheap carbon rod and it will certainly be more serviceable. Carbon, or graphite, is a much 'softer' material so that the ferrules are certainly prone to wear quite quickly: they must be well waxed in order to slow this process down. Despite the obvious advantages of carbon as a rod building material, a second rate carbon blank will not only perform badly, it will also break quite easily on impact with some obstacle, or when false casting energetically with only a little line beyond the rod tip. Thus, it does not pay to settle for very cheap carbon rods, not only because they will be found wanting in the cast (particularly as far as presentation is concerned) but also because they will not stand up to the kind of wear imposed by fishing under difficult conditions. Do not despise glass rods. Purchase a good one if you are likely to fish from difficult banks, where trees may perpetually cause snagging for example, and the rod will take an amount of stick. A really good glass rod *will* cast sweetly, accurately and delicately: it will achieve distance and it will wear well. It may be heavier than carbon rods of similar length and line rating, but at a shade over four ounces, that should not be a very great imposition. On the other hand, a cheap quality glass rod will undoubtedly be heavy and crude; it will be tiring to use and will undoubtedly be far too clumsy in the cast for delicate dry-fly work.

REELS

It is strange how we become attached to our favourite reels, and how much money we are prepared to pay for them despite knowing that cheaper reels would be quite adequate. Basically, a reel is little more than a line store although the angler is advised to play his fish on the reel which allows a much tighter control than the practice of hand lining the fish in. We have already said something of specialised fly-reels, although there are still one or two points worth considering.

Even when fishing the dry-fly, it is quite common for the fly to drift with the breeze so that we have to 'mend' the line in order to avoid 'dragging' the fly on the surface: as a result, an amount of slack is left at our feet. When a fish rises to the fly, and we tighten into it, the slack line poses a problem and must be quickly gathered on to the reel before we can begin to play the fish with complete confidence. Then again, if a fish moves towards us during the fight, we may have slack line which could result in him freeing himself unless we can maintain tautness. One of the methods which may be employed is to walk backwards up the bank, taking the slack line on to the reel as we do so. Well, this is all very well, until we trip up, fall backwards into the mud and lose contact with the fish into the bargain. The reel must therefore assist us in maintaining a tight line.

A few years ago I thought that a particular fly-reel had answered all my prayers and would put an end to the problem of slack line: indeed I praised the reel in *The Art of the Wet Fly*. However, since then I have had to modify my opinions. Certainly, this reel retrieves the line on to the spool very rapidly when the trigger is depressed, whilst the automatic mechanism itself is extremely well made and very reliable. When fishing the wet fly with reasonably strong leaders the trigger can be pressed to take in the line at the start of the fight and may be left in the 'action' position so that any slack line, which occurs as a result of the fish's movements, will be removed immediately. However, with finer leader tippets, the spring-loaded retrieve can be far too severe. This was only one of the problems encountered with the reel. Originally, I had used it on rivers, where light lines were the order of the day, or on reservoirs, where weight forward sinking lines had been used: with these lines it could cope. When I intended to use double-tapered AFTM 6 and 7 floaters it was impossible because of the reel's restricted line capacity (and on stillwaters it is also important to have a considerable store of backing in addition to the fly-line itself).

Thus, I have abandoned the use of automatic reels although I have not done so essentially because of their most common criticism – weight. They are certainly much heavier than conventional fly-reels and this can eventually provide fatigue, although on some rods they do stabilise the butt and handle, thus actually improving the casting action.

Given that I required a reel rapid enough to remove the hazard of slack line, and possessing a capacity adequate for the use of double-tapered lines, plus backing, I then turned quite naturally to multiplying reels. In the majority of cases, not only do multiplying reels possess gears, which allow a greater amount of line to be retrieved per turn of the handle than single-actioned reels, but also, they are manu-factured with reasonably narrow spools, which also aids rapid line retrieve. Accordingly, I would certainly recommend the use of multi-plying reels for stillwater dry-fly work.

LINES

In the matter of fly-lines, I suppose that I am as guilty as many other people of using cheap lines from time to time which often results in a loss of casting potential. Certainly, it does not make sense to purchase expensive stillwater tackle and then to use it with a sub-standard line, although I doubt the validity of claims that the line should be the first consideration. Some claim that you should choose your line first of all and then choose the rod and reel to go with it: such claims are invariably made by line manufacturers who naturally have a vested interest in this kind of argument. It is true that well-balanced tackle will only reach its optimum performance with a top quality fly-line, but, whereas a good rod will make reasonable casts even with a poor quality of line, an inadequate rod will not achieve reasonable casts even with the highest quality of line. Thus, the quality of the line is not our foremost consideration, although the weight of line to be used is, since that will condition the type and line-rating of rod to be purchased.

As I have already claimed, apart from floss dapping lines, the line sizes most valuable to stillwater dry-fly fishing are double-tapered 5, 6 and 7 lines; weight forward 6 and 7 lines. So far, I have taken it for granted that most anglers will be acquainted with the AFTM line rating in use today. However, a brief explanation may be useful to beginners in the sport although I do not propose to offer much more than a superficial consideration.

First of all, the AFTM line rating system was developed by the American fishing tackle industry in order to standardise the weights of fly-lines and make it easy to match a line to a rod. Rods prefixed with the inscription ♯ 6 are designed to be compatible with an AFTM 6 line.

Lines are rated from 3 to 12, so that a 3 weight line is very light, and a 12 weight line very heavy (and only likely to be used for heavy salmon fly-fishing). The weight divisions are standardised by the weight of the first thirty feet of line, so that if a double-tapered line weighs the same in its first thirty feet as a weight forward line, then the lines will be given the same classification. However, this system is by no means perfect simply because most competent casters are capable of aerialising more than thirty feet of line and this produces certain problems based on the differences between double-tapered and weight forward lines.

When casting with more than thirty feet in the air, the angler will be adding the weight of more line belly to the strain of the rod when using double-tapered lines, whilst with weight-forward lines, he will merely add the lighter weight of the very thin running line. For this reason, if a double-tapered AFTM 6 line will get the best out of a similarly rated rod, the same rod is capable of taking a greater weight of weight-forward line in the hands of an average caster. A beginner using an AFTM 6 rod will therefore find it easier to cast with a weight-forward 7 line than with a weight-forward 6 line. As a result of this kind of discrepancy, and with an acknowledgement that modern anglers often aerialise more than thirty feet of line, certain line manufacturers have developed weight-forward lines with a longer fat belly to them.

What is the real difference between double-tapered and weight-forward lines? Why do we need different types of lines?

Initially, my simple approach to these questions is to suggest that double-tapered lines are most commonly to be used because they cast beautifully (and will facilitate difficult casts, such as the roll cast) and present a fly delicately. In addition, since a double-tapered line possesses the same taper at each end, it is very economical to use: when one end begins to wear out, you simply reverse the line on the reel. However, the double-tapered line does have its restrictions both in terms of windy weather and long-distance casting.

It is difficult to 'shoot' a great deal of line with a double-tapered floater. This is where the weight-forward line comes into its own. It should not be used all the time because it does not present a fly with the delicacy of a double-tapered line and when the forward taper wears out, the line cannot be reversed and is finished.

Fly-lines, unfortunately, do not possess a very long life and if the fishing budget is restricted, a double-tapered line is a better bet. However, weight-forward lines are ideal for the job which they were designed to do. Since the bulk of the weight comes in the first section of the line, this enables the belly to pull out a long length of the thin 'shooting' line allowing the angler to reach distance by shooting line even though he has only aerialised the forward taper and 'belly' beyond the rod-point before the cast. Accordingly, the weight forward line will 'cut' better into a wind than a double-tapered line and is the line to use on such occasions.

If an angler normally fishes with AFTM 6 lines, he would be advised to choose a weight-forward 7 line for fishing under rougher conditions. One final point worthy of consideration is that double-tapered lines facilitate a quicker 'strike' when a fish has risen to the fly than do weight-forward lines, so that although weight-forward lines allow long distance casts, hitting the fish at such distances can sometimes pose something of a problem, particularly on upland stillwaters where the wild fish often rise quickly to the fly and eject it again at lightning speed.

Today, it seems almost irrelevant to compare the performances of silk and synthetic lines because silk lines are almost impossible to obtain. The great advantage of silk lines was that they were so supple, allowing beautifully smooth and delicate casts, while their diameter was much thinner than plastic lines which allowed them to cast better into a wind. Having said this, they did have the disadvantage of sinking unless you continually re-greased them, whilst the grease tended to clog the rod rings and reduced the possibility of 'shooting' line. At the time of writing, new silk lines are being produced in France and America although, as yet, I have not had a chance to test their quality and performance. I somehow doubt whether they will achieve the high standards of the old English 'Kingfisher' lines. (Silk lines are now being produced in Britain again. Appropriately, they are called 'Phoenix'.)

In the meantime, we are limited to plastic lines, which at their best are *nearly* as supple as silk and *nearly* of the same diameter. At their worst, they continually coil like springs, refusing to straighten out adequately in the cast, and are very bulky, which negates the possibility of delicate presentation.

As an illustration of the last point, I once purchased a cheap AFTM 6 line which was as bulky in the belly section as a Cortland 444 line rated at AFTM 8. Of course, you generally have to pay for quality, although certain expensive lines are by no means perfect and do not possess hard wearing properties, while certain budget lines not only perform well but also last a number of seasons. As with most items of tackle, it is wise to experiment until you discover the best buy – and do not believe all that you read in advertisements. There are many fine lines on the market today but, from my own experience it is difficult to beat the quality of certain American lines. I have used some of Hardy's lines for a number of years and found them excellent. The lines are sky-blue in colour and are produced with a matt finish which is of critical importance: highly polished lines which have a shiny finish may shoot well (although often too quickly, which makes them difficult to control) yet they cause a flash during the cast which is very likely to scare fish.

The ultimate dry-fly fishing line, however, is in my opinion, the mahogany-coloured Aircel Supreme. It is expensive, yet, regularly cleaned and lubricated, with 'Permagrease', it will last for many seasons. Being brown, it is less susceptible to the effects of light and does not crack as easily as lighter coloured lines. Some anglers argue that brown lines are less likely to scare fish although I am not completely sold on this argument.

Whatever lines you decide to buy, make sure that they are supple and have a reputation for being hard wearing – a reputation, that is, among anglers rather than from tackle shops. I have had two expensive lines from a well-known manufacturer which contained a number of flaws and which soon began to crack during use. Perhaps it may be argued that I might have misused them, yet I used them in precisely the same manner that I use other lines which show very little sign of abnormal wear and tear.

How significant a matter is colour when buying a fly-line? As far as I am concerned, for dry-fly fishing, where you watch the fly for a sign of a rise, the colour of the line doesn't really matter at all. (However, if you intend to use the same line for fishing the nymph, it pays to purchase a reasonably visible line which will enable you to detect takes more easily.) Today, floating lines are available in many different colours. It makes little difference. As far as I am concerned, trout are only likely to see the line as a dark silhouette against the sky (unless you fish in very shallow water where the colour of weeds may be reflected back on to the line). On the other hand, even the finest of fly-lines will appear as thick as a tree trunk to a fish which suggests that the fly line should be separated from the fly by a nylon leader as long as conditions will allow.

A further matter of importance concerning fly-lines is their protection during normal usage. Naturally enough, a fly-line will eventually wear and crack, which will result in it sinking or even breaking. However, its life will be prolonged if it is treated well. One of the greatest problems lies in the cast itself. An angler who cannot cast correctly may easily damage his line by beginning the forward thrust too early so that the line cracks like a whip – no line can take this kind of usage for very long and will eventually begin to crack at the point of maximum stress. Storing the line in tight coils on a reel spool (particularly throughout the close-season) will also damage the line and prevent the line from straightening out nicely when it is eventually used. From time to time the line should be taken off the spool and stretched in order to get rid of the coils, although it is important to use gloves during this process since the line can easily cut the hand or produce friction blisters. Poor quality lines all too readily develop into coils which are very difficult to remove and ultimately spoil the casting properties of the line.

A further matter which is detrimental to the longevity of a fly-line is the use of silicone-based floatants (which some anglers use to prevent the fine tips of lighter lines from sinking) and the action of dirt and solvents on the plastic coating. There are perfectly safe and reliable floatants for fly-lines and leaders on the market. They help to lubricate the line, which enables you to 'shoot' further, and seem to keep the line nice and supple, but make sure that you buy a silicone-free grease.

Because of the general pollution content of the atmosphere and rivers, stillwaters often produce scum which not only makes a fly-line dirty, but also reacts with the chemical structure of the plastic coating, thus destroying it. In addition, the dirt on the line may also collect minute particles of grit which will have an abrasive effect on the line, particularly when it is 'shot' through the rod rings. Worn rod rings themselves are quite often the cause of line failure. For this reason, it is important to clean the line as often as possible either with a rag and clean water (but not detergents which have a harmful effect) or with a manufactured fly-line cleaner.

Attaching the line to the leader can be achieved in a variety of ways and although nail-knots (often covered by a coat of varnish) are very popular, they have never seemed ideal to me. The essence of the nail-knot is that a heated needle is passed through the core of the fly-line and out through the plastic coating so that the nylon leader may be passed through and whip-knotted around the line. Although this produces a very neat finish it often produces a weakness in the plastic coating which may fracture under the pressure of a heavy fish. Plastic line-connectors are ideal and add little bulk to the join. Often I resort to a simple knotted loop at the end of the fly-line which is simply attached to the loop of the nylon cast. This may seem a little bulky yet I am convinced that it adds momentum to the tip of the line thus aiding the turnover of the line during the cast. It also seems to help the cast to straighten out particularly if the butt section of the nylon is a little on the stiff side.

LEADERS

As normal maxim, it is worth adopting as long a leader as possible when dry-fly fishing in order to put the greatest distance between the fly and the fly-line. In reasonable conditions, I normally use leaders of 15 or 16 feet in length which are rather awkward to cast until you get used to them. Because most commercially sold leaders are generally only 9 feet in length, it will be necessary to join the leader to the fly-line with a further 'collar' of nylon line in order to achieve the required length. This nylon collar ought to be quite thick in diameter (I use 20lb breaking strain) as this will help to create a natural taper from fly-line to leader point, thus aiding the leader to turn over nicely in the cast — this matter being essential to the delicate presentation of a dry-fly. There are some very long knotless tapering leaders available commercially: they taper nicely to a fine point (so that you cut it at whatever point produces the correct breaking strain) but tend to be rather expensive.

For dry-fly fishing, leaders with droppers on them must be rejected except when combining the dry-fly with nymphs or pupae (this technique is outlined at a later stage). When presenting the dry-fly, the droppers will cause surface disturbance (particularly in calm conditions) and they will cause a great deal of line wake when using the moving dry-fly (for example, when imitating sedge flies). Leaders made up from various thicknesses of nylon, knotted together, will suffice for general fishing but will again cause too much disturbance when the water is calm or when the fishing technique involves the moving dry-fly. When conditions are relatively calm, knotted leaders must be avoided and you must purchase the rather expensive continuous-tapered leaders.

Another problem with knotted leaders, is that under calm conditions, the knots invariably gather scum, become very obvious, and are likely to scare fish. Equally, when you desire to grease the leader, in order to improve its buoyancy, the knots will clog the grease into obvious fish-scaring blobs. It is important to remember that a fine leader appears far bulkier in diameter when viewed from an underwater position.

As far as the strength of the leader point is concerned, it is a matter of weighing up certain variables: the size of the fish likely to be encountered, the weather conditions, and the size of the fly. In general, it would seem foolish to attempt to catch double-figure fish on a nylon point of only two pounds and it is hardly fair to risk breakages which result in fish having hooks in their mouths and nylon trailing from them. For this reason, fisheries often have rules about the minimum breaking strain of nylon to be used. When the water is calm, however, the nylon point needs to be as fine as possible if we are to avoid scaring fish. Conversely, you can get away with thicker and stronger nylon under windy conditions, when the water is quite rough. Incidentally, windy conditions will also call for a shorter leader (about 10 feet in length), since the long leader will be impossible to cast and will undoubtedly fall in a heap rather than turn over nicely. Finally, tiny flies call for fine points, not only because thick nylon would never go through the eye of the hook, but also because a small fly will not float naturally when attached to thick nylon. Equally, since small flies are really only fished during calm conditions, thick nylon would also scare the fish. When using large flies, the nylon can logically be thicker and stronger. This is often essential since large flies sometimes provoke large fish into smash-take rises.

Under normal conditions (when the weather is breezy, but not rough, and the fly is of medium size) I use leader points of $3 - 3\frac{1}{2}$ pound breaking strain, although I would increase this a little if I expected to encounter very large fish. When using small flies under calm conditions, the leader point may be reduced to $2 - 2\frac{1}{2}$ pounds and alternatively increased to as much as 5 pounds when using large flies under rough conditions, or when fishing large flies to large fish. In terms of size, I would class flies tied on 16 to 20 hooks as small; tied on 12 to 14 as average and on size 10 and upwards as large.

A number of other points must be made when considering nylon leaders. First of all, there is the matter of whether to grease or not. I think this matter may be resolved quite simply. If you are going to move the dry-fly, then the leader must be left ungreased. A sinking leader will cause little disturbance whilst a greased floating leader will produce a great amount of line-wake.

The object of grease is to ensure that the leader floats, but it also has the unfortunate effect of making the nylon appear much bulkier.

Thus, whenever grease is used, it ought to be applied thinly and smeared evenly over the whole leader. It is better to grease quite often rather than ensure that the leader floats for a long time by applying a lot of grease which will undoubtedly scare fish.

When do you need to grease the leader? In essence, it is only necessary to grease the leader in order to allow you to tighten quickly (since it takes longer to pull nylon up through the water if it sinks) or when a sinking leader is likely to pull the fly under water. If you only need to tighten in a leisurely manner, then you need not grease the leader. For rapid takes, the leader must be greased. For large flies, liberally applied with floatant, it is only necessary to grease the stoutest part of the cast, yet you must grease to within a foot of the fly when using small flies. Small and delicate flies will soon be pulled under the water if the leader begins to sink and when using such flies, greasing is essential.

There are many good leader floatants on the market including 'Mucilin' and 'Permagrease' although I have always used 'Alcock's Linefloat' which I purchased in bulk many years ago. This line grease, when warmed in the fingers, melts nicely so that it can be thinly spread over the leader, and it possesses a unique smell which became, for me, part of the poetry of dry-fly fishing. Unfortunately, I am now down to my last tin, and since the demise of the old Alcock's firm occurred many years ago, I shall never be able to replace it.

Today, many commercial leaders are made up of nylon which is very shiny: such leaders ought to be anathema and avoided like the plague. Not only do they create a flash during casting, they also reflect too much light when lying on the surface of the water. Shiny nylon may be rubbed gently with a scouring agent although you stand every chance of ruining the strength of the line. If the nylon has a dull surface, then it is adequate for my purposes yet some anglers go a step further and dye their leaders a variety of dark colours. If you desire to do so, dyes are readily available and very effective.

Ultimately, the leader is the most important part of your equipment for it effectively forms the weakest link. It must be thin enough not to scare fish before they rise, but it must also be strong enough to hold them once they are hooked.

Breakages are a disaster so that you must continually check the leader for signs of wear and damage produced by chafing against obstacles and so forth. Wind knots must also be avoided, since they weaken the strength of the nylon severely. Once nylon has been stretched, which will occur if you catch a few fish, it loses strength. Although it may seem unnecessarily expensive, dispense with a leader after a day's fishing. Wear and weakness in a leader is not necessarily visible to the human eye. By all means leave the thick nylon collar attached to the fly-line between fishing trips, but never attach the leader itself until you get there. After all, until you can assess the conditions, and decide what kind of fly or technique to use, you cannot possibly decide either on the length or the strength of the leader.

OTHER ITEMS OF TACKLE

We parked the car and walked down the pathway to a wooded creek. So this was Rutland water. Morning mists rolled out over the water and water fowl splashed along the surface before take-off — it was magical. A fish rose almost eerily and my excitement became almost religious as I stood before this stillwater fly-fisherman's mecca. Then I saw him. . . .

Carrying an array of rods, staggering under the weight of an over-full tackle box, and almost dragging a green fishing umbrella behind him, a worried-looking fat man struggled to the waterside. His rods fell on to the ground in a sickening clatter, the tackle box collapsed in a rattling heap and every self-respecting rainbow and brownie bolted for cover in a state of terror. Oblivious and undeterred, this son of Isaac assembled the sections of his umbrella, opened the huge green canopy and rammed it into the ground. Then, with the furtive glance of a mating peacock, he assembled a gigantic landing net, waded carelessly into the water like a hippo, and sank the net into the muddy ooze. With a sigh of relief and a victorious belch he waded back for his rods, safe in the knowledge that his territory had been staked out, claimed and defined. I didn't approach him — perhaps he might only growl, but I had a sneaking suspicion that he might also bite!

So much for the sophistication of the modern reservoir fisherman. Of course, this man was by no means typical, yet he was similar enough to many of the fishermen whom I encountered gracing the banks of this lovely water. The stillwater dry-fly fisherman must not load himself up with gear, or shackle himself to a single fishing location. He must travel light and be prepared to move around in search of his quarry. At times, he must stalk his fish as stealthily as the most cautious of river fishermen, for there are times when fish will be discovered rising quite near to the bank. At such times they are likely to be caught only by those who practise a very careful approach, and such an approach is only possible if you are unburdened with extraneous gear. Accordingly, I believe that an essential piece of equipment (or rather clothing) is a fly-fisherman's waistcoat, or, as the Americans call it, a wading vest.

Excellent waistcoats are supplied by a number of specialist companies, whilst cheaper imported waistcoats, though less well made, will serve the same purpose. I possess a very cheap waistcoat which has been ripped many times, stitched up with nylon thread and will undoubtedly rip again. Nevertheless, though by no means elegant, I am peculiarly attached to it and it possesses all the pockets I require. At the back, there is a large pocket for storing light waterproof clothing and a similar pocket on the inside. On the outside (which zips together), there are two zips which lead to additional, capacious inner pockets. There are also two large outer pockets and a series of eight smaller pockets. The waistcoat is completed with a sheepskin pad, for drying flies, and a 'D' ring on which a collapsible landing net may be clipped. The waistcoat is light and comfortable and capable of carrying all the articles which are required for mobile stillwater dry-fly fishing. It may, in fact, be useful to consider the contents of my waistcoat pockets.

In one of the large inner pockets I usually carry spare reel spools with spare floating lines of different sizes, thus allowing me to adjust my techniques to the conditions at any given time. Other pockets contain fly-boxes, a cast wallet, small spools of nylon line, scissor-pliers, a marrow spoon or hand pump, a priest, a carborundum stone for sharpening hooks, tins of line grease, a container of fuller's earth mixture (when sinking the line during nymph fishing), aerosol containers of dry-fly spray and polarised spectacles. These are all my necessary items and I find no need for any other items which are advertised in the angling press as being essential.

Fly-boxes are a matter for personal choice and budget, and it must be stated that I am often guilty of carrying too many boxes and too many flies. However, when travelling light, it is best to carry only one box with all the necessary dry- and wet-flies contained within. For this purpose, my ideal fly-box is a lightweight metal box which has sixteen spring-lid compartments for dry-flies and foam pad on which I carry a selection of nymphs and wet-flies. The spring lids are invaluable on windy days. Cheaper plastic boxes usually possess a number of compartments making it possible to carry a nice selection of dry-flies: however, as soon as the single lid is lifted on a windy day, it is not unusual for the entire contents of the box to be borne off on the wind.

I always carry a leather cast wallet which contains grooved plastic discs holding made up casts in various lengths and strengths. Changing the casts then becomes a reasonably straightforward matter, although it is often the case that only the point needs replacing (either through damage or reduction in length because of the continual changing of flies) and for this purpose I carry a number of small spools of nylon in various breaking strains. Recently, an ideal spool dispenser has come on to the market which will hold several spools and prevent them from tangling in the pocket.

A pair of scissor-pliers is useful and there are a number of reliable models on the market. This implement will not only enable the angler to cut nylon, but will also allow him to remove flies from the mouths of fish without damaging either the fly, or the fish (if you intend to return it to the water).

A 'priest' is also a necessary item because it is only fair to despatch a sporting fish with alacrity and without undue suffering. Many of the priests which I have examined in tackle shops have heads which are far too light: my priest was made for me by a friend and, being made of brass, it is heavy enough to kill any fish with two sharp blows to the head. One 'priest' available today possesses a handle which doubles as a marrow spoon.

The marrow spoon is a very long-bowled scoop which is pushed into the fish's mouth, twisted around and then withdrawn again. When it is withdrawn, it contains the entire stomach contents of the fish, making it possible to define the exact food form which the fish has been feeding upon. Ideally, when a fish has been scooped, the stomach contents should be placed in a little white dish containing a small amount of water, where the insects will divide and become clearly defined (unless they have already been partially or entirely digested by the fish's stomach juices). Suitable white plastic dishes may be purchased from the artist's supply shops. An alternative to the marrow scoop is a small hand pump which operates according to the principal of a syringe.

An invaluable item of equipment (though perhaps even more important when nymph and wet-fly fishing) is a hook sharpening stone which may be purchased very cheaply. Many commercially tied flies and many hooks supplied for fly-tying, possess rather blunt points which do not purchase a good hold on the fish when you tighten into it. Hooks must be sharpened to a very fine point before use, and must be inspected during use (particularly after the capture of a fish) for signs of damage. Damaged, blunt and bent hook points will only result in the loss of a fish. An equally important item in my wading vest is a pair of polarised spectacles which will not only cut out glare when trying to locate the fish, but also allow you to concentrate on the floating fly without undue eye-strain. Continual concentration on a stillwater dry-fly can easily result in headaches, a subsequent loss of concentration and loss of fish.

Finally, it is essential that the stillwater dry-fly fisherman carries a supply of good floatants both for the cast and for the fly itself. As far as line greases are concerned, several good line greases are available although I am rather conservative and tend to stick to my old traditional brands.

There are various ways of ensuring that the dry-fly floats well, although the principle matter of importance is to tie them yourself using buoyant materials, light wire hooks and stiff cock hackles. However, the fly will have to be annointed with *something* since the construction of the fly and continual false-casting (to rid it of moisture) will not maintain permanent floatation. Various oils have long been available, yet the most convenient method is to spray the fly with a modern aerosol floatant.

Our equipment is completed with a good quality folding net which may be clipped onto the waistcoat ring (the kind of net which may be 'flicked' into position) and comfortable waders. Naturally, I have argued that wading ought to be kept to a minimum although it will be necessary on occasions. However, when stalking fish, it is sometimes necessary to crouch on wet grass which necessitates the use of comfortable thigh waders unless we wish to suffer damp trousers and a touch of rheumatism. Try to purchase a pair of waders which are as light as possible, since stillwater dry-fly fishing will demand an amount of walking around, and if you have to wade over stones, make sure that the waders have hob-nails in their soles.

Now I will deliver my last piece of advice concerning equipment, with devastating hypocrisy. Always check that all the necessary items needed for a day's fishing are stored in the pockets of your waistcoat before you set off from your car for the long walk to the other side of the reservoir; indeed, check before you leave home. It is always a good idea to keep each item in the same pocket for each expedition so that you can select what you need as quickly and efficiently as possible.

Why did I refer to hypocrisy? . . . It was a lovely summer evening and the reservoir displayed just a hint of a ripple in places. I set up my rod and threaded line through the rod rings as I viewed the numerous circles of rising fish with eager interest. Pond Olives were hatching prolifically, taking to the air like miniature helicopters and a dry Greenwell's Glory seemed an obvious choice. Having unzipped my waistcoat pocket, I plunged my hand inside to grab my fly-box . . . it wasn't there!

3

A note on casting

This is simply a note on casting. To say that I am not an expert at casting a fly would be an understatement. I cannot cast phenomenal distances and only occasionally have I ever shot the entire length of a weight-forward fly-line through the rod rings. Nevertheless, this does not worry me particularly and in some respects my lack of distance-casting has been a positive advantage. For one thing, my inability to cast at a distance inclined me towards more delicate forms of fishing such as the traditional wet-fly, the nymph and the dry-fly whilst it also taught me to seek accuracy as a compensation for loss of distance.

My deficiencies in casting do not qualify me to offer much instruction on casting although there are a number of points which I believe worth making. Should you wish to improve and develop your casting then you would be well recommended to seek out a reputable instructor or study any of the books which provide instruction. Three books spring readily to mind − T. C. Ivens's *Stillwater Fly-Fishing* (although Ivens concentrates on distance), F. M. Halford's *Dry-Fly Fishing* and Charles Ritz's *Fly-Fisher's Life*.

Whatever your personal standard of casting, do not seek to make distance your top priority when stillwater dry-fly fishing. The top priorities are accuracy and delicacy of presentation, and no matter what anybody else says, these qualities are only achieved consistently with reasonably light double-tapered floating lines. On windy days, however, a weight-forward line may be called for, and under such conditions, delicacy will not be quite so important.

You must try to land a floating fly with real delicacy in order to avoid putting down feeding fish. Delicacy and distance do not go together easily. Although distance casting may allow you to reach more rises, it is always more difficult to 'hit' fish at a distance unless you use a longer rod which will allow you to pick a longer length of line off the water more easily. When you attempt to reach longer distances you will inevitably forsake the double-tapered line for a weight-forward one, and then perhaps even abandon that in favour of a floating shooting taper or head. As you move away from the double-tapered line you move away from delicacy of presentation, whilst making it increasingly difficult to set the hook home.

While the weight-forward line is difficult enough to pick off the water when 'striking' (because the greatest weight is displaced at a distance from the angler) the backing of a shooting head makes that line even more unwieldy to pick up.

As far as I am concerned, the shooting head is certainly out when dry-fly fishing. Naturally, by forsaking distance in the cast, the dry-fly fisherman must in some way compensate. First of all, the increased delicacy and accuracy will be a great compensation. Secondly, compensation for not being able to reach trout rising further out will be achieved by moving around cautiously in order to discover fish feeding within a reasonable range. Stalking, in other words. Thus, mobility will counterbalance distance. Finally, the greatest bonus gained by restricting casting distance will come in the form of a higher proportion of hooked fish to rises.

When fishing at any distance up to 20 yards, I find that I hook the optimum number of fish; up to 25 yards and the proportion is reasonable (even then, only about 50 per cent) — beyond 25 yards and many rises will be missed, even if they are reasonably slow and leisurely. Clearly I do not subscribe to the school of thought which puts distance

A dull day and a good wave. On this day a large red palmer did the trick.

above all other casting considerations when fishing on stillwaters: that philosophy best suits the use of the lure and attractor. If you are used to double-haul casting in order to achieve distance for your lure fishing, you may find it difficult to readjust your casting. The dry-fly, intended to float, simply cannot be presented in the same manner as a lure intended to sink — surface disturbance does not matter in lure fishing but it does with the dry-fly. At first, the shorter cast in dry-fly fishing may frustrate you and you may well feel yourself reaching out for distance and thus marring presentation: resist the temptation.

Before casting a dry-fly for the first time in earnest, practise casting on the lawn. Simply tie a piece of red wool to the end of the cast and try landing it as delicately as possible on a variety of targets, at a variety of distances. When a degree of proficiency has been achieved, then you are ready to fish the dry-fly and give it a fair trial. Too often, I have seen anglers slapping down the fly-line when trying the dry-fly during a rise, then blaming the dry-fly technique for their lack of success, rather than their own low casting standards. The dry-fly only succeeds when a suitable artificial is cast to the surface feeding trout (or other trout likely to take the floating fly) and when the presentation of the fly is of a reasonably high standard.

While distance certainly isn't one of the stillwater dry-fly fisherman's overwhelming objectives, a flexibility of casting technique certainly ought to be. It is not simply a matter of chucking out a lure (which may be weighted appropriately for windy conditions) and then leisurely retrieving it. It is a matter of presenting a lightweight dry-fly in a variety of difficult environments and with a need to cast, re-cast and change direction sometimes with remarkable rapidity. In truth, I am an intuitive kind of caster likely to make up casting techniques on the spot and as conditions dictate. I am not an instructor and, therefore, cannot hope to teach you how to perform all the casts which will become necessary in the course of your fishing. Nevertheless, it may be worthwhile if I outline very briefly a number of casting techniques which ought to be learned and practised by the aspiring dry-fly fisherman.

Unfortunately, too many modern fly-fishermen tend to plunge into the sport without serving an adequate apprenticeship. Instead of experiencing a variety of fishing styles, they are likely to start with the lure, succeed in catching fish and thus stick with this method. Accordingly, the demands on casting are negligible and the result is that the majority of stillwater anglers are only able to perform the conventional overhead cast and the double-haul, which is simply a variation of it. It follows, therefore, that faced with the necessity of casting in front of a variety of obstructions, they will simply take to the water and wade out as far as possible. The following notes simply offer a guide to the basic techniques which need to be mastered in order to improve our efficiency as dry-fly fishermen.

Assuming that the angler is reasonably accomplished in conventional casting and used to casting heavy lures with heavy tackle, under windy conditions, what happens when he turns to the light dry-fly and tries to drive it into a stiff breeze? Undoubtedly, the line piles up in a heap and our angler stalks off to find a bank from which fishing is possible with the wind blowing from behind. This need not be the case. When driving a dry-fly into a breeze, the 'downward cut' cast may be used. This cast (in its classic form) is described in great detail within the pages of Halford's *Dry-Fly Fishing* and I propose only to outline my own version of this cast in brief. The object is to cast in the normal overhead manner, ensuring that the back cast is high and that the line gathers sufficient momentum. Then, move smoothly into the forward thrust and as the rod moves forward of the angler at an angle of forty-five degrees, a further sharp thrust is imparted. This movement is best described as a 'downward cut' since the rod cuts sharply downwards in a quick and positive motion. The added momentum results in a quick unfurling of the line which will force it into the wind and keep it reasonably low so that the wind does not lift it upwards. This would result in a loss of power and distance. Unfortunately, this is a difficult cast to perform and demands a great deal of practice and impeccable timing. When fishing into the wind, it is also necessary to shorten the leader in order to allow it to unfurl correctly and straighten out, rather than fall in a heap.

Alternatively, when conditions are rough, you may cast with the rod parallel to the water (in a lateral plane rather than a vertical one) so that the backward and forward thrusts remain low. When you cast in this manner, the line is not caught by the full force of the wind. In addition, the line may be switched along the bank rather than backwards if space is restricted. This form of cast (sometimes referred to as the 'underhand cast') is also useful if overhanging trees prevent you from holding the rod vertically. If such casts are not developed, then lucrative fishing positions often have to be given a miss.

Bankside vegetation often poses an obvious casting imposition. One solution is to choose a longer rod, although I am not generally in favour of long rods for normal fishing − they lack delicacy of presentation when you need it most. The alternative is to turn your conventional nine-footer into a longer rod by extending the casting arm vertically, thus enabling you to throw a very high back cast. At the same time, by extending the arm as high as possible and by inducing a high line velocity, a greater distance may be achieved when needed. Traditionally, this form of casting is termed 'steeple casting'; it may also be of use when fishing from the dam wall.

There are many good fishing locations in front of a line of trees; sometimes you may fish such areas from a boat, but boats are not always available. Yet if you do fish in front of the trees, from the bank, the 'dry-switch' or 'roll cast' may be employed. This is achieved by drawing the line towards you on the water and then by casting the fly with a kind of roll outwards, off the water. First attempts will undoubtedly be clumsy until the technique has been mastered, but then it becomes invaluable. The 'roll cast' may also be used to change direction without the need for a back cast.

Changing direction with alacrity is one of the most important attributes of the dry-fly fisherman's casting technique, particularly during a rise when you may wish to cover several fish quite quickly. A quick change of direction in the cast is often an essential part of fishing the dry-fly from a boat. Although the 'roll cast' may be used, a simpler technique is possible if space permits. Imagine, you have just covered a rise, but no take has materialised. A fish shows ten yards to the right. You simply raise the line from the water in a very smooth draw, gradually gathering pace until the line is thrown up into the backcast. Then make a forward cast and with a flick of the rod change the direction of the cast towards the second rise. If line needs to be extended, false casting may be necessary (yet it must be kept to a minimum) and the false cast must come before the switch of direction. Though it often is performed quite quickly, the procedure of switching casting direction must ultimately be very smooth and controlled. As soon as the angler becomes anxious and panics into switching direction too quickly (in order to hit the ring of the rise) the cast will be bungled and the fish scared. Dry-fly fishing is exciting yet the excitement has to be controlled by a restrained approach.

When you are fishing from the bank and want to move along in order to cover a fish which has shown itself, a great deal of time will be wasted if you have to reel in and then start stripping off line again having reached the new casting position. A reel with a multiplying action may save a little time but that is only a marginal consideration. It is better simply to draw back the line and coil as much of the slack line as possible in the left hand (if you are a right-handed caster). Then move along the bank, false casting as you go so that you keep the line in the air. The false casts must be over land rather than water; you don't want to scare the fish. When the new casting position has been reached, you are ready to go straight into the cast with little time wasted. Once you make the cast, restrict the number of false casts and try to shoot as much of the spare line as you can.

These are just some of the casts which may be performed and, since necessity is the mother of invention, you will undoubtedly develop unusual casting techniques of your own. That is why I began by saying that my casting was in many ways intuitive. On occasions, because certain fishing locations have been so restricted and awkward, I have resorted to casting left-handed although I am normally a right-handed caster. I have even had to push my rod through a space between bushes and simply dangle a fly above a fish, without even an inch of the fly-line leaving the reel — this, however, could hardly be termed a cast. However, it did demand a high degree of stealth, thus illustrating how stalking your quarry may well be as important as your ability to cast — and sometimes even more so.

4

Strategy for locating and catching surface feeding fish

It was only a small reservoir and the brown trout rarely achieved a pound in weight, but they were game fighters and for the past few weeks had come readily to the floating fly. It was magical, so magical in fact, that I had left home before the FA Cup Final had ended in order to get there for the commencement of the evening rise. The best rises occurred at the head of the reservoir where a stone-strewn brook gurgled over a weedbed as it entered the impoundment and I strolled lazily yet nervously along the bank to this location. A sheep scurried away in front of me, the bilberry bushes and bracken rustling and crackling as it made for the hillside and safety. Martins darted to and fro after flies, occasionally dipping against the mirrored surface of the water and breaking the perfect reflection of the rugged granite hillsides which surrounded the valley. In the distance, the odd fish rose, and the splosh of its rise seemed to take minutes to reach me as if, in the stillness, time had stopped.

Eventually, I scrambled down an embankment and began to tackle up on a dried up moss bed, threading the silk line through the rod rings as patiently as I could. A few more fish began to show and I greased the line and leader before knotting on a roughly tied Blue Dun which had caught several fish during the last two weeks. Slowly, I crept towards the water's edge and worked out line ready for the first cast. A fish had been showing methodically in a circular feeding path and the very first cast almost miraculously landed the fly on target and only a second after the fish had disturbed the satin-smooth surface. Even for a badly dressed artificial, the fly cocked nicely and floated perkily as I tensed myself in readiness for the inevitable rise. . . . The fish disappeared and the fly fell over forlornly as a gentle breeze lifted it to one side.

Perhaps surprised, and certainly a little disappointed, I moved along the bank to cover another fish. By this time, there were so many apparent rises that the odd refusal did not seem to matter at all. Several fish rose in a line, no more than ten yards from the bank, yet a little further along. I dare not scare them so I inched along and knelt on a gravel spit to make my cast. This time, the fly was again refused although the fish kept on feeding as if it had not existed at all. On the fourth cast, a smallish fish splashed at the fly but did not take and I began to believe that my luck had run out. With an almost stupid naïvety I thought that it might have been some kind of judgement from above and almost began to plead with the deity for a rise: no rise came.

On the far side of the reservoir another angler had begun to work methodically along the bank and as his line slashed repeatedly across the water I thought with complacent amusement about his negative chances of success. I began to wonder who had won the Cup Final: then I noticed my brother angler bending forward with his net as a fish splashed around just out of his reach.

After a quiet smoke of my pipe, I decided to anoint my fly with oil. Suppressing my increasing sense of frustration and injustice, further casts were made but without any success, although a myopic swallow almost mistook my fly for the real thing before swooping away disdainfully and leaving a tiny white deposit dissolving in the water. Eventually, I retrieved my fly violently and ensnared it in the blade of a bullrush. As I tugged to free the fly, the rush bent sharply over and the fly disappeared underwater before tearing away. The bullrush bent upright again, its greenery flapping over in acknowledgement of the battle. The fly was by this time thoroughly wet through and my spirits

Early one morning in May. A fish rises only two yards from the bank. Stalk it and fish fine and far off.

were dampened beyond belief. With an optimistic belief in the 'last-cast-syndrome' I flicked the fly out into the reservoir as a prelude to my journey home.

The sodden Blue Dun sank gently. There was a swirl and I tightened instinctively into the miracle of a hooked fish. As it turned out, it couldn't have weighed much more than eight ounces – but it was a fish. With a power of logical analysis, some way beneath the perception of a Descartes or a Spinoza, I reasoned that if a drowned fly could work once, it might work again. Accordingly, I moved back to my original casting position, squeezed the fly gently in the water and made a cast of consummate indelicacy. Ironically, no sooner had the fly begun to sink that the cast juddered and I had struck into a second fish, marginally larger that the first. And so it went on . . . .

As the sun slid behind the dark shadow of the Pennine range, a happy angler began to walk home with a limit bag of golden brown trout. On an evening of apparent promise for the dry-fly, a sinking fly had succeeded in achieving the impossible. Without knowing it, I had discovered the importance of the nymph and I have no doubt that you are questioning the relevance of such an anecdote in a book on the stillwater dry-fly. Believe me, it is certainly relevant because it emphasises the difference between appearance and reality. To me, those fish had given all the appearance of rises to floating adult flies, yet, quite clearly, they must in reality have been feeding just beneath the surface. One may fish the dry-fly at all times if so wished, but one will only fish it effectively when trout are prepared to feed on surface flies. To ensure whether they are, or are not, one must read rise forms like a sleuth will read finger prints. In my days of innocence, any surface disturbance produced by a fish would trigger off the use of dry-flies: how wrong I was.

Almost paradoxically, one of the first principles of stillwater dry-fly fishing is to understand when not to use the dry-fly. Stillwater dry-fly fishing is perhaps most commonly discredited when it is used at the wrong time and found to be wanting: from such an experience, unfortunate generalisations are drawn. As we have considered at an earlier stage, the absence of any form of rise does not necessarily signify that the dry-fly will prove fruitless and I have had too many successes with the dry-fly, even when the surface of the lake has seemed to be as barren as a desert, to believe that fish will only take floating artificials when they are actually feeding on floating naturals. Conversely, and with an equal degree of importance, the dry-fly will not always succeed when fish are apparently rising. It may seem rather obvious to use the dry-fly when fish show themselves at the surface and the air is full of winged sedges or olives, but it just could be that the fish are feeding upon nymphs or pupae so near to the surface that the disturbance is hardly distinguishable from a conventional rise form. Therefore, our first consideration should be an analysis of those 'rise' forms which only signify subaqueous feeding.

The first 'negative rise' as far as the dry-fly is concerned, is what I have come to term 'the Polaris missile rise', which is an exceptionally dramatic event often performed by large rainbow trout. All of a sudden, the surface is shattered as a huge fish shoots right up into the air and then flops with a nerve-tingling splash back into the water.

I was once told by an old fisherman: 'You see, they do that to get rid of fish lice. You can't catch 'em when they're jumping.'

'Oh,' I said, suitably impressed and remembered his advice long enough to impart it to a good many other unsuspecting souls.

What began to sow the seeds of doubt, was the fact that none of the fish I had ever caught from that particular water had any lice on them. On the other hand, most of the trout I had taken from a small, stocked urban reservoir did show evidence of fish lice − yet I had never seen them jump so dramatically from the water. Why did they do it? A likely enough theory was that they rose very quickly from a deep position in order to secure a floating fly which their instinct told them was about to escape. Having risen from the depths with such momentum, it would only seem natural that the fish would carry on moving upwards through the surface film and into the air. Good, I had solved that one − until I began to flog such 'rises' with dry-flies to no effect at all. Perhaps that man had been right after all. Eventually, however, by the process of *reductio ad absurdum* I managed to catch one of these spectacularly rising trout − on a nymph. To be precise, I caught it on a leaded nymph which was allowed to sink almost to the bottom and was then raised quite rapidly towards the surface with a pull of the line and a raising of the rod. As far as I can now ascertain, that seems to be the solution: trout which rise like 'Polaris missiles' are chasing ascending nymphs to the surface, where they engulf them and then rise out of the water with the momentum of their initial efforts. I might easily be proved wrong yet I am reasonably satisfied with this solution and conclude that this 'rise form' does not indicate the use of the dry-fly. However, it is impossible to claim that the dry-fly will never work under such circumstances although it has certainly never worked for me.

There are other 'rise' forms which seem to signify the use of a nymph or wet-fly rather than the use of the dry-fly. One obvious sign that trout are not feeding on floating flies is when they rush around near the surface and produce evident bow-waves. This normally occurs in the shallows and is a product of trout herding fry into a small area and then rushing in on them: it is often the case that several fish will be feeding together in the same area. The initial attack may result in a number of fry being caught although trout often show a preference for the weaker members of the shoal who have difficulty in escaping, or for the fry which are damaged by the initial attack. These fish may be devoured in a more leisurely manner which, therefore, allows the trout to expend a minimum of energy.

Such a feeding pattern is usually encountered towards the back-end of the season when fry seem to be most numerous in the shallows and have gained in size from the egg stage (often, they will be coarse fish fry which have hatched from eggs shed some time between March and June). Bow-waving trout are usually tackled with attractors (such as the Butcher, Alexandra, Peter Ross and Teal and Silver) or with lures (such as the Baby Doll, Sinfoil's Fry, White Lure and Polystickle), yet there are many occasions when this style of fishing does not seem to work and produces an amount of frustration.

For some reason, conventional lure fishing techniques did not succeed very well with fry-feeding fish during the 1981 season and I was very interested to note that a number of enterprising individuals (not including myself, I must add) decided to give the dry-fly a chance and succeeded in catching fish. In general, large flies were used (such as large sedge patterns or palmer-dressed flies) and for some reason, the fry-feeding trout rose to them quite readily. Just why fish, and large ones at that, should rise to a floating fly when apparently preoccupied with large subaqueous items of food, I have no idea, but what this teaches us is that the dry-fly is *always* worth trying when other techniques fail. One word of warning, however, if you do have occasion to try a floating fly when fish are bow-waving, since they are feeding close in, exercise caution and try to stand well back from the water when you make your cast. Admittedly, 'bow-wavers' are feeding in a rather more indelicate fashion than usual and tend to be somewhat rash, but they can be scared and particularly by injudicious wading.

Bow-waves are produced by trout moving in quick darts and must certainly not be confused with gentler V-shapes produced by fish cruising quite steadily near the surface. Such 'rise' forms are normally produced by trout feeding upon a plentiful supply of minute life forms – perhaps plankton, perhaps tiny pupae in the surface film and perhaps emerging and floating flies. Trout sometimes cruise along in this manner when feeding on small gnats, minute adult biting midges and the dun and spinner stages of *caënidae*. The tiny caënis mayflies have a very rapid final life cycle and can metamorphose from mature nymph, to dun, to spinner in a very short time. As a result, it is quite possible for fish to feed on duns and spinners simultaneously. On some stillwaters, the resident species of *caënidae* tend to 'hatch' into duns and change into spinners during the night, so that it is not uncommon to find trout mopping up spent female spinners in the early daylight.

When trout are cruising and taking tiny flies they often browse along just under the surface with their mouths almost continually open rather in the manner of a basking shark feeding on plankton. All that exists in their feeding path is engulfed and under such conditions they are feeding blindly since their window of vision is restricted so near the surface. If you can estimate the feeding path, and can drop your fly just in front of them, it may well be taken along with a host of naturals. However, although you may catch such a fish on a tiny floating fly, in all honesty you haven't caught it by an imitative approach since it did not make an individual scrutiny of your artificial. Further, under such circumstances, the fish may easily brush against your fly and become foul hooked − perhaps even in the eye! Fishing tiny artificials is a more satisfactory ethical method when trout are feeding on *individual* naturals and are revealing themselves with sipping rise forms. More of this at a later stage.

At the moment, our principal concern is to understand the restrictions imposed upon the dry-fly by our interpretation of rise forms and those 'rises' which generally signify nymphing trout must be understood. A characteristic of certain trout feeding on nymphs, and particularly upon chironomid pupae, is the 'head-and-tail' rise form, although this rise form is sometimes occasioned by floating food forms such as snails and ephemeropteran spinners. Naturally, it is important to define the food form before deciding upon the approach and if you do suspect snails or spinners, there should be a number of such naturals floating around for you to observe. Spinners will necessitate the dry-fly technique and a greased cast although it is important that the fly rests right in the surface film and does not float high on the water.

A number of floating snail patterns have been devised and on waters such as Rutland, where snails are not only plentiful but also a favoured diet of the fish, it is wise to carry copies with you. At certain times of the season, snails seem to migrate to the surface and although trout do feed on them at other times, this presents us with a perfect chance to use the dry-fly technique even if the pattern is in itself a little unusual and unconventional. A simple enough pattern is produced by attaching a suitably shaped cork to a size 10 hook and then winding partially stripped peacock herl quite roughly over it. A clipped down black cock hackle may be added in front of the 'body' in order to represent the snail's 'pad'.

However, 'head-and-tail' rises to floating food forms are not as common as they are to fish feeding on pupae and emergent nymphs.

The 'head-and-tail' rise is produced as a trout's head breaks the surface and then goes under again as the back arches over in a roll — the trout disappearing with a flip of the tail. Although the floating fly or snail just might occasion such a rise form, it is normally to be associated with trout feeding on nymphs and pupae and a nymphing technique is generally called for. Trout rising in this manner are often feeding in a preoccupied manner and, if they are feeding on nymphs and pupae, the dry-fly is unlikely to achieve very much success. A more likely offering would be a midge pupa pattern fished under the surface on a greased cast and a floating line. I have known times when trout have revealed themselves in 'head-and-tail' rises only to switch to more conventional rise forms once the 'hatch' has been well underway: this suggests a change in the feeding pattern and a switch to the dry-fly since the fish have probably changed their attentions from nymphs or pupae to adult fly. Why such changes in feeding pattern occur is sometimes hard to explain, particularly when under almost identical conditions on another occasion, the fish will look at nothing other than the mature pupal stage.

'Head-and-tail' rises also occur when trout are feeding on the intermediate stage between pupa (or nymph) and fully-fledged adult fly; that is, they become preoccupied with the insect at the very stage of emergence. In a sense, this is a matter which falls half-way between conventional nymphing and dry-fly tactics and as such, it is often either misunderstood or ignored completely by the angler. Thus, although the use of 'emergers' may not strictly come under the provinces of the dry-fly it is worthy of consideration in the present book and I will devote a certain amount of attention to it at a later stage.

The next 'rise' form which I must deal with isn't really a rise form at all since trout which produce it are certainly feeding below the surface and are unlikely to break the surface film with any part of their bodies. This sign of feeding fish is most definitely a sign of fish feeding on active pupae and nymphs. Both pupae and nymphs, though perhaps inert just prior to the act of emergence, are often very active so that trout which feed on them must also move quite quickly in order to catch them. As a result of the quick turns and movements of the fish, water is displaced at the surface in the form of a 'bulge' or 'boil' which is easily distinguished from conventional rises to adult flies even if the beginner may initially confuse the two. The strength or definition of the 'boil' will give some indication of the feeding depth whilst trout feeding very close to the surface will create a distinct humping or bulging, which in rougher water often appears as a swirl.

Although it may be easy to pinpoint the whereabouts of a trout feeding close to the surface in this manner, it is a little more difficult to detect if the 'boil' is caused by a fish lying deeper down since the whirl of water will be largely dissipated before it reaches the surface. A fish feeding a couple of feet below the surface may only provide the slightest evidence of its activity particularly if there is something of a wave on the water. Under such conditions, look for a saucer-like calm zone within the rough and broken water. Incidentally, I feel that I must clarify one point. Although nymphs of the *Baëtis* group of mayflies are known to be very active swimmers (and were referred to by Oliver Kite as 'agile darters') the more laboured swimmers of other mayfly groups are also active prior to emergence and, therefore, are capable of inducing boiling 'rises'. Equally, although chironomid pupae may hang vertically suspended in the surface film prior to emergence, they can also wriggle quite rapidly in a lateral plane and thus demand more energy on the behalf of pursuing trout. Thus, midge pupae do produce boiling 'rise' forms which thus makes nonsense of the theory that midge pupae always ought to be fished statically or worked as slowly as possible. Pupae fished rather more rapidly in little darts and spurts do catch fish and there is nothing particularly unnatural in fishing them in this manner.

I do not propose to deal with the capture of bulging and boiling trout (I have covered appropriate techniques in *The Art of the Wet Fly*) because my essential concern is with the dry-fly, which is generally of little use when trout are feeding in this way. However, I will make one exception to this rule. In rougher conditions swirls sometimes appear when there is a good wave on the water. These are produced by fish feeding subaqueously on adult flies which have become drowned by the rough water. If fish *are* feeding on drowned flies, rather than nymphs and pupae, it is usual to see the occasional splashy rise form as well as a boil or swirl. Such a rise will be occasioned by fish which pick off the odd insect as it floats along at the surface prior to being swamped. Under such conditions it pays to try a large buoyant fly such as a palmer and, since visibility may be a little poor, a bi-visible is a good bet. The bi-visible is simply a conventional palmer fly (such as one possessing a red seal's fur body, red-brown cock hackle wound all down the body and ribbed with oval gold tinsel) with a light coloured, or even white, front hackle. This makes the fly far easier to see.

Let us now turn to the rise forms which signal a more effective use of the dry-fly although by no means an exclusive use of it. In the circumstances I am about to describe, a wet-fly will sometimes catch fish just as easily as a dry-fly, yet it is only natural that in this book I should deal exclusively with the dry-fly. I have made this point simply in order to emphasise the fact that an angler does often have a choice as to which method he wishes to employ.

Having already made some reference to 'splashy' rise forms, I will attempt to expand this theme by means of my first consideration. During rougher conditions, most surface rise forms are likely to be splashy, rather than delicate. However, this is not simply a matter of the effect produced by a wave hitting the head of a rising fish, it is also likely to be related to the size of the food form which occasions the rise in the first place. Small insects rarely hatch under rough conditions, I imagine because they would be swamped before they have had chance to dry their wings and take off from the water. Therefore, rough water hatches on stillwaters are only likely to involve large flies such as the Mayfly (*E. danica* or *E. vulgata*) or large sedges, and are sometimes not 'hatches' at all but involve many terrestrial creatures such as moths or crane flies which are blown on to the water. If splashy rises do occur during conditions of wave, it is often a good bet to use a large floating artificial pattern, the precise identity of the pattern being a matter of selection according to our observation of the natural insects in evidence at any given time.

Although the kind of 'dry-fly' rise form, described so far, is associated with windy conditions, similar rise forms may occur when the water is quite calm or when there is little more than a ripple on the surface of lake or reservoir. What we are considering is the slashing rise of a large or reasonably sized fish which we must not confuse with the youthful and somewhat unnecessarily energetic rises of small fish who often splash vigorously at anything. The slash take of a good fish is induced only by floating insects which themselves produce a surface disturbance, either as they struggle to free themselves from the surface film after emergence or in the case of terrestrials, as they attempt to avoid drowning. In the evening, sedges skitter along the surface thus creating a wake or disturbance which trout find very attractive, whilst the evening is also the time when fluttering moths may fall on to the water. As these insects struggle against the grip of the surface film, especially in calmer water, a series of vibrations are apparent both to trout and angler alike. Large mayflies may also induce slash takes, while at different times during the season struggling terrestrials such as daddy-longlegs, hawthorn flies and drone flies may be seen buzzing and struggling when blown on to the surface of the lake. Even more outlandish terrestrial creatures may be responsible for this kind of rise form and I know of one little bay in a reservoir, surrounded by long grass, where high winds will deposit various beetles and grasshoppers on to the water. At such times, the water may almost explode with dramatic rises.

The common feature of all insects referred to above is that they are not only large, but likely to struggle violently or awkwardly or move quickly on the surface of a stillwater. Trout are attracted to them by *movement* and this triggers off the kind of violent rise form which we have depicted. I have no doubt that trout also react instinctively in this manner because the movement suggests to them that the creature might soon escape and be lost forever.

For our purposes, when using the dry-fly to combat such rise forms, standard hackled and winged patterns are of little real value because they offer little impression of movement, and if we do try to work them, they will become drowned and less effective. A palmer-dressed fly (so long as it is dressed with good, stiff cock hackles) is not only a good floater, which will stand twitching across the surface, it also possesses a good impression of movement even when it is quite still − this is because of the pattern of surface disturbance produced by the many hackle points which pierce the surface film. The observations, on palmer-dressed flies, made by the great G. E. M. Skues are as true today as they ever were and there is nothing simply old-fashioned about the palmer fly even if they were in use as long ago as 1651. Skues observed:

> A good deal of cheap scorn has been wasted upon the excessive number of legs given by fly dressers to the artificial fly to ensure flotation, particularly to the sedges. I would ask, how often is it that the hackles of flies are taken for legs? Many of the sedges flutter upon the surface; and may not the saying that they are dressed 'buzz' be wiser than it looks? The effect of fluttering and the effect of a bush of hackles may not look dissimilar to the trout. . . . . *The Way of a Trout with a Fly* (1921)

So, for this style of fishing we have palmer-flies, although other styles of dressings may be appropriate for this type of stillwater dry-fly fishing. However, the palmer, when dressed on light wire hooks is ideal on breezy evenings when we may invert a golden rule of dry-fly fishing and encourage our artificial to 'drag'. As our line is caught by the waves it will bow round and will pull the fly across the surface, particularly if we do not 'mend' the line and keep the rod point in a fixed position, which may well induce a dramatic take. Palmers also offer good representations of moths: in this case, the fly need only be twitched occasionally. However, another method is actually to *retrieve* the dry-fly along the surface and a number of more modern dressings are ideal for this type of fishing. Such a fly is the deer-hair sedge which is extremely buoyant and will remain afloat even when given this kind of treatment: the dressing of this fly is given in a later chapter.

When slash takes occur to daddy-longlegs, artificial imitations utilising plastic mayfly bodies are very buoyant although the natural insects merely struggle erratically so that a more conventional dressing, such as Richard Walker's Daddy-longlegs, will suffice if we only intend to 'work' the fly by twitching it with movements of the rod tip.

Large mayflies may be imitated with any of the dresssings provided in this book, whilst buoyant imitations of bluebottles, drone flies, beetles and grasshoppers will also be found at a later stage.

If we can fish from a boat when slash takes are in evidence, and particularly when there is a stiff breeze and a good wave on the water, then 'dapping' proves the ideal technique for catching fish feeding on large flies in this manner. Of course, as we discussed in the chapter on tackle, a long rod will be necessary and a floss line, or one of the new synthetic blow lines connected to the fly by a long nylon cast. Line is paid out into the wind and the rod is held almost upright so that maximum lift can be gained from the wind. The fly will settle on the waves and be lifted off again with each gust; all the movement necessary for full mobility and attraction will be supplied by the wind. At any time, often when least expected, large trout may rise dramatically and desperately to the fly as though afraid that the fly may escape its grasp. Undoubtedly many rises will be missed, yet this doesn't really seem to matter when the fishing is as exciting as this. Naturally, the technique will only work properly if the right kind of fly is used and the *wrong* kind of fly is a heavy one. Your artificial must be as light as possible and this will necessitate a light up-eyed mayfly hook which is long enough in the shank to provide for the construction of a large fly. The fly itself should be a bushy palmer-dressed artificial constructed out of top quality cock hackles which are quite long in the fibre; the kind of hackles which are often cast aside as useless when dressing more conventionally-sized flies. The best possible fly for dapping possesses no body as such – you simply rib the hackles in close turns all the way down the shank of the hook, which may well mean that several hackles are used in the construction of each fly.

In summary, as is evident from their rise form, trout which slash at natural flies have a feeding instinct which is generally triggered off by the movement of their prey. As a result, they too move quickly and will feed with less caution than is normally the case, but you will only catch them if your artificial behaves in the same manner as the natural. This is the one occasion when the movement of the fly may be just as significant to the dry-fly fisherman as it is to the wet-fly fisherman, nymph fisherman or lure stripper. When trout are feeding on darting nymphs, even the most realistic nymphal dressing that is simply allowed to sink slowly and pathetically to the bottom, will enjoy little success, and it makes no more sense to use a static dry-fly when the surface of the lake is alive with sedges skittering to and fro.

Slashing rises are common enough, but we will now turn to the most obvious of rise forms which are often associated with dry-fly fishing, even in the minds of non-anglers — I am referring to the conventional rise form which is so delightfully captured in the title of Vincent Marinaro's recent book: *In the Ring of the Rise*. I was about to say that we all recognise the widening concentric circles produced by a fish rising to a floating fly, and then I remembered one poor angler who I saw repeatedly casting to rings produced not by fish, but by expulsions of marsh gas from the bottom ooze.

The dimpled ring of the rise is certainly part of the poetry of trout fishing and it is almost synonymous with the dry-fly. In the middle of a lean and cold winter, when I begin to long for the warm evenings of summer, a picture evolves of a gently rippled lake, dappled with the rises of numerous fish. On such actual occasions, success may in truth be limited, for we do not always catch as many fish as we imagine that we will catch, or indeed ought to have caught; but the spirits are never low, the fish are there, we can actually see them. It is strange that we may also experience a greater sense of success from a brace of fish caught on dry-fly during an evening rise, than from a limit bag caught on wet-fly on a day when no fish actually showed themselves at the surface.

The rings produced by fish rising to floating flies differ in magnitude, not simply because the fish themselves differ in size (though this sometimes conditions the rise form) but essentially because the insects which induce rises either differ in size or are positioned differently in relation to the surface film. Thus, the rings produced by a fish rising to a reasonably sized mayfly will differ in scale from those produced by a fish rising to a tiny fly; the rise form of a fish engulfing a natural fly floating on the surface will differ from that produced by a fish rising to take a spent spinner lying flat in the surface film. Reading these rise forms will help us, to a degree, in detecting what insects trout are actually feeding upon, but there are always surprises. When the surface is flat calm, trout will sometimes rise to pupae lying motionless in the surface film in a manner which is largely indistinguishable from bona fide rises to floating flies.

The most common surface rise is what Skues describes as 'the kidney shaped double whorl' and is a rise to large or medium mayflies, stoneflies, hawthorn flies and many other species of insects. The form of the rise is a distinct circle (or whorl) within a circle and is accompanied at times by a noise which is by no means easy to define yet is recognised by all fly-fishermen. With experience, it is often possible to judge the size of the fish from the rise, for whatever sound is produced will vary in tone from bass to treble, and the higher the tone, the smaller the fish. The rise form of a good fish is a ring which appears almost leisurely and is accompanied by a solid slurp or 'splosh' whilst a small fish will often rise far more quickly and produce a noise which may be described onomatopoeically as a 'splish'. However, the ring of a rise may just as easily appear without any evident noise.

One very important factor is that small trout rise quickly and reject the fly quickly, necessitating a rapid reaction on the behalf of the angler, whilst larger fish rise in a leisurely manner so that a rapid 'strike' will only result in pulling the fly out of the fish's mouth. You have got to give a good fish time to turn downwards with the fly and the usual sequence when a fly has been taken is to recite something like 'one – two – three tighten!'

In general, it is perhaps wise to rehearse the leisurely tightening of the line so that if you do miss fish, you will only miss the smaller ones. The large ring rise form is usually a sign that trout are taking floating flies which are positioned above the surface film (rather than in it) and is a signal that the dry-fly must be used rather than the wet-fly. Indeed, if you observe this rise form very carefully it is often possible to detect the fish's nose breaking the surface film. On occasion, the whole mouth will be visible although trout often seem to open their mouths under the surface of the water, thus sucking in both water and the fly which means that they hardly need to break the surface. At such times, and particularly if the water is calm, a single bubble may appear in the middle of the widening circles of the rise form.

Although conventional rise forms may be produced by trout feeding on terrestrial insects, terrestrials are most likely to appear on the lake in windy conditions, thus resulting in a more splashy rise form. I normally associate the 'ring-rise' with trout feeding on aquatic insects and particularly the mayfly group (Lake Olives, Pond Olives, Sepia Duns, Claret Duns and the like) the smaller sedge flies, and adult Chironomid midges (which are taken rather more frequently than most anglers seem to believe). The precise insect which has conditioned any particular rise of this nature should be easily observed and thus copied accordingly with a dry-fly.

'Ring-rises' are also most likely to be produced when the water is calm or contains little more than a good ripple, for the medium-sized aquatic insects which induce this kind of feeding are only likely to hatch when they can guarantee an adequate chance of drying out their wings before flying off: rougher water would give them little chance and might easily drown them. It is not uncommon, therefore, to witness the sudden appearance of ring-rises when, on a day of stiffish breezes, a prolonged lull takes place. It is surprising how often the wind will settle down towards evening, and I suspect that 'evening rises' are not merely conditioned by temperature changes but also by equable conditions of calm water. On rough days, calm zones are often common parallel to, or at a slight angle to the bank, and hatches may be concentrated in this calm water thus making it an obvious area to explore with the dry-fly.

Fishing to conventional ring-rises is certainly a matter of 'matching the hatch', and hackled and winged floating patterns of a traditional design are excellent for our purposes if they are dressed on hooks of the right size and made up from materials of the correct colour. Suitable flies for the imitation of various insects are offered in Chapters 7 and 8.

Many people get by with a minimum of imitations, indeed, some people only use a single pattern. The beginner might do worse than adapt such a tactic since 'matching the hatch' is a matter of some sophistication and necessitates a collection of many different patterns of flies. As general purpose dry-flies, the Grey Duster, Greenwell's Glory and Blue Dun take a great deal of beating. You may do quite well by using only a single pattern (dressed in various sizes) throughout the season although there are times (particularly when there is a flat calm) when fish become ultra-selective and will scrutinise the fly carefully. A 'precise' imitation may, therefore, produce the required results whereas general patterns may only result in the fish rising short (that is, coming to the fly and then neglecting to take it at the very last moment). Whatever pattern is used, it must be presented correctly so that it cocks nicely on the water, and in the style of fishing, 'drag' is anathema. The fly is likeliest to be taken shortly after it has landed, for at this time, it will look its best and will not be affected by surface pull or the whims of the breeze. It is possible to say a great deal about presentation and tactics, but at this stage I would like to concentrate simply on the recognition of rise forms and leave tactical approaches and techniques to a time when I can concentrate on them more fully.

The next rise form is essentially little more than a scaled down version of the previous one and may best be described as a 'sucking' rise particularly since that kind of sound accompanies it. This is only present under calm conditions when trout are feeding on hatching insects of medium and small size or on the smaller species of terrestrials. It is a rise form which I generally associate with the use of the dry-fly, even when chironomid midges are hatching in profusion, although most anglers would probably approach this form with a team of pupae particularly when the banks are littered with the empty pupal shucks. Nevertheless, trout do feed on the floating adult chironomid and particularly if a hatch occurs under calm and humid conditions. At such times, the emergent adult fly may float on the water for some time

54

as it waits for its wings to dry out. The adult fly thus becomes an easy target for the trout and a Grey Duster, Blue Quill, Beacon Beige or any other good general dry-fly will often do the trick.

However, calm conditions can mean that the trout will become very selective so that a more precise chironomid dry-fly may become necessary. 'Sucking' rise forms are also produced by fish feeding on insects in the very act of emergence and I will devote an amount of attention to this matter in due course. Trout are most likely to feed on emerging flies when the process of emergence takes longest to complete, for example, when an oily scum reduces the surface tension which the fly uses to escape from its pupal case; at such times, not only does the fly attract the trout's attention by the movement of its prolonged struggle, but also because of the amount of time which it spends in one position, thus presenting a leisurely meal.

The final dry-fly rise form of real significance is the 'sipping' rise which is often the most frustrating rise form of all. Sometimes, a lake may be covered by tiny dimples and rings, some of which may be produced by tiny minnows or fry, some by flies alighting to lay their eggs, some by corixidae collecting air at the surface before diving down again and some by large trout!

Elsewhere, I have described trout cruising around like basking sharks as they mop up tiny naturals, but in this case, however small the fly, they rise delicately to individual insects – and unfortunately, they often become completely preoccupied in their feeding and unlikely to accept any larger artificials. Sipping rise forms may be frustrating yet their greatest fascination is that they are sometimes produced by the largest of fish which, therefore, creates an amount of suspense and excitement. Tiny duns (such as the *Caënidae*), tiny stoneflies and midges (including the minute adult biting midges) spent spinners, and even tiny pupae are capable of producing sipping rise forms under the calmest of conditions and the stomach contents of fish at such times may reveal a dense mass of small insects with not one insect of another species among them. As a result, it is often necessary to have a pretty good idea what food item is obsessing the trout and be able to present a fair imitation.

Although some anglers advocate the use of a contrasting large fly, I have little faith in this gambit although it is sometimes worth using a multi-hackled pattern which may imitate a 'clump' of insects. For example, trout may even feed on greenfly and a useful pattern to use is a fly dressed on a fine wire size 10 hook, with a bright green floss body and a series of white or pale hackles dressed along the body. However, in most cases, the most useful pattern is a very tiny artificial fly presented on a very fine leader. Fishing such tiny patterns often results in eye-strain and it is difficult to synchronise a sipping rise with the disappearance of your own artificial: it is often necessary to tighten whenever a rise occurs in the vicinity of where you believe your fly to be. A great number of fish will be missed in this manner, a great number of strikes will be made to rises that have not even been to your fly and a hooked fish will need to be played with great caution. You may be lucky, but no matter how good an angler you are, a limit bag under such conditions is rather unlikely.

In terms of floating patterns, three flies stand out among all others under such conditions (the Grey Duster, the Black Spider and the Blue Dun) when a general pattern is required rather than a precise imitation. At one time, I always used a tiny Grey Duster when struggling against sipping rise forms, although in recent years I have found it very difficult to obtain good quality Badger cock capes. I now use Cree cock hackles instead of Badger. It seemed reasonable to call this variation the Cree Duster. As a result, a tiny 'Duster' dressed with a soft or substandard cock hackle is likely to become easily drowned and is, therefore, of little use when fishing in this style. Recently, a tiny Blue Dun has become my favourite small general pattern both on lakes and river. The appropriate dressings of the three flies are as follows:

Grey Duster
Hook size: 18 – 22.
Tying silk: Brown.
Hackle: Badger cock (black centre with creamy white tips).
Body: A dubbed fur mixture of three parts hare's ear and one part blue rabbit fur (or mole).

Black Spider
Hook size: 18 – 22.
Tying silk: Black.
Hackle: Black cock (very small and dressed lightly).
Body: Black floss silk or seal's fur.
(The pattern is also effective when dressed as a knotted midge and given a second hackle at the end of the body. This pattern then suggests coupling insects and may be dressed on size 16 hook.)

Blue Dun
Hook size: 18 – 22.
Tying silk: Primrose yellow.
Hackle: A tiny Blue Dun cock hackle.
Tails: Blue Dun spade hackle. No more than three or four fibres.
Body: A dubbed fur body made up of three parts blue rabbit fur and

one part mole fur. The body should be dressed very lightly over the primrose tying silk.

Wings: Pale starling. Tying wings on such a minute pattern is by no means an easy task and the wings certainly do not aid the killing properties of the fly. However, wings do make the fly far more visible to the angler and this can be very useful, particularly for those anglers who either suffer poor eyesight or are prone to headaches.

The Blue Dun seems as likely as any pattern to tempt fish no matter on what minute natural flies they are gorging themselves. The Grey Duster is an excellent imitation of the upwinged Caënis and any other tiny pale flies; and the Black Spider succeeds with tiny dark naturals which are usually of the *Diptera* order. Further specific patterns, representing particular insects, will be offered at a later stage.

Tiny artificials must always be made of the highest quality materials (this is particularly true of the hackle), dressed on fine wire hooks and dressed as sparsely as is practical. It is not unusual to find that the most successful fly possesses a short, slender body and only a single turn of the smallest cock hackle available — in itself, this provides a great challenge at the fly-tying bench. I feel that I really must emphasise yet again the importance of a top quality cock hackle when tying minute flies. Your artificial must not only sit nicely on the water but it must also be buoyant enough to avoid constant drowning. A badly-dressed fly, or a fly made up with poor quality hackle may even become waterlogged when you are simply lifting the line off the water for a re-cast. At such times the fly is bound to drag a little over the surface and will readily absorb water if the hackle is soft. The practice of using large hackles for small patterns, and then trimming the hackles down to size, should be avoided since the butts of the hackle fibres will be too thick in relation to the size of the fly. This will certainly result in a loss of translucence and will produce a very clumsy fly.

One point to remember is that 'sipping' rises are sometimes produced by fish feeding on a fall of ephemeropteran spinners and in this instance the conventional dry-fly tends to stand too high on the surface film and thus offers the wrong kind of silhouette to a fish. A suitable pattern for spinners is to dress a fly with lateral bunches of feather fibres projecting at right-angles from each side of the hook. This fly is held in the film by the 'wing' fibres and by a bunch of tail feather fibres which should be fixed in place so that they splay out fan-like. One advantage of sipping rise forms induced by a fall of spinners is that, with the exception of Caënis spinners, the natural insects are larger than the minute insects which normally produce this form of rise. However, it is naturally important that you recognise the fact that trout are actually feeding on spinners for at such times, they are likely to reject conventional dry-flies riding high on the water.

During the process of writing this section, it was suggested to me that the working title ('Rise forms and the location of fish') was rather tautological. That is to say, if it was about rise forms, there was no need to refer to 'the location of fish' since the rise form itself would betray the trout's whereabouts. Naturally, this is seemingly quite true, and yet it must be pointed out that the observation of a rise form certainly does not guarantee the location of a fish when fishing on still waters. Fish in rivers do tend to hold a fixed position and they rise consistently in the same place. The flow of water both produces a constant supply of food (making it possible to feed 'in position') and provides a current of oxygenated water which will flow through the trout's mouth and gills. On the other hand, stillwater trout need to move around in search of their food (particularly during calm conditions when there is no wind to produce a current) and in order to maintain a reasonable supply of oxygen to the bloodstream. For these reasons, when a trout rises in a stillwater, his rise form may mark the position which he has already vacated. Thus, if you delay your cast to the ring of the rise, the trout may well have moved elsewhere. Similarly, anglers often get the impression that there are several fish rising in a certain area when in truth there are only a couple of fish, or perhaps even one fish. Unless two separate rises occur simultaneously, you must always be aware of the possibility of those separate rises being produced by the same fish.

During a 'rise', fish often move quite rapidly from one position to another and before the cast is made it is necessary to plot the feeding path of the fish so that the fly may be landed a little in front of it. Casting to the rise can be quite frustrating when fish are on the move, yet, if timed correctly, it can be profitable since the fly remains perfectly cocked on the water for only a short time. The trout has little chance to inspect the fly which in any case is presented in its most efficient form. Fishing the water (that is, casting to the general feeding area) may be less frustrating, yet it is only really successful if the fly continues to cock perfectly. If the fly is allowed to float for any length of time it is necessary to mend the line continually in order to avoid any drag occurring.

'Fishing the water' with a fly which is allowed to float for some time tends to work best when several fish are feeding in a limited area.

It is also possible to locate fish when there are no rise forms in evidence and sometimes such fish will be willing to take a dry-fly. In the introduction we referred to the remarkable success of certain anglers who use little other than the dry-fly throughout the season and their success often lies in their ability to visually locate fish or to fish in areas where fish are most likely to be present at any given period during the season. Particularly in small lake fisheries, fish may be located with close observation and with the aid of polarised spectacles which will cancel surface glare. Once a fish has been observed, it is partly a matter of personal choice, I suppose, whether the dry-fly or nymph is employed. On the other hand, there are certain significant features of fish which are more likely to take a nymph rather than a dry-fly: they will be swimming around in a business-like manner and their mouths will open much wider on occasions as they engulf a nymph, shrimp or the like.

When fish are feeding in this manner, they tend to become preoccupied with their present item of food and tend to remain at that feeding depth. If they do rise in the water, they will only do so in pursuit of an escaping creature which is ascending to 'hatch'. On the other hand, a fish which is observed swimming around in a leisurely manner or which remains largely in a fixed position and does not open its mouth appreciably wider than normal, may be prepared to rise to a dry-fly unless satiated.

When fish are located by observation, and this is naturally easier in a small fishery, it is certainly not true that fish lying deep down are least likely to rise to floating flies. As discussed in the introduction, fish lying deeper in the water (so long as it is not too deep to allow the penetration of adequate light) can see a greater surface area than fish lying close to the surface, so that the cast need only be made in the general direction of the fish. On the other hand, if you observe a fish lying close to the surface, an accurate cast into its window of vision will be necessary or else your fly is likely to be ignored simply because it hasn't been seen. It is often the case that trout will rise to even a tiny fly when lying deep, whereas they will reject every weighted nymph fished at the depth in the water at which they are actually positioned. Even so, in order to obtain more consistent results when angling for such fish it makes sense to make their ascent worthwhile by offering them a more substantial 'item of food' in the form of a large artificial fly.

Even when fish cannot actually be seen, the dry-fly is by no means useless although I am certainly not advocating the use of the dry-fly at the expense of other methods. I am simply attempting to define the possibilities which the dry-fly provides: possibilities which are all too often ignored even when all subsurface techniques have been fruitlessly tried. However, when the water is very murky, the dry-fly often proves to be of limited value since the silt (or other matter) suspended in the water, prevents adequate light penetration so that the trout are not able to see a surface fly. Equally, the broken surface pattern of light produced by rough conditions also limits a trout's vision of a surface fly although a large bushy artificial stands a better chance of being seen and, indeed, often does extremely well when there is a wave on the water. Of course, most anglers would be unlikely to use small flies under rough conditions anyway, since such patterns do not possess adequate buoyancy. Incidentally, I have often had rises when using a bushy dry-fly in windy conditions at the beginning of the season.

The speculative dry-fly is a method to hold in reserve, perhaps for those occasions when the nymph proves unproductive, although it may be used more frequently on smaller lakes. Small lakes provide a psychological boost since the angler can cover the whole expanse of the water from either bank or boat. In contrast, larger expanses of water cannot be fully covered so that the location of fish is a difficult proposition: we may get the impression that large surface areas are completely barren of fish and accordingly, loss of faith in the speculative dry-fly may occur quite quickly. Equally, once your concentration has lapsed, you may guarantee that a fish will rise to your fly and be missed. Thus, the speculative dry-fly is only worthwhile on larger waters if it is applied to known fish holding areas, for example, sheltered bays and creeks, summer shallows (particularly if there are weedbeds present) and calm lanes when it is windy. The dam wall is capable of producing good dry-fly fishing as is a point or promontory between two bays — the latter location also providing the additional possibility of allowing the angler to cover a greater surface area than is normally possible from one fixed position.

The word 'speculative' may well communicate an impression of luck, a kind of hit-and-miss gambit, though this should not really be the case. Hopefully, a reading of later chapters will help to elucidate my use of the word 'speculative' and outline approaches of a more specific nature.

5

Dry-flies and aquatic hatches

This chapter is intended to introduce the reader to the natural stillwater flies which induce rises from trout of sufficient intensity to be worthy of the angler's attentions. Although certain flies are less common than others, they are included since they may appear in considerable numbers in certain locations and at certain times of the year. If an angler encounters them, he must be prepared, and although his usual patterns may well suffice in the case of certain less common species, it will be found that some are distinctive enough to command individual imitations in their own right. Specific imitation, or 'exact' imitation as it is often inappropriately termed, is most likely to be necessitated by flat calm conditions when trout are most easily scared and in their most annoyingly selective moods.

Before considering the main aquatic orders and species themselves, a few brief introductory remarks need to be made about aquatic hatches. First of all, it is fair to say that aquatic hatches are often overrated by stillwater dry-fly fishermen and that the much awaited 'hatch' often results in poor dividends and abject misery. Naturally, this is a generalisation (the mayfly on an Irish lough may well produce a veritable bonanza) but it is still a generalisation which is of value. When a breeze blows hawthorn flies on to the surface of a lake, it is quite common to find the water erupting with rising fish which must be likely to take a floating fly unless the majority of naturals are being swamped and drowned. However, an aquatic hatch works in a rather different manner since the emerging adult fly merely represents the tip of the iceberg. For each adult fly in existence on the surface of the lake or reservoir, there will be many more mature nymphs or pupae awaiting emergence. Thus, trout may well prefer to feed lazily on the easily accessible mature aquatic stages. Indeed, the frustration produced for the fly-fisherman who has waited all day for an evening rise only to find his dry-fly completely ignored, may be explained in terms of nymphing trout which are feeding so close to the surface that they appear to be indulging themselves on floating flies. Even when adult flies may be present in numbers, the dry-fly may well lose out to the accurately fished nymph. I am the last person to advocate a blind faith in the dry-fly as a kind of stillwater fly-fisherman's panacea; when it works, it works well, but when it doesn't, the nymph or wet-fly must be brought into play.

From generalisation, let us move on to arguments of a more specific nature. So far, it has been intimated that trout may prefer the aquatic insect stage to the adult fly, yet this is not an exclusive rule. For instance, trout generally prefer the chironomid pupa to the adult midge, yet those who conclude that trout *never* take adult midges, and that dry-flies are *never* of any use during chironomid hatches, are making a critical error. They may well succeed nine times out of ten with their pupal patterns, but on the tenth occasion, they will draw a blank since they have failed to recognise the fact the trout are feeding on adult chironomids. The exact details of this illustration will be discussed later in the present chapter, but, for the moment, we will merely emphasise this general statement on the chironomid − that it offers the dry-fly little more perhaps than a thirty per cent chance of success. Against this insect we can offer the contrast of the mayfly (*E. danica* and *E. vulgata*) which produces exceptional sport with the

Three fish for breakfast. These trout succumbed to a small Cree Duster within twenty minutes and were caught close to the bank, in the vicinity of the rise form shown in the photograph on page 42. The rainbow in the middle of the picture is actually the fish responsible for the delicate rise form in the previous photograph.

dry-fly and as far as lake fishing is concerned, offers the nymph fisherman only marginal chances of success. The contrast of these opposed poles (the chironomid and the mayfly) emphasises the importance of studying each individual species when considering the significance of aquatic hatches.

The need to have a full appreciation of each aquatic species may be further highlighted by reference to two very closely related species of flies, namely the Pond Olive and the Lake Olive. It is normally assumed that being so similar, each species offers an equal opportunity for the use of the dry-fly: in my experience, this is not so. When Pond Olives are hatching, they are capable of appearing in considerable numbers, yet trout often prefer the mature nymphal stage because the dun often leaves the water very quickly. On the other hand, in very similar conditions of weather and atmospheric pressure, I have observed the Lake Olive dun floating along with the breeze for some time before leaving the water and thus not only inducing a considerable surface rise but also providing a greater chance of success with the dry-fly.

Similarly, the spinner stages of the two stillwater olives cannot be considered in an identical manner. The Lake Olive spinner returns to lay her eggs on warm evenings in such numbers that trout will gorge themselves, particularly on the spent females which lie inert after having shed their burden of eggs. An appropriate pattern may well reap rich rewards, although there is often the problem of one's artificial fly having to compete with so many natural flies for the trout's attentions. However, with the Pond Olive spinner it is a little different. The Pond Olive spinners tend to appear rather more spasmodically and in smaller numbers until light fades in the very late evening. Indeed, many stillwater fly fisheries will have closed for the day when they appear and they may well continue to oviposit well into the night. On the other hand, all this may result in offering the dry-fly fisherman a chance of success with his quarry if he is able to fish very early in the morning when the trout may still be mopping up the accumulation of spent flies. Indeed, this may produce particularly good fishing if a breeze has resulted in the spent flies drifting against a certain bank where the rises of fish will reveal that they may be caught without the exhaustion of long casting.

Apart from the distinctions between individual species, varying conditions of weather will often play a part in deciding the relative success of the dry-fly during an aquatic hatch. For example, let us consider the Pond Olive again. Although the nymph is often preferred to the dun in dry weather conditions, wet weather conditions can make all the difference since the dun has greater difficulty in drying its wings and remains on the surface of the lake for a longer duration. Accordingly, since it then provides the trout with an easier target, the trout can feed on it without expending a great deal of energy and he can be caught on the dry-fly. Even so, wet weather conditions vary so much and although light rain has often produced my best dry-fly fishing, heavy rain only results in both natural and artificial fly being obscured from the trout's view by the disturbance caused by the raindrops on the surface of the reservoir. Floating flies are recognised as a mirror image in the surface film. When it rains very hard, the mirror is shattered and the image fragments completely.

There are other times when the weather and water conditions are likely to produce optimum chances of success with the dry-fly. For example, when the surface of the lake or reservoir is oily calm or covered in scum, flies have difficulty in breaking away from the surface, or indeed, have difficulty even breaking through the surface film. In fact, the most successful dry-fly under such circumstances is likely to be the pattern capable of floating in the film rather than a design which will float high above the surface. At times such as the one under consideration, even the chironomid pupa may come second to an emerger pattern fished in the film.

One of the greatest mistakes made by anglers is to make blanket assertions covering an entire lake or reservoir, and whilst it is easy to appreciate that large expanses of water such as Rutland are made up of numerous micro-habitats in the form of bays and creeks, the same may often be said of smaller lake fisheries. There are many occasions when some fish will feed subaquatically in certain areas of a fishery, while others will rise to dry-flies in a different location.

Rises to floating flies are often concentrated in areas such as calm lanes, or in other areas away from the breeze and rougher water. When a breeze blows directly into a bay, it may well result in a concentration of floating insects being trapped within the bay, which in turn may produce a localised rise. Such bays may differ also from other parts of a reservoir in that they actually support a different ecosystem so that what happens in the bay at any given time will not be true of the reservoir as a whole. If for example, the bay is relatively shallow and weeded, it may attract nymphs of the Pond Olive and produce reasonable dry-fly fishing in season. On the other hand, a neighbouring exposed shoreline is less likely to support Pond Olive nymphs and equally unlikely to produce good dry-fly fishing at times when the sheltered bay will. What this proves, of course, is not that an angler should automatically fish in the bay, but that if he does so, he would be well advised to use a floating artificial and conversely, a sunken fly when he tackles the exposed shoreline.

Above all, it seems necessary when talking about aquatic flies to avoid drawing rigid and dogmatic conclusions. Some general guidelines to the effectiveness of dry-flies, when faced by aquatic hatches, have been provided so far, and although it may only scratch the surface of the subject, I do not propose to go much further. Each angler will arrive at his own conclusions as a result of his fishing experiences, and often, as a result of new experiences, he will feel obliged to change them. To put it simply, there are times when trout are 'on' floating flies rather than 'on' nymphs, and there are times when they prefer nymphs to the adult insects. There are times when a good general dry-fly will catch fish feeding on floating naturals, and there are times when a more specific imitation becomes necessary — usually during calm conditions when trout have a greater chance of studying the imitation before pronouncing it good.

Then again, there are times when trout are most definitely feeding on floating insects when nothing will seem to tempt them. Such occasions are indeed frustrating and maddening yet they remain good for the sport since they retain its overwhelming sense of mystery. A true fly-fisherman would undoubtedly tire of his sport if his success were overwhelmingly constant.

Finally, in describing a variety of insects during the pages of the present chapter I must stress that the artificials presented to the reader are a personal choice based on my fishing experiences, and are not put forward as a cure for all ills. Undoubtedly, many efficient and killing imitations have been omitted and I certainly would not claim that I am attempting to offer any 'exact' imitations. The traditional equation between dry-fly fishing and the supposed school of 'exact' imitation is at best ludicrous. Indeed, it isn't necessary to have much more than a working knowledge of entomology since general patterns will produce reasonably constant success throughout any given season. Who can guarantee what 'exact' imitation really is anyway? After all, no matter how we empathise, we will never be able to see a fly exactly as a trout sees it.

THE UPWINGED FLIES

The upwinged flies, day-flies, mayflies or ephemeroptera — call them what you will — are the most storied and romantic flies of the fisherman's year. Nevertheless, on stillwaters at least, they are by no means as important as their history in angling literature might suggest. The reputation of these flies evolves greatly from their significance on the chalkstreams where a good hatch may well cover the surface of the stream. On stillwaters, though good hatches do occur, they are often localised rather than widespread. Trout may prefer to feed on the nymphal stage of these flies yet the dun and spinner stages can provide the angler with good sport.

So much has been written about the upwinged flies that it is not necessary for our present purposes to include a detailed account of the insect's life cycle. The upwinged flies are so called because they hold their wings together in an upright position when at rest. The wings themselves are quite large, and behind the upright main wings there is usually a small pair of hindwings although they are absent in some species. In the dun stage, the wings may be transparent or opaque yet they are generally bright and transparent in the spinner stage. The wings are attached to a plump thorax, which also holds three pairs of legs, and then the segmented abdomen tapers to the tails which may number two or three.

When mating has taken place, females lay their eggs over water, directly on to the surface of the water, or in the case of the Baëtidae, the females actually crawl beneath the surface in order to oviposit. The eggs either sink to the bottom or attach themselves to weeds where they hatch into larvae which are actually tiny, immature nymphs. The nymph grows through a series of moults (known as instars) until it is ready to emerge as the adult fly. It is with the nymph that we find the greatest variations of appearance and habit: some nymphs can dart around in an agile manner, some swim in a very laboured fashion, some develop flattened bodies and cling to stones, while others bury down into soft mud and gravel of the lake bottom. When the nymph is mature, it swims to the surface where the nymphal case splits and the adult fly emerges, stretches its completed wings, dries them and flies off from the water. At this stage, the adult fly is often taken by trout, though it depends on the length of time that the fly rests on the surface before flying free. This time not only varies according to the type of fly, but depends also upon weather conditions: when the surface film is covered with scum, or when it is a little cold or damp, the adult fly remains on the surface for a greater length of time. If this is the case, then dry-fly fishing is often very lucrative since fish will concentrate on the adult fly. They can pick them off in a leisurely manner.

The dun stage normally lasts a day or two (much shorter in the case of the Caënidae) and in this stage the fly normally rests on vegetation awaiting the next metamorphosis. Since it possesses no mouthparts as such, the fly cannot drink or feed and is simply designed to become a breeding machine. The next development is from dun to spinner. The dun is often a dull coloured insect, but when its skin splits again

Figure 2: A Typical Ephemeropteran Spinner

down the middle of the thorax, the bright and beautiful spinner emerges. It is now ready to mate. Apart from its brighter appearance and shinier wings, the abdomen usually changes colour whilst the tails and legs are longer than those of the dun stage.

The spinners mate in flight, the female (normally the larger of the two) supporting the weight of the male as it lies beneath her, their abdomens joined together. For this purpose, the male spinner possesses a small pair of 'claspers' attached to the penultimate body segment. When the female is 'ripe' and conditions are right, normally in the evening, the female lays her eggs and the whole life-cycle begins again. Trout will feed avidly at this time, picking off egg-laying females or leisurely devouring spent females and exhausted males. The spent fly characteristically lies flat and inert on the surface of the water, its wings no longer erect but projected laterally and quite flat. Although some flies may have more than one life-cycle during a fishing season, the life-cycle is generally an annual affair. However, weather conditions have a great part to play in this time span and if the spring and summer are cool and damp, the Mayfly (*E. danica* and *E. vulgata*) may even develop a biannual cycle.

There are fewer types of upwinged flies on stillwaters than there are on rivers and although such flies as Ditch Duns, Blue Winged Olives, Large Summer Duns, Dusky Yellowstreaks and Autumn Duns are to be found on various stillwaters, they tend to be only of localised importance. Some upwinged flies, such as the March Brown, are found only on rivers and never on stillwaters. Because we are dealing essentially with a restricted variety of common flies, and because they are all similar in appearance (varying only in colour and size) it is not necessary to produce a separate artificial for each individual species. The exact imitation-school may hold sway on chalkstreams yet stillwater trout tend to feed less selectively. Thus, it seems sensible to begin with a selection of artificial flies which will cater for all our needs, then we can turn to a more detailed consideration of individual insects.

A SELECTION OF PATTERNS TO IMITATE THE UPWINGED FLIES: DUNS

These patterns are illustrated in Figure 3.

Blue Dun
Hook: Size 14.
Silk: Primrose Yellow.
Body: A mixture of mole's fur, blue rabbit under fur and grey seal's fur dubbed on yellow silk.
Wings: Starling (a variety of shades).
Hackle: Medium blue dun cock hackle.
Tail: Fibres from a blue dun spade hackle.
   This pattern is a good fly to use for a variety of duns.

Pheasant Tail
Hook: Size 12 – 16.
Silk: Brown.
Body: Pheasant tail fibres ribbed with gold wire.
Hackle: Honey dun, red game cock, ginger cock or blue dun cock.
Tail: Either the same fibres as the hackle or pheasant tail fibre tips.
   This is an excellent general pattern and although it will take fish feeding on Pond Olives or Lake Olives, it is one of the best imitations of the Sepia and Claret Duns.

Greenwell's Glory
Hook: Size 14 – 16.
Silk: Primrose Yellow.
Body: Waxed primrose silk or primrose silk soaked in cellire varnish. This turns the silk a delicate pale olive shade. Rib the body either with

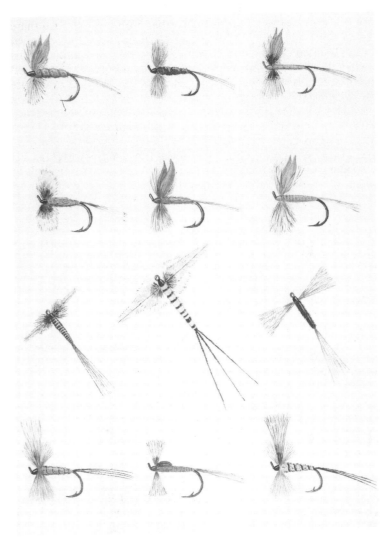

Figure 3: Upwinged fly patterns

        1st Row . . . Rough Olive, Pheasant Tail, Greenwell's Glory
        2nd Row . . . Grey Duster, Blue Dun, Yellow Olive
        3rd Row . . . Lunn's Particular, Mayfly Spinner,
                      Pheasant Tail Spinner
        4th Row . . . Grey Wulf, Kite's Apricot Spinner,
                      Yellow Wulf

unwaxed primrose silk or with gold wire.

Wings: Dark starling or hen blackbird.

Hackle: Furnace cock.

Tails: The same fibres as the hackle.

This is a wonderful dry-fly and will catch fish feeding on most of the upwinged duns. It is a particularly good imitation of the Pond Olive and will serve for the Lake Olive when tied with a slightly paler wing.

Rough Olive 1

Hook: Size 12 – 16.

Silk: Olive.

Body: Medium olive green heron herl or seal's fur ribbed with gold wire.

Wings: Medium starling.

Hackle: Medium green olive or brown olive cock hackle.

Tails: As per hackle.

This is a good imitation of the later Lake Olive Duns.

Rough Olive 2

Hook: Size 14 – 16.

Silk: Brown.

Body: Dark Olive condor herl or seal's fur ribbed with gold wire.

Wings: Dark starling.

Hackle: Dark brown-olive cock hackle.

Tails: As per hackle.

This pattern is a good representation of the early summer Lake Olive Duns and a good general fly for any darker duns.

Yellow Olive

Hook: 14 – 16.

Silk: Yellow.

Body: Light olive-yellow heron herl ribbed with gold wire.

Wings: Light starling.

Hackle: Yellow or golden olive cock hackle.

Tails: As per hackle.

This pattern is good for paler Pond and Lake Olives, the Yellow May Dun and perhaps even any of the Pale Watery Olives which sometimes appear on stillwaters.

Grey Duster

Hook: Size 14 – 18.

Silk: Grey or brown (depending on how light or dark you intend the pattern to be).

Body: A mixture of hare's ear and blue rabbit underfur.

Hackle: Badger cock (normally a small hackle feather).
Tails: As hackle (optional).

Although a good general dry-fly (some anglers use this fly alone for all their dry-fly fishing) it is an excellent imitation of the Caënis when tied in small sizes. A darker or lighter fly may be produced, depending upon the mix of the dubbing. Grey heron herl can also be used for the body whilst the darker patterns may be tied with a blue dun hackle instead of the badger cock.

Mayfly (Grey Wulf)
There are many patterns tied to imitate the male and female duns of *E. danica* and *E. vulgata*; the reader is free to choose from any published within the pages of hundreds of books on fly-fishing. Mayfly imitations are often excellent dapping flies. My own favourite fly is the Grey Wulf, a hair-winged fly designed by the famous American angler Lee Wulf. A yellow version of the same fly is also a killing pattern.
Hook: Size 10 long-shanked mayfly hook.
Silk: Grey.
Body: A mixture of blue rabbit and grey-seal's fur ribbed with brown tying silk.
Wings: Brown fibres from a buck tail, divided and either tied upright or inclined slightly forwards.
Hackle: Blue dun cock.
Tails: Pheasant tail fibres.

SPINNERS

Although it is possible to produce precise imitations of all the ephemera spinners, my personal feeling is that general patterns will suffice. Having said that, the spent Mayfly spinner is such a large and distinctive insect that it does merit individual attention.

Lunn's Particular
Hook: Size 14.
Silk: Crimson.
Body: Undyed stripped hackle from a natural Rhode Island Red cock hackle. This produces a neat tapering and segmented body.
Wings: Pale or medium blue dun hackle tips tied 'spent'.
Hackle: Bright natural red cock hackle. This should be a small feather so that the pattern floats close to the film.
Tails: Natural red fibres from a large hackle, quite long.

This is a beautiful looking pattern and a personal favourite. I bought a stock of these flies in 1959 and still have a few left. They are so perfectly tied and fashioned out of excellent materials and serve to underline the recent decline in standards of commercially tied patterns by means of contrast. The Lunn's Particular is an excellent general spinner pattern.

Pheasant Tail Spinner
Hook: Size 14.
Silk: Crimson.
Body: Pheasant tail fibres ribbed with bright copper wire (it must be fine).
Wings: Any pale cock hackle (usually blue dun, cream or ginger) tied in the usual manner and then trimmed so that only lateral fibres protrude from the hook. No additional hackle is used for the purpose of floatation.
Tails: As per hackle. The tail fibres should be splayed out into a fan shape in order to aid floatation.

Red Spinner
Hook: Size 14.
Silk: Crimson.
Body: Crimson floss silk or wool ribbed with white gossamer tying silk.
Wings: White cock hackle trimmed above and below so that the fibres project laterally in the manner of spent wings.
Tails: A fan of white cock hackle fibres.

Apricot Spinner (Oliver Kite)
Hook: Size 14.
Silk: Golden olive.
Body: Swan primary herls dyed apricot.
Thorax: The same herls doubled and redoubled.
Hackle: Palest honey dun (trimmed above and below).
Tails: Pale yellow cock fibres.

For those of you who do not mind a little extra time at the fly-tying bench, it is worth including a few fluorescent fibres in the spinner patterns which employ hackle fibre wings. A few fluorescent green, orange and red fibres may be obtained from fluorescent floss silk and then tied in with the wings. In this instance, it is better to tie in bunches of hackle fibres for the wings rather than hackle the fly in the conventional manner. What is the reasoning behind this?

When a natural spinner's transparent veined wings rest flat on the lake surface, the light shining through them is deflected to create a little rainbow halo of light which the trout sees under the water. The fluorescent fibres create a good impression of this phenomenon.

Mayfly Spinner

As with the Mayfly dun, there are many tyings of the spinner or spent gnat. The following pattern is an excellent imitation although the reader may well discover several other patterns of similar effectiveness.

Hook: Size 10 – 12 long shank Mayfly hook.
Silk: Brown.
Body: White floss silk, wool or seal's fur ribbed with a single pheasant tail fibre or dark copper wire.
Thorax: Pheasant tail fibres.
Wings: Blue dun hackle points tied spent.
Hackle: Badger cock hackle.
Tails: Pheasant tail fibres.

Badger Spinner

Hook: Size 14 – 18.
Silk: White.
Body: Pale white swan herl.
Wings: Badger hackle tied spent (i.e. as with the Pheasant Tail Spinner).
Tails: Badger hackle fibres tied in a fan shape.

This pattern will imitate any very pale natural spinners.

So much for the artificial patterns. The natural flies may be encountered throughout the season and normally emerge during the daytime (thus their alternative name of day-flies) when a good hatch may produce excellent fishing. When the weather is very hot, hatches may incline towards the cooler evenings and become part of the oft-mentioned 'evening rise'. The evening rise is just as likely to be produced by a fall of ephemera spinners, since egg-laying usually takes place in the evening, and, in the case of the Caënidae perhaps even during the night-time. Thus, fish may actually feed on the spent Caënis spinner at dawn.

From time to time, most, though certainly not all upwinged flies, may appear on stillwaters. I intend simply to treat those species, which in my own personal opinion, are most commonly to be encountered – the Sepia Dun, Claret Dun, Pond Olive, Lake Olive, Yellow May Dun, Mayfly and Caënis.

The Sepia Dun (*Leptophlebia marginata*) (Figure 4) is a medium-sized upwing fly which is quite common and may be encountered throughout the fishing season (although hatches are generally sparse from August onwards). Its greatest merit is that it is the first upwinged fly to emerge and can produce good dry-fly fishing from the beginning

Figure 4: Sepia Dun. Leptophlebia marginata: female subimago or dun

of April. Particularly towards the beginning of the season, hatches tend to occur towards the middle of the day when the temperature is warmest. The Sepia Dun is a very distinctive fly with its fawn wings and the dark sepia-brown body and perhaps could only be mistaken for the Claret Dun. The Sepia Dun is a three-tailed fly and its legs are dark olive-brown in colour. Thus, the pheasant tail, dressed on a size 14 hook, provides an admirable imitation although, during the early part of the season, it takes a good 'rise' in order to produce exciting dry-fly fishing. Generally, the soundest approach is to cast the pattern directly to individual rising fish. The spinner is similar in appearance to the dun, possessing a dark red-brown body, transparent wings and longer dark brown tails. However, it is not of much consequence as an angler's fly, perhaps because the spinners tend to oviposit in small numbers rather than in hordes.

The Claret Dun (*Leptophlebia verspertina*) (Figure 5) is very similar in appearance to the Sepia Dun but is a little smaller in size. It too may be imitated by the pheasant tail pattern. There are many who would argue that the fly is incorrectly named and point out that the abdomen is not claret but a very dark brown. That would originally have been my opinion when I first caught a specimen whilst sitting beside a Scottish loch. However, a closer examination of the natural fly in various conditions of light did reveal a distinct claret tinge, which would seem to vindicate whoever it was first christened this fly. It is a fine point really and the angler need not split hairs. The dun's wings are dark grey (although the hindwings are a little paler), the legs almost black and the three tails, a dark-grey brown. The female spinner has a general brown appearance (again tinged with claret) including the

Figure 5: Claret Dun. Leptophlebia vespertina: female subimago or dun

wings which, though transparent, are distinctly brownish. Claret Duns are very common on stillwaters (more so than the Sepia Duns) and start to emerge around the beginning of May, lasting to the end of August. The heaviest hatches seem to occur on May and June afternoons when excellent dry-fly fishing may be had, particularly on upland reservoirs and lochs. The nymph of this species seems to thrive in peaty or acidic water, and since much of my fishing is done in the Pennine reservoirs, the Claret Dun must figure as one of my favourite natural insects. On warm evenings in late spring, female Claret spinners may congregate in numbers to lay their eggs, thus producing dry-fly fishing of the highest order. The pheasant tail spinner is an admirable imitation of the spent female fly.

Pond Olives (*Cloëon dipterum*) (Figure 6), as their name implies, are commonest on small lake fisheries since the nymphs prefer shallow water. Although they are to be found on larger reservoirs they are unlikely to emerge from deep open expanses of water and will be encountered in shallow and sheltered bays.

The Pond Olive is in many ways one of the great enigmas of stillwater fly-fishing. It is a very common insect and occurs in great numbers: its greatest period of emergence is from May to the end of July although it may be encountered well into September. On the one hand, it may emerge in vast numbers, yet, on the other, the dry-fly will often be singularly ineffective during a good hatch (which generally occurs during the afternoon). The reason for this is quite simple: the dun emerges from the mature nymph and leaves the water very quickly so that trout will often prefer the mature nymph to the adult fly. Thus, the would-be dry-fly fisherman repeatedly casts to

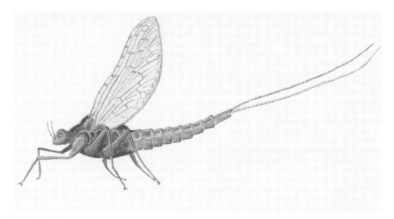

Figure 6: Pond Olive. Cloeon dipterum: female subimago or dun

apparent 'rises' without success and eventually concludes that the dry-fly is universally useless on stillwaters: he then turns to the nymph with success.

In many ways the dun is not a dry-fly fisherman's fly unless conditions are right. If the air is a little moist, or the water is flat-calm and scummy, then the dun struggles to emerge quickly and dry its wings in readiness for flight. Trout may then feed on it in a leisurely manner. At such times, the dry-fly is quite deadly. But what size and pattern do we employ? The enigma continues.

As the season progresses, the emergent dun lessens in size: early season flies being relatively large and late summer flies no more than small-medium. Whatever pattern you choose to use, have a stock of flies from size 12 down to size 16. Another problem with the Pond Olive is that its coloration varies enormously both in relation to location and time of the year. I often encounter duns with a distinct yellow-olive body (perfectly imitated by the Greenwell's Glory) yet in other areas, the abdomen is commonly grey-brown in the male and brown-olive in the female. The thorax of the dun is brown-olive, the wings are grey, the legs a dull yellow-olive and the tails, similar in colour to the legs, possess red-brown rings. Pond Olives do not have a pair of hind wings and possess only two tails. Because of the colour variation, I would suggest four patterns for the Pond Olive − the Greenwell's Glory, Rough Olive 1, Rough Olive 2 and Pheasant Tail.

If the dun is sometimes a disappointment to the dry-fly fisherman, the spinner certainly isn't. This beautiful creature has an apricot coloured body, whilst the wings have deep yellow bands on their leading edges. The female apricot spinner descends in great numbers in the evening to lay her eggs. She may be taken by trout as she dips against the surface, if not, she will certainly be devoured when she lies spent with exhaustion after egg-laying has been completed. This may occasion a great late evening rise and produce good sport if the angler possesses the correct pattern − Oliver Kite's 'Apricot Spinner'. Ovipositing seems to continue well into darkness and it is always infuriating when fishery officials 'blow the whistle' at dusk, just when a full-scale rise is beginning to develop.

The Lake Olive (*Cloëon simile*) is very similar to the Pond Olive and is also a very common stillwater fly. It begins to appear in May and can be seen throughout the season, although it emerges in greatest numbers in May and June, and then again at the end of August and into September. Between these two periods, hatches tend to be less intense. Lake Olives may appear from the same areas as Pond Olives, yet they will also hatch over deeper and more exposed water since the nymphs are able to withstand colder conditions. The dun of this fly is like enough to the Pond Olive dun for the same artificials to be used and, therefore, for angling purposes, they may be treated as one and the same fly. Emergence generally takes place in the afternoon or evening (odd flies will also emerge during the morning) and the dry-fly is more consistently effective with the Lake Olive than it is with the former species.

In appearance, the Lake Olive dun is rather like a slightly duller version of the Pond Olive dun and the only real difference is that the rings on the Pond Olive's tails are darker. The Lake Olive's wings are essentially grey (sometimes with a tinge of olive), the thorax is a dark olive-brown and the abdomen either grey-brown or olive-brown. The female spinner has transparent wings (suffused with an amber shade) and a dark chestnut abdomen: the Pheasant Tail spinner is a good imitation and particularly useful on June evenings. At this time of the year, a great number of female spinners return to stillwaters to lay their eggs and trout will feed avidly on spent flies, thus occasioning a tremendous evening rise. That does not mean that trout will be easy to catch because your artificial will have a great deal of competition. It is important that a quick cast is made to the ring of a rise (even then the trout may have moved on) or is made to intercept a fish in its feeding path. This is true of rises to spinners, but it is even more true of rises to duns. Spinners are inert so that fish only need to swim around slowly in order to feed, however they tend to move more quickly when feeding on duns which at any moment may fly away and escape them.

My inclusion of the Yellow May Dun (*Heptagenia sulphurea*) as a common stillwater fly may well evoke the odd raised eyebrow.

However, I have witnessed many hatches of these flies in the North of England and in Scotland and believe that they are reasonably common in those areas — perhaps also in other areas of Britain. Although they are unlike other upwinged flies in coloration, I have known anglers to confuse them with the Yellow Sally Stonefly — simply because of colour. The beautiful Yellow May Dun is essentially a fly of late spring and early summer; it is a medium to large sized dun and has yellow wings, sulphur yellow body and legs and two greyish-yellow tails. The Yellow Olive pattern (see the section on artificials) tied with a medium-yellow dyed cock hackle is a good artificial representation of the dun. Strangely, although I have encountered good hatches of duns (on Loch Awe, for example) the spinners of this fly remain something of a mystery to me. I doubt whether they are of much consequence to the angler.

The largest upwinged flies on stillwaters are those flies commonly known as Mayflies (see Figures 7 and 8). There are three species of Mayflies although the only common ones are *Ephemera danica* and *Ephemera vulgata*, the former is by far the commonest. Although the Mayfly is widely distributed there are few stillwaters these days which have Mayfly hatches of any real significance. On many waters the fly no longer appears at all. Those anglers lucky enough to fish lakes and reservoirs where decent hatches still occur, may have excellent dry-fly sport with such flies as the Grey Wulf. However, when hatches are only sparse the mature nymph is often taken in preference to the adult dun — this also occurs generally at the beginning and end of the hatching period when duns do not emerge in large number. The famed Mayfly hatch rarely lasts for more than a couple of weeks and normally takes place towards the end of May or at the beginning of June, the exact time of emergence depending upon weather or conditions.

The dun of *E. danica* has large, almost triangular forewings and relatively large hindwings. The dark veined forewings are a greenish-yellow in colour and have darker patches: it is the wing colour principally which has led to the dun being called the Green Drake. Nevertheless, there is often a yellowish green tinge to the body though the principal coloration is straw yellow; there are darker patches on the dorsal surface and the thorax is a dark olive-brown. The legs of the dun are dark brown and the three tails a dark grey. It will be noted that the Grey Wulf does not possess the same coloration as the natural dun: nevertheless, it still catches fish during a mayfly hatch. For those of you who might prefer a closer imitation, in terms of colour, the following Yellow Wulf is a pattern worth trying:

78

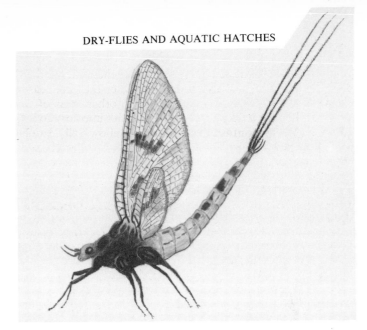

Figure 7: Mayfly. Ephemera danica: male subimago or dun

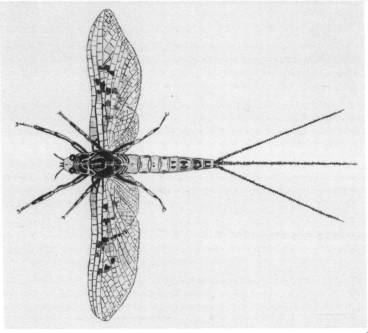

Figure 8: Mayfly. Ephemera danica: female imago or spinner

79

Yellow Wulf (Mayfly)

Hook: Size 10 long-shanked Mayfly hook.
Silk: Primrose yellow.
Wings: Dyed yellow fibres from a bucktail, divided and either tied upright or inclined slightly forwards.
Body: Pale lemon yellow angora wool ribbed with a pheasant tail fibre.
Hackle: Yellow-olive cock hackle.
Tails: Pheasant tail fibres.

Whilst the Mayfly nymph is often preferred to the dun during a hatch, the spinner has no 'competition' from the nymphal stage when it falls on to the water in the evening. The spinners devoured by trout are as likely to be males as females (differences in appearance are minimal) and may be imitated by the Mayfly spinner pattern mentioned previously. The male spinner, with its cream-white body, black thorax, legs and tails is known as the Black Drake; the female spinner is similar, though it possesses a brown thorax and legs, and greyish-brown tails. The female spinner is commonly called the Grey Drake, before it lays its eggs, and the the Spent Gnat after egg-laying has been completed.

The final upwinged flies for consideration are the tiny Broadwings or *Caënidae* (which have been referred to as the 'Fisherman's Curse'). Although there are six British Caënidae, only two are commonly encountered on lakes and reservoirs: *C. robusta* and *C. horaria*. *C. robusta* (the Dusky Broadwing) differs little in appearance from dun to spinner: the dun has broad, pale grey wings, a creamy-grey abdomen and dark brown thorax. The legs and tails are dirty white. The dun of *C. horaria* (the Yellow Broadwing) is similar in appearance to the former insect although it is a little smaller and has a creamy-yellow abdomen. For both flies, a size 18 Grey Duster is an adequate imitation although even a fly tied on a size 20 hook is by no means too small – the naturals are very tiny creatures.

Broadwings are very common on stillwaters and appear in vast hordes in the evenings; there are often so many emerging duns and egg-laying spinners around at the same time that you might be excused for believing in summer snowstorms. The transposition from nymph-to-dun-to-spinner, and finally to spent fly, can occur with amazing rapidity. Evidence seems to suggest that the whole process will often carry on well beyond the first hours of darkness. Broadwings first appear in May and continue throughout most of the season until the end of August.

The simultaneous presence of so many duns and spinners ensures a vast evening rise on many waters although the fish are notoriously difficult to catch. The Grey Duster may well be an excellent imitation yet if it is placed directly in front of a feeding fish, the chances are that it will still be ignored. On occasions, a large Palmer fly may succeed where tiny artificials fail, but this tactic by no means guarantees success. The trouble is, that when Broadwings are around, trout are often 'high' in the water. Rather than rising to individual insects, they tend to swim 'blindly' along gulping in many insects in one go. So close are they to the surface that the zone of vision is very limited and it is impossible to expect them to actually *see* your fly. A good 'hatch' of Broadwings certainly occasions the need to fish the dry-fly, yet it is a very frustrating business and you will be lucky to catch the odd fish, let alone a limit bag. On the other hand, the wet-fly will stand absolutely no chance at all!

SEDGES OR CADDIS FLIES

The sedge or caddis flies (*Trichoptera*) (Figure 9) are supremely important to the stillwater dry-fly fisherman; they are present throughout the entire season but are most significant on warm evenings in spring and summer. On such evenings, sedges will skitter across the water in droves and the fish will respond with lusty rises. The whole lake appears explosive and exciting, and the dry-fly is deadly.

Fortunately, sedge flies do not produce selective feeding according to individual species, since, on any evening and at any water, there will be many species of sedge present simultaneously. In essence, they all look the same, varying only in terms of size and colour, which means that impressionistic patterns will usually suffice − exact

Figure 9: Adult sedge fly

imitations are unnecessary. Indeed, the most realistic of imitations will often prove useless if fished statically. Sedge flies usually cause a commotion on the surface which may effectively be emulated by actually retrieving the fly. This is a particularly good ploy when using palmer-dressed artificials which possess a natural 'buzz'.

Trout love sedges to the extent that imitations will kill fish during the day when there are few natural sedge flies around. The artificial sedge will kill fish at times when none are actually rising, also when trout are apparently feeding selectively on other kinds of flies. The use of the artificial sedge at such times represents a kind of gratuitous angling: you offer trout an item of food that they would love to eat if they could get it. When trout are feeding selectively on tiny insects, and are notoriously difficult to tempt with any small artificials, a calculated switch to a large bushy dry-fly may just produce the goods.

Perhaps it will be clear by now that my own approach to the sedge flies does not relate to the imitation of individual species. Indeed, I would readily admit that I can only recognise a limited number of species from the couple of hundred species which actually exist, but that in no way prevents me from catching fish.

Sedges are easily recognisable since they rest with their wings folded above the body, giving the impression that they have their own little roof to keep them dry. They are not unlike moths in appearance (particularly in flight) although the sedge's wings are covered by tiny hairs rather than scales. Sedges have four wings (the front pair being slightly larger) whilst their bodies are slimmer than those of moths. There are no tails although sedges possess distinctive antennae, projecting from the head, which in some species are very long indeed (for example, the appropriately named Longhorns).

Whilst sedges do emerge during the daytime (usually sparse hatches of the smaller flies) most sedges appear during the evening. In terms of size, the sedges vary considerably from tiny flies which are of little interest to the angler up to the Great Red Sedge (*Phryganea grandis*) which is well over an inch in length and presents the trout with a fine meal. In terms of colour, sedges fall into four categories – brown (from a pale fawn to cinnamon or deep red-brown); grey (from a pale silver-grey to grey-brown or silvery charcoal); mottled (normally fawn or pale brown with darker blotches) and black (from silvery-charcoal to an obvious black). The black sedges, for some reason or other, do not seem to have as much appeal, as far as trout are concerned, as do the other colours of sedges. Some years ago, for example, I used to fish a small reservoir which produced thousands of Black Silverhorns on summer afternoons and evenings, yet I never once saw a fish rise to an adult fly, nor did autopsies reveal the presence of such flies in the stomach. Black imitations caught no fish at all. On the other hand, trout always fed avidly on small cinnamon sedges and the corresponding artificial would always catch fish. Nevertheless, I do always carry a few black palmer sedge imitations with me just in case.

And now to artificial flies. There are many popular sedge patterns, some of them centuries old and some of them modern. Personally, the traditional palmer flies are my favourites and I find them hard to beat. However, choice of pattern is always to some extent a subjective matter and it seems only fair to include two of the really good modern sedge imitations: the Richard Walker sedge pattern (*Fly Dressing Innovations*, published by Benn) and 'G and H' Sedge developed by Cliff Henry and John Goddard (made popular by John Goddard's *Trout Flies of Stillwater*, published by A. and C. Black).

Richard Walker's Red Sedge (Figure 10)
Hook: Size 8 or 10 long shank round bend.
Silk: Brown.
Body: Either clipped chestnut coloured ostrich herl or pheasant tail fibres with a tag of arc chrome daylight fluorescent floss.
Wings: A bunch of natural red cock hackle fibres, clipped square level with the hook bend.
Hackle: Natural red cock hackle.

If this pattern is to be used in a retrieve-method of fishing, then it must be well proofed for it is not naturally a good floater.

The G and H Sedge (Figure 11)
Hook: Size 8 or 10 long shank round bend.
Silk: Green.
Underbody: Dark green seal's fur dubbed on to silk and tied in at the bend. After the body of deer hair has been tied in and shaped, the seal's fur is stretched along under the body and tied in at the eye.
Body/Wings: Several bunches of deer hair trimmed to shape to represent the roof-shaped wings of the natural fly.
Hackle: Two rusty dun cocks tied in together at the eye and wound slightly down the body. The top of the hackle is then trimmed off to approximate the head of the natural fly. The stripped butts of these two hackles may be left to form the sedge's antennae.

This is a good representation of the paler sedges (though a little bulky in appearance) and is particularly buoyant so that it is an excellent pattern to use when imitating the skittering motions of the natural fly. You never need to oil this pattern.

The following palmer-dressed flies cater for all my needs. If you wish, you may add an additional white hackle at the eye of the fly in order

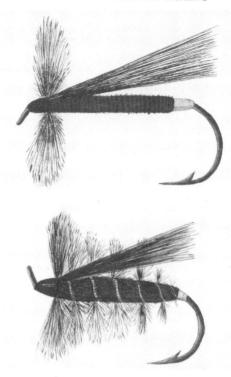

Figure 10: (Top) Richard Walker's sedge
(Bottom) Palmer sedge with hair wing

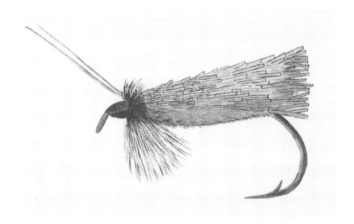

Figure 11: G & H sedge

84

to improve visibility at dusk (such flies are known as Bi-Visibles). More realistic patterns may be created with the addition of hair wings (squirrel or bucktail) or wings made out of hackle fibres (see Figure 10). Normally, I include wings for the statically fished patterns, since trout have more chance to assess their realism, and dress wingless palmers for fishing the moving fly. To be quite honest, I do not really think that the wings add a great deal of effectiveness, though they might boost the confidence of the angler in his artificial fly. Dress your patterns on light wire hooks in order to improve buoyancy.

The Ginger Palmer
A good imitation of any of the pale or fawn-coloured sedges.
Hook: Size 10 to 14.
Silk: Orange.
Body: Ginger seal's fur ribbed with oval gold tinsel.
Body hackle: A medium-fibred ginger cock hackle.
Front hackle: Two ginger cock hackles tied bushy. Add a white cock hackle instead of one of the ginger hackles to create a bi-visible.
Wings: Optional. Ginger cock hackle or squirrel tail hairs tied in to slope backwards.

The Brown Palmer
A good general sedge imitation particularly for the cinnamon sedges.
Hook: Size 8 to 14.
Silk: Brown.
Body: Fiery brown seal's fur ribbed with oval gold tinsel. You may include an optional tag of lime green DF silk to imitate the prominent green egg sacs of certain species.
Body hackle: A medium-fibred brown cock hackle.
Front hackle: Two brown cock hackles tied bushy or two brown hackles with a white hackle next to the eye.
Wings: Brown bucktail or brown cock hackles trimmed square.

The Red Palmer (or Soldier Palmer)
This is a particularly good imitation of the large and small Red Sedge. The latter fly is over an inch in length and in the North of England is often known as the 'buzzard' or 'bustard'. The Red Palmer is also an excellent general stillwater dry-fly.
Hook: Size 8 to 14.
Silk: Crimson.
Body: Medium to dark crimson seal's fur or wool ribbed with oval gold tinsel.
Body hackle: Natural red game cock or dark ginger cock, medium fibred.

Front hackle: Two natural red game cock hackles tied bushy or two red with a white hackle next to the eye.
Wings: Red game cock hackle fibres, or bucktail, or squirrel, or even pheasant tail fibres trimmed square.

The Mottled Palmer
A good imitation of any mottled sedges, marbled sedges or grouse wings.
Hook: Size 10 to 14.
Silk: Fawn.
Body: Ginger seal's fur ribbed with fine oval gold tinsel or three strands of mottled turkey tail feather twisted together and wound along the body.
Body hackle: Cree or ginger cock hackle, medium-fibred.
Front hackle: Two cree or grizzle hackles tied bushy.
Wings: Natural grey squirrel hairs or a few deer hair fibres.

The Black Palmer
This fly represents the black sedges, black silverhorns, silver sedges and so forth.
Hook: Size 10 to 14.
Silk: Black.
Body: Black seal's fur ribbed with oval gold tinsel.
Body hackle: Black or dark slate coloured cock hackle, medium-fibred.
Front hackle: Two black cock hackles tied bushy.
Wings: Squirrel tail or bucktail dyed black.

These patterns are excellent floaters when tied with good quality cock hackles, although I tie them differently for really rough weather. Indeed, the rough weather patterns are simplicity itself to tie. All you need to do is rib four or five hackles from the eye to the bend of the hook and fix them in place with a rib of tying silk. As the hackle stalks are ribbed along the shank they produce a reasonable body and the entire pattern is extremely bushy, light and buoyant. With a good chop on the water, these flies float well and the trout get little chance to examine them closely. Being light and buoyant, the simple hackle palmers make excellent dapping flies when tied in the larger sizes.

For angling purposes, it is worth taking a closer look at the natural sedge fly. After mating, female sedges lay their eggs in a variety of ways: some lay their eggs in bankside vegetation; some lay eggs on reeds and lilies; some oviposit by crawling beneath the surface of the lake, whilst others drop their eggs directly on to the water. By far the most common form of egg-laying is directly on to the surface of the water, which, as it turns out, is a good thing for the dry-fly fisherman. Egg-laying may occur at any time during the day yet it most frequently occurs during the evening. Female sedges fluttering along the surface to deposit their eggs are a prime target for trout; they are attracted by the surface disturbance and it makes sense to use a moving rather than a static fly.

If there is a breeze, then you can simply allow the fly to drift (although the odd twitch helps to add attraction) and if a belly develops in the line, so that the fly skates quickly across the surface, all to the good. The dragging fly is certainly very effective at sedge time. On calm evenings, the fly may be retrieved in pulls and jerks with pauses in between; takes may come at any time and they will often be quite violent, which means that a strong leader point is necessary. In the evening, a slightly thicker leader will not really put the fish off. If you decide to employ the moving dry-fly, then avoid leaders with several knots in them since these will produce unnecessary line-wake. The wake created by the fly itself, however, as it drags along the surface, will not put the fish down in the evening − it will seduce them into taking the fly.

When the eggs have been deposited, they sink and cling to underwater vegetation and stones. The eggs then hatch out into the famous caddis larvae which build a variety of cases out of sand, stones, debris and vegetable matter, although some species are free-swimming and do not build cases at all. These creatures are fascinating but are of little concern to the dry-fly fisherman. Imitations of caddis larvae are particularly useful in cold weather, towards the beginning of the season, when the fish may be lying deep and are unwilling to rise to the floating fly or nymph fished near to the surface.

After the larval stage, the next metamorphosis produces the pupa which trout love to eat. Trout feed on the pupa either in its free-swimming ascent to the surface or when it migrates to the shallows, where it changes to the adult stage among stones and aquatic vegetation. Particularly during the day, trout may prefer the pupal stage, yet it is often difficult to estimate which life-cycle stage is being preferred. (At such times a pupa-dry-fly combination is worth trying. This method is discussed at length at a later stage in the present book.) Generally, when adult flies are being preferred, it will be a result of those species which emerge from the pupa in open water. The adult fly emerges quite quickly yet it does not become rapidly airborne like the upwinged flies. It skitters along the surface of the water either in order to take off or reach dry land. In either case, it may well cause a commotion on the water for quite some time which will attract the trout's attention. In the adult stage, the sedge presents a ready meal.

Once again, a moving artificial seems called for and if it is fished from the bank, its retrieve suggests an adult fly seeking the safety of dry land after emergence.

Rise forms are a good clue to the preferred life-cycle stage. If trout are selecting the pupal stage, then you may expect surface boils, or head-and tail rises: if trout are rising noisily, or are 'slashing' at the surface, the reasonable bet is that they are taking surface flies as they skitter around. From June onwards, particularly in the evenings, the adult fly seems to be preferred to all other life-cycle stages. Not only will there be emergent adults, but also egg-laying females and even adult flies simply attracted to the surface of the water. The larger sedges, in particular, are essentially nocturnal creatures, and whilst they may be absent during the daytime, they become fully active as soon as the light begins to fade. Sedges of many different species will appear at the same time, and as far as the choice of pattern is concerned, it either means studying the most common species (which is difficult when it is quite dark) or trying various palmers in sequence. In general, my first preference is a large fly since it is my belief that large artificials do tend to attract the larger fish. For daytime fishing, unless conditions are quite rough, a smaller size of fly may be called for.

On summer evenings, the surface disturbance produced by myriads of adult flies renders the pupal artificial a poor second to the dry-fly imitation. In any case, as the evening darkens, it is impossible to see the leader which means that fishing the pupal pattern will be of little use: it will be almost impossible to detect takes. On the other hand, large dry-flies are more readily visible − and especially if you fish into the sunset so that the fly may be seen in silhouette.

It may be advisable to choose a bi-visible palmer pattern in order to increase the visibility of the fly. However, as long as you have a good idea where your fly is fishing, the dry-fly may be used effectively when it is even too dark to be able to see it. The logic behind this is quite simple and concerns inducing the fish to break the surface of the water in a noisy fashion, which is achieved by using a moving floating fly. As a trout rises to the fly at the surface it will produce quite an audible slashing sound which is your cue to tighten. Naturally, you will argue that similar sounds will be produced nearby as trout take natural insects. Whilst this is quite true, with experience, and by making sure that you know the position of your own fly, it becomes possible to discern the difference. You will of course, make mistakes − it is impossible to prevent that − but you will also catch fish. Detecting takes by sound alone is easiest when fishing at short range and in the evening long casting is rarely essential since fish will come quite close in unless you scare them. Indeed, they will often swim right up against the bank as they pursue escaping sedge flies. Dry-fly fishing after dark is both rewarding and exciting as long as fishery rules permit it. Unfortunately, it is an all too frequent occurrence for the rules to terminate fishing at dusk, as a result of which the best fishing is lost to all.

It is necessary to stress the uniqueness of dry-fly fishing at sedge time, since all the conventional and traditional rules of the dry-fly purist may well be broken. Sedge patterns *may* be fished statically (during the day they are effective when cast to rising fish, no matter what they are feeding on) but in the evening the static fly is often relatively ineffectual. It may take fish, yet fish will be more likely to be attracted by the moving natural rather than the static artificial. Thus, the moving artificial stands a much better chance of success. Fishing dry-flies to trout taking sedges is really not that much different from wet-fly tactics in that both methods incorporate movement — in a breeze, cast out and allow the fly to swing round before retrieving almost parallel to the bank. However, it is best to twitch the fly from time to time rather than to employ a complete dead-drift. Concentrate throughout, for takes will often occur at the seemingly 'deadest' point of the drift when you least expect them. If there is little breeze, allow the fly to float statically for a while and then retrieve in a series of erratic little pulls with long pauses in between. At times, even a speedily retrieved fly will produce explosive takes, particularly when little daylight remains.

Trout are certainly attracted by the wake created by the moving fly and may even rise to the knots on the leader if they produce a disturbance. However, it is not a good general policy to put fish down by creating unnecessary line-wake. (For this reason, experimenting with dapping tactics from the bank would seem worthwhile if you can fish with the wind at your back.) Our intention is simply to attract trout to the artificial fly. Accordingly, the moving dry-fly necessitates the use of a light and delicate fly-line; some anglers prefer a size 4, although a double-tapered size 5 floater is suitable and a size 6 double-tapered line is certainly manageable. Anything above that line weight is certainly too heavy while weight forward fly lines create far too much disturbance when retrieved. Those who long-cast with heavy weight-forward size 8 lines (or even heavier!) may project their flies a considerable distance, but they will catch few fish. Since it is well to avoid line-wake, the fly-line should be separated from the fly by a long leader (at least fifteen feet) whilst the leader itself should be left ungreased or even treated with fuller's earth so that it sinks below the surface. A greased leader will often cause far more surface disturbance than the fly itself.

It is well to remember that sedge time really is time for the dry-fly! Artificial sedge fly patterns are good general stillwater dry-flies. On small lakes, they will produce fish when there is no apparent feeding activity and when the surface is mirror calm. All of a sudden the mirror will be broken like shattered glass as a large fish rises to take the juicy offering and then bores deep, shaking his head in anger and disbelief. When conditions are breezy on larger waters the speculative sedge pattern will induce fish to rise from water as apparently barren as the Gobi desert. On those occasions when the nymph or lure does not produce a fish, whether trout are rising or not, try a bushy dry-fly; I have even caught trout on palmered sedge flies when they have been obviously fry-feeding and have rejected all the usual lures and fry imitations. Why this should be, I have no idea.

When speculating with sedge patterns during the daytime, a change of tactics is called for: the moving fly is nowhere near as deadly as it is at dusk, and indeed, is more likely to scare fish than attract them. On the other hand, it is rather fruitless if you simply become a reservoir heron, root yourself to the spot, and cast repeatedly to exactly the same place. Travel light and move around searching the water as you go. If there is a breeze (particularly if it blows parallel to the bank) then the dry-fly can be drifted over a considerable area of water with a single cast. As a general pattern, the Red Palmer is difficult to fault. It is often a good tactic to use this fly rather after the manner of a coarse fisherman's float, by placing it on the point and then knotting midge or sedge pupae on to the droppers of the leader. The Red Palmer will not only support the pupae near to the surface, it will also move when one of the pupae has been taken and stand a good chance of catching fish in its own right.

One final note of caution with reference to large sedge patterns. It is a rare thing, particularly if the trout are of reasonable size, for the flies to be taken and ejected quickly. Once the fish has the fly, allow a pause before tightening, otherwise you may well pull the fly right out of his mouth or prick him and put him down. Finally, since large trout rise to large artificials, do not indulge in an over-enthusiastic strike, which will undoubtedly result in a smashed leader and a terribly frightened fish likely to spread panic far and wide.

STONEFLIES

The Stoneflies (*Plecoptera*) are rarely considered to be of much importance generally on stillwaters and are considered even less significant as far as dry-fly fishing is concerned. Certainly, stoneflies are not the most important aquatic flies on stillwaters and are more likely to be associated with rocky upland streams, yet they do appear in numbers where lakes and reservoirs are of the upland variety as opposed to the lush reservoirs of the Midlands and South. Thus, if you fish stillwaters in Wales, Scotland, the Lake District or amid the Pennines, then stoneflies must not be neglected. However, even on these waters, you will not encounter 'hatches' of stoneflies as such, since they change from nymphs to adult flies on dry land: the only adult flies readily available as trout food are egg-laying females.

Adult stoneflies (Figure 12) possess two tails and hard and shiny wings. The wings are held very close and flat over the top of the body when at rest and in the smaller species are even wrapped over and round the body. Members of this order of flies differ greatly in terms of size, and although some species are much more slender than others (for example, the willowfly), the general appearance is quite similar. The nymph of the stoneflies is rather like an earwig and differs little from the adult fly with the exception of wings. The fly has a thorax made up of three segments and a body of ten segments. In some species, the length of the thorax is almost equal to that of the abdomen. Stoneflies have distinctive antennae which are often quite long.

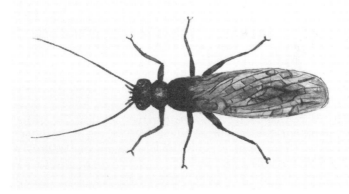

Figure 12: Adult stonefly

Stoneflies are not particularly accomplished fliers and the flight pattern of the female flies is a characteristic straight line travelled at a very slow speed. For this reason, even a moderate breeze may result in numbers of females being deposited on the lake where trout will feed on them. At such times anglers are often under the mistaken impression that they are witnessing a hatch. If the females are poor fliers, the males are *very* poor fliers and although this may suggest that they are likely to be blown on to the water, this is rarely so, essentially because male stoneflies often avoid flight completely. Indeed, the males of certain species of stoneflies are completely incapable of flight, their tiny atrophied wings giving the appearance of little more than wing stubs. Not surprisingly, stoneflies do not mate in flight but at rest on dry land.

Adult flies are very pale creatures when they first appear from their nymphal shucks although they gradually darken to their normal adult colour in a few hours. The nymphs crawl along the bottom until they reach the rocks and stones above water level where the nymphal skin splits and the adult fly emerges safe from the jaws of marauding trout. Some species even climb laboriously into bushes before the transposition takes place.

Being able to drink (and in some species to eat also) stoneflies can exist for longer periods in the adult stage than upwinged flies, although few species exist for much longer than a couple of weeks. During this time, adult flies spend their lives hiding among bushes and trees, or under the stones from which they metamorphosed. Their actual habitat seems to be related to the coloration of the fly so that the Yellow Sally (Figure 13), being a yellowy-green, will hide among the greens and yellows of vegetation, whilst other species will be of a colour that provides camouflage when hiding among stones and boulders. Quite obviously, since adult flies tend to hide away, and are only occasionally blown on to the water before mating, they are of little real value to the angler and are rarely encountered by trout.

After the nymphal stage, the only time an adult stonefly returns to the water is when the ripe female returns to lay her eggs. Females lay their eggs in a number of different ways: some dip against the water in order to release their eggs; others drop down on to the water and release them in one mass, whilst others actually swim along the surface depositing eggs as they do so. Whatever method is employed, when a number of females are simultaneously involved in egg-laying quite a surface disturbance is produced with the result that trout are triggered into feeding activity. At such times, the dry-fly is called for, and, as in the manner of sedge imitation, a moving fly is often more successful than a static fly. Nevertheless, the static fly will suggest spent females and may therefore catch its fair share of fish.

There are a limited number of stoneflies (less than forty) and only a few of them are of any significance to the stillwater dry-fly fisherman. Nevertheless, it is well worth taking note of the following species and tying a few patterns whenever you choose to fish an upland reservoir, lake, loch or tarn.

THE LARGE STONEFLY

The most distinctive stonefly is the Large Stonefly which comprises three separate species (with completely unpronounceable Latin names) all rather misleadingly referred to as 'Mayflies' in the North of England. These common insects have a wing span of almost two inches and although the insect may resemble a large sedge fly when in flight, when at rest, the wings are folded flat across the top of the body so that the fly gives an impression of being very broad and flat.

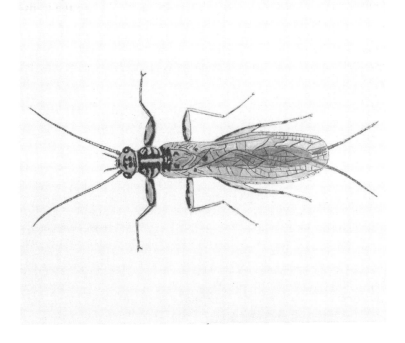

Figure 13: The yellow Sally stonefly

The Large Stonefly is most populous in any upland region of Britain, and although it may be commonest on rivers, it is also fairly common on lakes and reservoirs, both alkaline and acidic. The large and carnivorous nymph of this species (normally referred to as a 'creeper') was once greatly prized as a bait for bottom fishing and this seems in part to have led to the neglect of the adult fly. The adult fly has a long and thick body which tapers very little from thorax to tails. The body is a rich brown colour banded with yellow and tending to be much yellower on the belly than the back. There are two pairs of wings of a similar colour to the body, only darker, which are folded up and held flat over the back when the insect is at rest. The Large Stonefly has two tails and two antennae and is normally encountered in May and June. At this time of year, the Large Stonefly female will often become a subject of the trout's attentions, either when she paddles along the surface of the water to deposit her eggs or when she lies spent and exhausted at the end of this process. She offers quite a juicy morsel and is worthy of imitation. My own favourite pattern, developed from tyings published in the nineteenth-century by Bainbridge (*The Fly-Fisher's Guide* (1816)) and Theakston (*British Angling Flies* (1853)), is dressed as follows:

Hook: Size 10 long shank.
Silk: Brown.
Body: Yellow seal's fur with a dubbing of brown seal's fur ribbed along it.
Hackles: Three cree or grizzle cock hackles wound from behind the eye to a third of the way down the hook shank.
Wings: Mottled hen pheasant or partridge tied flat over the top of the body.
Tails: Two pheasant tail fibres.

Figure 14: Yellow Sally dry-fly

YELLOW SALLY STONEFLIES

The next stoneflies of any consequence are the distinctive Yellow Sallies which have greenish or brownish-yellow bodies and yellow wings. There are two Yellow Sallies, a medium-sized fly (*Isoperla grammatica*) and a small fly (*Chloroperla torrentium*); the former is commonest in May and June, the latter from late April to July, although they may appear throughout the conventional fly-fishing season. Where Yellow Sallies exist, they often appear in considerable numbers and when the adult females return to the water in order to lay their eggs, the trout often become crazy for them and feed in a very preoccupied manner.

The indolent adult flies normally hide in bankside vegetation before mating, which takes place at rest. This stonefly frequents stony streams and stillwaters (generally in upland regions) although it is sometimes found on limestone lakes in considerable numbers. The nymph does not seem to be greatly affected by the relative acidity or alkalinity of the water. Yellow Sallies may be quite important at the beginning of the season when fly-life is generally sparse; egg-laying normally takes place during the afternoon, when fish may take active egg-laying females, or exhausted and spent females, quite avidly. Because of its colour, this fly is easily recognised and it is easy to discern when trout are feeding on it. At a pinch, the patterns offered for the Yellow May Dun will kill fish feeding on the Yellow Sally although it is not an upwinged fly, which means that artificial wings tied in an upright position are not singularly realistic. Whilst few, if any, Yellow Sally patterns have emerged from the South of England, this fly has been imitated for centuries in the fly-fishing literature of the North. The following pattern (Figure 14) is a development from a fly invented by Alfred Ronalds (*The Fly-Fisher's Entomology,* (1836)) which he thought extremely profitable 'on very hot days when it is busily employed laying its eggs upon the water'. It may be fished either as a hackled pattern, or as a winged pattern, with equal success:

Hook: Size 12 or 14 (depending on which of the Yellow Sallies is in evidence).
Silk: Yellow.
Body: Amber-yellow seal's fur with a little brown and green seal's fur mixed in. Rib with brown tying silk.
Hackle: Dark yellow cock hackle tied bushy for the first third of the hook length.
Wings: Optional. Any slip of pale feather dyed a pale yellow colour and tied in to lie flat over the body.

Most of the other common stoneflies encountered on stillwaters tend to be very small, slim and brown in colour: varying from red-brown to dark brown, almost black. They differ very little in appearance and for angling purposes may be regarded as one and the same insect. They are much slimmer in profile than the larger species of stoneflies and include flies which wrap their wings around the body when at rest, making them appear very slim indeed. For this reason, one species gained the popular name of Needle-flies. Any of the small brown stoneflies may be imitated by using the Pheasant Tail dry-fly. One of the most important of the smaller stoneflies is the Willow Fly (*Leuctra geniculata*) which is widespread in its distribution and common on stillwaters in the month of September. These flies are just less than half an inch in length, are slender, and brown-olive in colour. In flight, their clumsiness makes them appear quite large in size. One of the best imitations of the Willow-fly is provided by a dry-fly called the *Beacon Beige*, which I tie as follows:

Hook: Size 14.
Silk: Brown.
Body: Stripped peacock herl, which should produce a dark brown/fawn ribbed appearance.
Hackle: A red game cock hackle and a cree or grizzle hackle wound together.
Tails: Optional (they may help the fly to float nicely), fibres of cree or grizzle hackle.

The Beacon Beige will also succeed as an imitation of any of the small brown stoneflies including the common Needle-flies which produce reasonable rises on stillwaters, even in the South of England. Unfortunately, these insects are often neglected simply because they are mistaken for other flies, midges or gnats for example; it is an understandable error considering how small they are. There are two flies popularly termed needle-flies, *Leuctra hippopus*, which is common at the beginning of the season, and *Leuctra fusiventris* which is common towards the end of the season. Both flies are very slender brown insects and differ very little in appearance. Needle-flies often appear in great numbers in order to lay their eggs and thus provide good rises although the trout are often difficult to catch. Because your artificial fly will be in competition with a host of naturals, it is worth giving a little twitch from time to time in order to attract the trout's attentions.

MIDGES

The midges (*Chironomids*) are the most common and populous of all the stillwater aquatic hatches and few anglers would argue against their importance. On the other hand, whilst it is readily accepted that trout feed extensively on the larvae and pupae of midges, it is usually agreed that the adult fly is of little importance and, as a result there are few dry-fly imitations of the adult midge. Whilst I accept that the pupa, in particular, is more important than the adult fly, I do not accept that imitations of the adult chironomid are of no value. Thus, as far as I am concerned, there is a place for the dry-fly when imitating this family of the Diptera order. Even during daytime hatches of midges, the emerging fly, or even adult fly after emergence, may be preferred to the pupa or eaten along with it. In the evening, the rise may be occasioned entirely by trout feeding on egg-laying females which may render the pupa quite useless (since no natural pupae are actually ascending to the surface at that time). At times such as this, anglers see midges flying around and conclude hastily that they are hatching; they reach for pupal patterns and then flog the water with them becoming perplexed when no takes materialise. Quite simply, the artificial midge pupa is not a panacea.

For some strange reason, I have not had the kind of success with the midge pupa that I seemed to enjoy in former years. The reason for this is by no means clear, although I sometimes wonder whether stocked fish become over-exposed to pupal patterns which have increased enormously in popularity over the last decade. We are all aware of the fact that popular lures often lose their effectiveness when they are over-used because trout begin to get wary of them. Accordingly, it is often worth turning to the dry-fly when the pupa fails to work adequately: a new tactic will often work simply because it is different and less likely therefore to scare the fish. It is also true to say that dry-flies rarely catch fish during midge hatches simply because they are rarely used and enjoy little publicity. There are times during the daytime when dry-flies will catch fish just as well as pupal patterns; it is simply a matter of personal choice which to use. Generally, adult flies emerge very quickly from the pupal shuck so that it is easier for trout to pick off the mature pupae. However, some adults do fail to become airborne and trout will devour them gratefully. For this reason, a static dry-fly may enjoy a measure of success being taken in mistake for an unfortunate natural. Paradoxically, therefore, the dry-fly will take fish when trout are seemingly feeding on pupae rather than adult flies.

I remember fishing from a boat at Packington a number of years

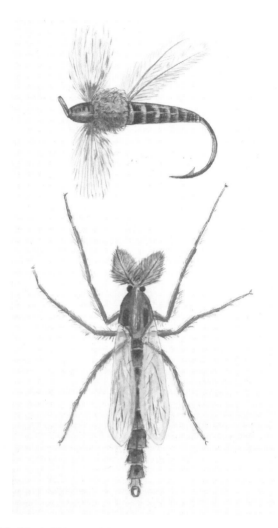

Figure 15: (Top) Chironomid dry-fly
(Bottom) Adult male chironomid

ago. I caught rainbow trout during a hatch of midges by fishing a team of pupal imitations; my boat partner fished pupae on the droppers and a Grey Duster dry-fly on the point. He caught an equal number of fish, yet they all fell to the Grey Duster, and a point of general interest was that his fish were all brown trout. Thus, although I would never argue that the dry-fly is generally better than the pupal imitation, it is worth using the dry-fly if you prefer fishing it.

Midges are members of the huge Diptera order, referred to by entomologists as the 'true' flies – this order includes crane flies, gnats, hawthorn flies, bluebottles and the like. The word 'Diptera' means 'two wings' which thus distinguishes the true flies from the sedges, stoneflies and ephemeropterans which normally possess four wings.

Chironomids (or non-biting midges) are known locally by many names including 'Black and Blaes', 'Duck Flies', 'Harlequin Flies' and 'Buzzers', whilst they are wrongly referred to as 'gnats' in a number of old angling books. There are about four hundred species of chironomids although many are of little value to the angler, either because they are too minute or too rare in their distribution. Not only are most species aquatic by nature, but also they appear throughout the trout season in huge numbers which serves to underline their importance. From the early days of stillwater angling, such 'giants' as Dr Bell, who fished the reservoirs of Chew Valley in Somerset, have offered imitations of midges – generally imitations of the pupa. Nevertheless, midge imitations have existed for an even longer period of time although the older patterns imitated the adult fly. For example, Alfred Ronalds tied an imitation of the Golden Dun midge which he made popular in 1836.

In profile, the adult flies are all rather similar, possessing long and quite slender bodies which have a characteristically humped thorax. In the smaller species, the bodies are proportionately slimmer than those of the larger species. The fly's thorax includes the wing roots and the body segments from which the long legs of the fly emerge. Midges do not possess slender antennae but two distinct 'plumes' project forwards from the head. The fly's wings are relatively slender and are normally held in a flat backward position over the body when at rest. They project backwards in a V-shape and are not folded completely over one another like the wings of a stonefly. The body is notably longer than the wings, which, when viewed with the long spidery legs, makes the midge resemble a small crane fly. The bodies of many species have a distinctly ribbed appearance which may be perfectly imitated with a material such as stripped peacock herl or hackle stalk.

Chironomids only really vary in terms of size and colour. The early season species tend to be smaller and are often black in body colour although various black midges do appear throughout the season. Whilst some of the black midges do possess completely black bodies, certain species possess lighter bands around the divisions of their body segments, thus giving them a distinctly ribbed appearance. Various

99

green midges are also common throughout the season: some like the Blagdon Green Midge (by no means limited to that locality) have almost emerald green bodies, whilst other flies possess bodies of various shades of olive green. From mid-July to early September, a large olive green midge appears in numbers on warm days and provides good sport, particularly in the evenings.

Although various brown-coloured midges will be seen from time to time during the fishing season, they are most numerous from June to September and during this period the Large Red Midge makes its appearance. This strikingly beautiful fly seems to be a favourite of the trout. Its body colour is a light red-brown (as are the legs) whilst the transparent wings are also tinged with this colour. Being a large fly, the appropriate hook size for imitations is size 10 which gives the lie to the myth that the word 'midge' is synonymous with tiny insects. Other distinctive midges include the Orange-Silver Midge (which has a dull orange body ribbed with a silvery-grey) and the famous Golden Dun Midge (which is of a dullish golden-amber colour). The former insects are commonest from April to June (although later species also occur) while the latter normally appears from the middle of May to the end of August.

The above descriptions cover the commonest flies but it is important to be aware of local variations. For example, on one lake, huge numbers of tiny creamy-white midges emerged in April, the like of which I have never seen elsewhere. It may, therefore, be necessary to tie specific patterns in order to imitate species common only in your own particular area.

Midges normally hatch during the daytime although occasionally there are evening hatches. Evening is normally the time for mating to take place. Swarms of adult males often appear in huge numbers and look very much like columns of smoke swirling upwards. Females approach the swarms and coupling takes place in the air at which time a breeze will often result in coupled flies falling on to the water where trout eat them gratefully. The finest pattern at such a time is the Knotted Midge which is hackled both 'fore' and 'aft' and may be tied in a variety of colours.

After mating, many spent males will fall on to the lake surface. The females dip against the water to deposit their eggs and then again, often remain spent on the water. Thus, evening produces a good opportunity to fish the floating chironomid imitation. It should be fished statically and cast to the ring of a rise or in the path of a feeding fish. It is often difficult to work out a fish's feeding path although; if there is a slight breeze, you can guarantee that the trout will swim into the breeze which at least provides something of a clue. Generally, fishing dry midge imitations calls for delicate casting and perfect presentation; the leader should not be too thick whilst a light weight double-tapered fly line is essential.

Adult females lay a jelly-like raft of eggs directly on to the surface of the water and this 'raft' may float until the larvae hatch out and descend, or it may sink until the larvae have emerged. The larvae themselves usually remain in the bottom mud and are regularly eaten by deep-feeding fish. When the larvae become mature, they metamorphose into a free-swimming pupa which in coloration closely resembles the adult fly. The pupae are so well known that for our present purposes they do not beg close attention. They are particularly important as an item of trout food when they emerge to the surface before 'hatching' into adult midges. Certainly, when trout are really feeding on the pupal stage, the dry-fly will have to be abandoned in favour of the pupal imitation. A clue to preoccupied pupa-feeding is the characteristic head-and-tail rise form (which I often call 'the porpoise roll'). This is an obvious signal to adopt nymph-fishing tactics.

Although pupae may hang for some time near to the surface before the adults emerge, the emergence itself is often very rapid. For this reason, as discussed previously, the dry-fly is often held to be useless since adult flies soon become airborne. However, I hope that I have illustrated the point that dry-flies do work under such circumstances. Further, dry-flies are particularly successful under certain conditions, for example, when adult flies experience some difficulty in escaping from their pupal shucks. (At a later stage, I shall discuss particular approaches to adopt when trout are feeding on emerging flies.) Adult flies have difficulty in escaping from the pupal shuck when the water is very calm and oily, or covered with scum. For example, I once timed a number of emerging Red Midges under such conditions in early September and found that individual insects were taking over a minute to escape from the water. Many flies failed completely to free themselves either from the shuck, or from the surface film. As a result, trout fed avidly on emergent and adult flies without expending energy. They even preferred these stages to the pupa.

Hopefully, I have illustrated that the dry-fly *will* catch chironomid-feeding trout, *if* the right pattern is employed. It is now time to turn to appropriate artificial flies. As general patterns, the Grey Duster and Beacon Beige (described previouly) are quite satisfactory, dressed in a range of sizes from 12 down to 16. The Blue Quill is another general pattern which will catch trout feeding on midges.

Blue Quill

Hook: Size 10 to 16.
Silk: Brown.
Body: Stripped peacock herl.
Hackle: Dark blue dyed cock hackle.
Wings: Optional – Starling.

All three patterns will certainly catch fish, yet the chironomid is a distinctive enough creature to demand an artificial in its own right. Further, since the dry-fly will often be employed under very still conditions, and will be fished statically, it has to stand up to close scrutiny. Thus, it seems important to emphasise the most outstanding features of the chironomid when tying an imitation. First of all, it is important to note that the fly is quite slim and delicate, and possesses long, thin legs. For this reason, a bushily-dressed hackle seems most unsuitable. The hackle must be dressed quite lightly and must be reasonably long in the fibre in order to suggest the long legs of the natural – it must also be the same colour as the natural's legs (which means that it will usually be the same colour as the body). If the hackle is sparse, then the hackle feather itself must be of a very high quality or else the pattern will soon become waterlogged and sink. Secondly, it seems necessary to reflect the contrast between the natural's abdomen and thorax. This will be achieved by producing a reasonably slender abdomen out of stripped peacock herl, hackle stalk and the like, and then by producing a bulkier thorax out of a material such as seal's fur. Normally I include wings on my patterns, for the sake of realism, and use the narrow points of pale coloured cock hackles. These are tied in to lie flat and slope backwards in a V-shape. Because midges have slender and transparent wings, only hackle points seem suitable since light will pass between the fibres – opaque feathers from the wings of birds are far too bulky. According to these considerations, I tie the following flies which may be recommended to the reader:

Black Midge

Hook: Size 10 to 16
Silk: Black.
Body: Stripped black cock hackle stalk or dyed black condor herl.
Thorax: Black seal's fur.
Hackle: Black cock hackle, reasonably long in the fibre and lightly dressed.
Wings: White cock hackle tips.

Emerald Midge
Hook: Size 12 to 16.
Silk: Pale green.
Body: Bright green swan herl (dyed, of course).
Thorax: Light olive-green seal's fur.
Hackle: Medium green-olive cock hackle.
Wings: White cock hackle tips.

Olive Midge
Hook: Size 12 to 16.
Silk: Olive green.
Body: Various shades of olive-green stripped cock hackle stalk or dyed olive stripped peacock herl or condor herl.
Thorax: Olive-green seal's fur, a little darker than the body shade.
Hackle: Olive-green cock hackle to match the body shade.
Wings: Pale blue dun cock hackle tips.

Brown Midge
Hook: Size 12 to 16.
Silk: Brown.
Body: Stripped peacock herl or pheasant tail fibres.
Thorax: Medium brown seal's fur.
Hackle: Rich brown cock hackle.
Wings: Pale ginger or honey dun cock hackle tips.

Red Midge
Hook: Size 10 to 14.
Silk: Brown.
Body: Rich red-brown pheasant tail fibres or stripped peacock herl dyed red spinner shade or red-brown stripped hackle stalk.
Thorax: Dark red seal's fur.
Hackle: Natural red game cock hackle.
Wings: Pale ginger cock hackle tips.

Golden Dun Midge
Hook: Size 10 to 14.
Silk: Golden olive.
Body: Golden olive dyed swan herl, or stripped golden olive hackle stalk.
Thorax: Dark ginger seal's fur.
Hackle: Golden olive dyed cock hackle.
Wings: Pale ginger cock hackle tips.

Orange Midge

Hook: Size 10 to 14.

Silk: Hot orange.

Body: Grey heron herl ribbed in close turns with stripped peacock herl dyed a hot orange shade.

Thorax: A mixture of grey and orange seal's fur.

Hackle: Dark orange or ginger cock hackle.

Wings: Pale ginger cock hackle tips.

(As an alternative to the dressing of the bodies described above, a very realistic effect may be achieved by dubbing a slender body of the appropriate colour of seal's fur and then ribbing in close turns with stripped peacock herl dyed to the same shade as the seal's fur.)

6

Terrestrials, semi-aquatics and the dry-fly

What is a terrestrial insect? That's simple enough really, it is an insect which is bred on the land and only appears on the water by accident, generally when there is a wind strong enough to blow it on to the lake or reservoir. When a few terrestrials are blown on to the water, they may be picked off by trout along with whatever other insects are in evidence but, when terrestrials are blown on to the water in numbers trout often feed on them in a preoccupied manner and to the exclusion of all else.

What are semi-aquatics? That question, perhaps, is a little more difficult to answer and is somewhat subjective. For my own purposes, I regard semi-aquatics as those insects which have aquatic pupae or larvae (such as some of the crane flies, drone flies and certain moths) yet are likely to emerge as adult flies either in very shallow water or on dry land. They may return to the water in order to lay their eggs yet, like the true terrestrials, they are most likely to appear on the lake in numbers only when blown there by a stiff breeze.

Whether an angler fishes on stillwaters or rivers, terrestrial creatures are often more important to him than has sometimes been appreciated and they are very important to the use of the dry-fly. When trout feed on aquatic insects during a hatch, either wet or dry-flies may be successful since there will be plenty of nymphs or pupae rising in the water prior to the emergence of the adult floating insect. However, when trout are feeding on terrestrial insects, the case is somewhat different since terrestrials possess no subaqueous life-cycle stage which may either be preferred or eaten simultaneously with the adult fly. When terrestrials are around, trout are only interested in adult flies and they will feed on them at the surface unless such flies become drowned during choppy wave conditions. Thus, the dry-fly technique is usually very successful in the imitation of terrestrials.

It is surprising how often land-bred insects appear on the surface of stillwaters, and in what numbers, and although it is generally believed that they are simply blown there from the land, they also seem

105

to exhibit a fatal attraction for sheets of water. I often see them flitting backwards and forwards over the surface in droves, and for no apparent reason; the result of their activities, however, is clear enough, since many of them will be left struggling and dying on the water at the whim of the breeze. No doubt there is a reason for terrestrials being attracted to water and congregating in the immediate hinterland of lakes and reservoirs, but I am afraid that I do not know it. Nevertheless, it is a good thing that trout feed on terrestrials for they provide us with an excellent opportunity for using the dry-fly on stillwaters.

Fishing terrestrial imitations is often fascinating because it adds a new dimension to dry-fly fishing: that of actually working the floating fly. Classic dry-fly philosophy has always regarded movement of the artificial as anathema and the routine has involved an accurate cast accompanied by the patient observation of a static fly. Such a creed has been produced by the rich heritage of chalk stream literature since on the chalk streams, there are many upwinged aquatic flies and their imitation has been the central concern.

When an ephemeropteran dun emerges from its nymphal case it simply floats without movement until its wings are dry enough to

An offshore breeze and the trout are ready to take the floating fly where the calm water meets the ripple. Terrestrial insects have been blown there from the bank. The angler's fly-line is just visible in the bottom right-hand corner of the photograph.

enable it to fly free from the water. It emerges from the water and flies into the air. In order to dupe the trout into believing that our imitation has emerged from a mature nymph, the fly must be presented so delicately, and must alight so gently, that absolutely no disturbance whatsoever is produced. On the other hand, land-bred insects fall from the air and 'plop' on to the water so that delicate presentation is less significant. Indeed, there are times when an artificial fly falling rather clumsily on to the water can be a positive benefit since it not only emulates the natural insect but also attracts the trout's attention.

Trout are rather like Pavlov's dogs, their feeding instinct is a programmed reflex action, and if they are conditioned by a surface disturbance produced each time a natural terrestrial falls on to the water, they will react quite instinctively to an artificial presented in a similar manner. Further, whilst aquatic flies are likely to float passively until becoming airborne, terrestrials will struggle erratically in order to free themselves from the tension of the surface film. This struggle creates a pattern of vibrations at the surface which in turn attracts the trout's attention and thus acts as an important feeding stimulus. Accordingly, if we move our fly either by little pulls, twitches, or a slow retrieve, we can stimulate our quarry to take.

It is obvious that many terrestrials will become exhausted after a protracted struggle and will eventually lie quite still: they too will be eaten, but in a rather more leisurely manner. For this reason, a static dry-fly will also kill fish, yet it has one distinct disadvantage over a worked fly (apart from lacking the same stimulus of attraction) — it allows a fish time to inspect the imitation and reject it if it finds it wanting in any respect. Fishing a static fly will probably mean a longer wait for a rise after the cast has been made and even a statically fished Daddy-longlegs may be taken quite gently. Conversely, a Daddy-longlegs imitation which emulates the natural's desperate struggle for life, will probably induce more takes and these will be rather more violent and exciting than those with the static imitation. In many ways it remains a matter of personal choice although I have known times when only moving imitations of terrestrials have caught fish, whilst static flies have been ignored.

While we are considering the technique of using a moving dry-fly, it is important to underline the fact that trout do not behave with complete rash abandon and may easily become scared by the fly-line or by a 'bow-waving' leader cutting through the surface film. Two points emerge here; the first being that the leader ought to be as long as possible so that the thick fly-line is separated from the fly by as great a distance as possible; the second being that the last few feet of the leader ought to be left to sink rather than be greased. A greased nylon leader not only appears much thicker, it also causes a greater disturbance at the surface. In addition, a knotted leader will provide too much surface disturbance. In this style of fishing, a continuous tapered leader (which is a single length of tapered nylon) is preferable although such leaders are expensive to purchase. Even a continuous tapered leader will cause a wave at the surface, so that the last few feet must be allowed to sink since less disturbance is produced by drawing a leader along underneath the surface film. Another problem with leaders, and particularly leaders produced from expensive nylon, is that they often possess a shiny finish which produces a disturbing amount of flash, particularly on sunny days. Nylon which has a dull or matt finish is infinitely superior in this respect although shiny nylon may be dulled down with a liquid abrasive. Rubbing the leader with fuller's earth compound will achieve this effect although this will necessitate a thorough cleaning if the leader is to be re-greased since fuller's earth is used in making leaders sink. There are many anglers who prefer to dye their leaders black in order to make them less obvious to the trout (and this can be achieved quite simply) although I do not believe that the colour of the leader is all that significant.

Although I am firmly committed to the use of dry-flies when fishing for terrestrial-feeding trout (because I enjoy this experience) I am not suggesting that the wet-fly is useless, far from it. In very rough conditions, land-bred insects will become drowned and waterlogged so that trout will quite naturally feed on them below the surface, as well as at the surface in the case of naturals which are still afloat. It is agreed by many that imitations of the Drone fly succeed best when retrieved just under the water, although it is as likely that sunken Drone fly imitations catch more fish simply because this knowledge has been passed on, resulting in a greater percentage of anglers fishing this pattern beneath the surface. If an equal number of anglers worked their imitations at the surface, I doubt whether the results of the two techniques would differ markedly.

What an angler must be aware of, is the fact that terrestrial fishing often breaks many of the rules of stillwater fly-fishing. For example, although it is often considered best to fish into the wind, the opposite may be true concerning the subject of our present discussion. Normally, when a wind blows on to a bank, it not only tilts the thermocline of large reservoirs so that warm water forms against the windward bank, it also washes food items against this bank. Further, the waves and current produced against this bank disturb the bottom and wash around many creatures upon which the trout may feed. However, it will be noted that each of these considerations is of the greatest importance to subaqueous food forms. Terrestrial creatures will not be blown on to the water from the shoreline against which the wind is blowing and although they may drift there, on large expanses of water many will be drowned or eaten before they reach this bank. Thus, it may be of greater benefit to fish from a bank where the wind is at your back since land-bred insects will be blown on to the water from this bank and fish will congregate to feed on them when they land. Casting is easier but long casts may be necessary since the flies will be carried some way out before reaching the fish. Ideally, when the wind blows at a slight angle away from the bank good fishing conditions are often produced since the fish may feed quite close in. Calm lanes are also lucrative features under such conditions and often contain concentrations of struggling terrestrials and feeding fish. Equally, bays and creeks are productive and they often have the added advantage of making long-casting quite unnecessary.

While many terrestrials are blown on to the water from their airborne flight, or from grasses, bracken and bushes surrounding the reservoir, some simply fall from trees on to the water and may do so under relatively calm conditions. Always look out for trout feeding on terrestrials when fishing tree-lined banks or wooded bays, and be prepared to use outlandish patterns such as imitations of beetles and caterpillars. A word of caution however, although such creatures may drift out into the reservoir, many will be eaten close to the bank and whilst it is advantageous if fish are feeding close in (which they often do in the evening) they may be easily scared. Keep low, move quietly and cast along the bank some distance since the greatest distance possible ought to be put between the angler and the fish. It is possible to stalk quite near to such fish but this technique demands stealth, patience, discomfort and, at the end of it all, a very delicate cast, and casting beneath trees is never easy. Incidentally, many of the smaller lakes have tree shrouded banks which are rarely fished because of the difficulty of the cast, yet, with practice, such locations ought to produce some of the best results during the summer months, and some of the largest fish. The value of possessing a short rod, capable of casting under restricted conditions and presenting a very delicate line, should never be underestimated in stillwater fly-fishing.

Unfortunately, terrestrials have often been neglected by fly-fishermen who may regard them as unattractive Cinderellas when compared with the romantic flies such as Lake Olives and Blagdon Green Midges. Further, terrestrials belong to many orders and are as diverse in appearance as they are in classification which means that a series of different imitations is made necessary. This is obviously a problem for the angler who purchases flies on a strict budget or who desires to cut down on the selection of flies which he carries around with him. The reasoning also seems to be that since many terrestrials exist only for a very short period during any given season, they are not that important. Certainly, terrestrials may not seem to be as significant as midge pupae, yet terrestrials of one kind or another may be present during most of the season and individual terrestrials may dominate the trout's diet at any given time, thus becoming more important than the ubiquitous chironomid. There are times when hawthorn flies, drone flies and even the Coch-y-bondhu beetle are eaten to the exclusion of all else, and it would seem foolish to arrive at the water on such an occasion and be without an appropriate imitation.

Strangely, the imitation of terrestrials is sometimes thought to be a matter of recent innovation. This is not so. Certainly, the writings of John Goddard, Taff Price and others, in books and magazines, have attracted our attention to their significance, yet this was a matter which was never doubted by our angling forefathers. Terrestrials can be discerned in the *Treatise of Fishing with an Angle* (1496) and appear in numbers in the lists of flies offered by such men as Charles Cotton, Richard and Charles Bowlker and Alfred Ronalds. Terrestrial imitation reached its peak in the angling literature of the nineteenth century and even the high priest of the chalk stream, F. M. Halford, included terrestrial imitations such as Beetles (the 'Little Chap' and Coch-y-bondhu), Ants, Black Gnats and the Cowdung Fly. The trouble with many nineteeth century fly-fishing books, is that they included far too many patterns, so that when a movement developed for the reduction of patterns, and the standard lists were pruned, terrestrials were the first to go. I get the impression that some of these worthy gentlemen tried to imitate everything in sight so that if a fish rose to a dead sparrow they would have imitated it! Perhaps they did more harm than good in the long run, since their collection of patterns were far too catholic — yet they did produce some fine imitations of terrestrial insects.

Anyone interested in the imitation of land-bred creatures would benefit from a consideration of American angling literature which has dealt quite thoroughly with this subject. My own personal interest was stimulated originally by Vincent C. Marinaro's classic book *A Modern Dry-Fly Code* (1950), whilst some excellent patterns are offered in more recent books, such as *Selective Trout* by Swisher and Richards, and *Modern Fly Dressings for the Practical Angler* by Poul Jorgensen. However, the American tradition of terrestrial imitation reaches its zenith in a recently published book, *Tying and Fishing Terrestrials* by Gerald Alny, which is both informative and instructive.

110

It is hoped that the following notes will provide a sound introduction to the creed of imitating terrestrial insects with the dry-fly and provide enough food for thought to stimulate the reader into observation at first hand. For ease of treatment I have chosen to deal with terrestrials in alphabetical order, rather than in order of relative importance, which is by no means easy to assess.

THE ALDER

Although this is a very common and famous fly, I am not of the opinion that it is of very much importance as a dry-fly fisherman's fly. I include it simply as a matter of form.

The Alder (*Sialis*) (Figure 16) is a very distinctive fly, looking very much like a large dark brown sedge fly, with hard, heavily veined wings. It is really a semi-aquatic fly since adult females lay eggs on vegetation overhanging water. When the larvae hatch out from their eggs, they crawl off the vegetation and drop into the water where they

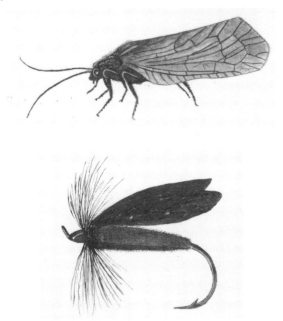

Figure 16: Alder-fly (Sialis lutaria)
(Top) Natural
(Bottom) Artificial

111

stay until mature. Then, the mature 'nymphs' crawl from their aquatic home on to dry land and, among shrubs and bushes, pupate for a week or so before emerging as adult flies. Adult flies appear in late April and continue to be in evidence until the end of June. Alder flies do seem to be attracted to water and often fly very low over it, although you will note that they do not hatch from it, nor do females make contact with it during egg-laying. In my opinion, although trout do feed on the aquatic larvae, they rarely devour adult flies. The fame of the Alder has perhaps been a product of the fame of the artificial fly tied supposedly to imitate it. This traditional fly was credited to Charles Kingsley (although he lifted it from Alfred Ronalds) who himself came to the conclusion that the adult Alder was of little real significance. Thus, I include the tying of the artificial Alder as a general dry-fly pattern and as a good imitation of the sedges – not as an imitation of the Alder!

Hook: Size 10 medium-long shank.
Silk: Mulberry coloured.
Body: Bronze peacock herl dressed over mulberry tying silk.
Hackle: Black cock hackle.
Wings: Speckled hen feather wing tied in the shape of a sedge wing.

You will note that shop-bought Alders are always wet-flies and several sizes smaller than a true Alder fly.

ANTS

Ants are members of the Hymenoptera order of insects and have been around this planet for at least fifty million years. To ensure such a successful history, ants have to mate, and that is where the interest begins to develop for trout and angler alike.

The great phenomenon of 'ant-falls' only occurs once a year, during a short period of dry weather, at any time from the beginning of July to the end of September. At such times, the great mating ritual takes place. Both males and females grow wings enabling them to migrate, swarm, court and couple. Male ants die soon after their intercourse with the females whilst the females rub off their now unwanted wings before laying their eggs, perhaps in the original nest, or in a neighbouring nest, or in a new nest which they establish themselves.

During calm conditions spent males may well fall on to the lake surface whilst even a slight breeze will result in falls of both males and females. They may fall in their thousands, providing trout with a feeding orgy and demanding that the angler choose a specific ant pattern since the fish will be feeding in a preoccupied manner.

Unfortunately, the angler's artificial must compete with many naturals so that the odds are stacked against success. For this reason, I do not think it a bad thing to retrieve the floating ant pattern in a series of tiny jerks and twitches — at least it will be noticed. If the fly begins to sink, it doesn't really matter at all, as long as it remains within inches of the surface it still stands a reasonable chance of being taken. When the weather is very rough, a wet pattern will indeed be more effective than a floater.

In 1676 Charles Cotton produced a nice little imitation of the red ant ('dubbing of brown and red camlet mixt, with a light grey wing') whilst standard copies of the red and black ants were included in F. M. Halford's *Floating Flies and How to Dress Them* published in 1886. Those of you interested in fly-fishing history may wish to look these patterns up although the following standard modern tyings will suit all occasions.

Figure 17: The Ant dry-fly

Red Ant
Hook: Size 14.
Silk: Orange.
Body: Two blobs of seal's fur (a 'red spinner' colour) representing the ant's bifurcated body.
Wings: Two blue dun or pale ginger cock hackle tips tied in sloping backwards and kept slightly apart.
Hackle: Red game cock, rather sparse.

Black Ant
Hook: Size 14.
Silk: Black.
Body: As above with the substitution of black seal's fur.
Wings: As above.
Hackle: Black cock.

Brown or Wood Ant
Hook: Size 12.
Silk: Brown.
Body: As above with the substitution of fiery brown seal's fur.
Wings: Blue dun cock hackle tips.
Hackle: Dark ginger cock, about three full turns.

The Wood Ant (*Formica rufa*) is about the largest of the ants and is very common on lakes and reservoirs which are bounded by woodlands, it may even fall from trees on to the water at any time during the season.

BEETLES (*COLEOPTERA*)

Beetles are eaten more frequently by trout than most anglers readily realise, although the majority are taken beneath the surface in either larval or adult forms. The whirligig beetle, however, which is a common enough sight as it describes circles on the surface of the lake, and many terrestrial beetles do provide a floating meal for his lordship. In particular, hordes of Coch-y-bondhu beetles often end up blown on to the surfaces of upland reservoirs where they are relished by the resident trout. In small tree-fringed lakes, large trout will often lie under the trees in wait for the many beetles which will fall from the leaves and branches and become easy prey. Strangely, modern anglers tend to ignore the beetle although its significance was rightly understood in the nineteenth century. For example, when Michael Theakston published his *British Angling Flies* in 1853 he included ten excellent beetle imitations.

Beetle patterns are often best fished in tiny twitches rather than statically and this point was emphasised by Courtney Williams in his excellent and comprehensive *Dictionary of Trout Flies* where he writes, 'there are, of course, scores of land beetles which accidentally get carried on to the water, where the buzzing disturbance they create serves to attract the attention of fish'. It is useful, therefore, to imitate beetles with moving dry-flies and a valuable tip is to improve the buoyancy of the artificial by including an underbody of either cork or Plastazote. The Black and Peacock Spider (dressed with a cock hackle) is an excellent general beetle pattern whilst my own Black Beetle is a good 'fly' when imitating whirligig beetles, staphs, ground beetles and the like.

Black Beetle
Hook: Size 10 to 16.
Silk: Black.

Body: Black seal's fur with a black cock hackle wound in palmer style along the body. The hackle is then trimmed close underneath in order to produce a flat profile thus allowing the beetle to float close to the surface.

Back: Black raffene, moistened and stretched over the back of the pattern and tied in behind the eye. Note that the raffene must be attached to the shank of the hook before the body is dubbed.

The Coch-y-bondhu beetle is often a very important terrestrial in hilly regions. I believe that the Latin name of this insect is *Phyllopertha horticola* although it often goes under other common names such as June Bug, Brechan Clock, Bracken Clock, Marlow Buzz, Hazel Fly and Shorn Fly. On breezy days, I have seen hundreds of such beetles blown on to a small Pennine reservoir; each gust of wind produced an aquatic explosion almost as if it were feeding time in a stew pond. My preferred dressing of the standard pattern is as follows:

Figure 18: Two good beetle imitations:
(Top) The Black Beetle
(Bottom) Claret hackled Coch-y-bondhu

Coch-y-bondhu

Hook: Size 14.
Silk: Wine coloured.
Tag: Gold Tinsel.
Body: Bronze peacock herl.
Hackle: Claret cock hackle.

During the summer months, soldier beetles, sailor beetles and cockchafer beetles may also occur in large numbers and are important enough for the dry-fly fisherman to keep a few patterns in reserve. Most of the soldier beetles are amber in colour (suggesting khaki army uniforms) and are aptly imitated by a pattern developed from one of Theakston's original designs.

115

Soldier Beetle
Hook: Size 12.
Silk: Brown.
Body: Amber seal's fur.
Hackle: Ginger cock hackle ribbed palmer-wise along the body and clipped close above and below.
Wing cases: A small amber feather with a black top from a pheasant's breast. The feather is tied in so that it lies flat over the top of the body.

During the spring and summer, another close relative of the soldier beetle, the sailor beetle, may also swarm and become important to the stillwater dry-fly fisherman. This beetle again, developed its popular name from its coloration, the wing cases being a deep blue. The following pattern is a good imitation:

Sailor Beetle
Hook: Size 12.
Silk: Black.
Body: Brown seal's fur.
Hackle: Black cock hackle dressed in the same manner as the Soldier beetle hackle.
Wing cases: A strip of 'Butcher Blue' mallard feather tied in to lie flat over the back.

Although I have never known a trout to eat a large stag beetle, they do frequently devour large cockchafer beetles which are about an inch in length. This fat juicy beetle possesses red-brown wing cases and grey-black underparts to its body; the following pattern is a good summer standby:

Hook: Size 8 mayfly pattern.
Silk: Black.
Body: Roughly dubbed black seal's fur with the fibres picked out to make the body appear fatter than it really is.
Hackle: Red-brown cock hackle tied palmer-style and then clipped above and below.
Wing cases: A mottled red-brown woodcock feather tied in to lie flat over the body.

BEES (*HYMENOPTERA*)

Occasionally, trout will rise to take bees as they buzz around and struggle on the surface of the lake. In actual fact, trout do not seem to relish these large insects although the following pattern will account for numbers of fish when the day is breezy and sunny.

116

Figure 19: (Top) Bee Fly
(Bottom) Ke-He

Bee Fly
Hook: Size 10.
Silk: Brown.
Body: Alternate bands of black and yellow seal's fur ribbed with a ginger cock hackle tied on palmer style. Clip the body hackle reasonably short.
Hackle: Ginger cock hackle tied bushy.

In *Fifty Popular Flies* (vol 2) Tom Stewart records a time when swarms of small black bees occupied the trout's attention in the lochs of Northern Scotland and the Orkneys. In the 1930s, an imitation of small black bees was developed by David Kemp and Bernard Heddle who christened their pattern the 'Ke-He'. Whether or not the fly is taken for a bee, it is a reasonably good stillwater dry-fly to use when conditions are rough and windy.

Ke-He
Hook: Size 12.
Silk: Brown.
Body: Peacock herl tied quite plump.

Tail: Golden pheasant tippets.
Hackle: Rhode island red cockerel.

Tied bushily, both patterns are good dapping flies particularly if a buoyant underbody of cork or Plastazote is included.

BLUEBOTTLES

These common flies are by no stretch of the imagination attractive or romantic creatures, yet, during the summer months, they are eaten quite frequently by trout. They are particularly common during hot weather when the water level is low enough to expose a muddy ooze or when the lake is bordered by a feature such as a farmyard or rubbish dump. Bluebottles relish rotting vegetable and animal matter and when drought conditions expose a wealth of rotting weeds, dead fish and other smaller creatures, these flies have a positive field day and lay their eggs everywhere. Many bluebottles end up on the water and are eaten greedily by the trout.

When the bluebottle lands on the water, its buzzing struggle is a signal to the feeding trout, which makes the palmer dressing very efficient. It is also worth twitching the artificial occasionally although static floating patterns are taken readily enough. The artificial bluebottle is certainly a very neglected pattern because it can be deadly during the summer months. It is also a good pattern to use when dapping.

My personal favourite dressing (Figure 20) is very buoyant (having an underbody of Plastazote) and although I include wings in the dressing (as an aid to visibility) it is just as killing a pattern when tied without wings.

Figure 20: The artificial bluebottle

Bluebottle
Hook: Size 10 or 12.
Silk: Black.
Body: Produce a Plastazote underbody and then dub 'iron blue' coloured seal's fur roughly over it. Wind a short-fibred body hackle of black cock over the seal's fur and then rib the body closely with blue metallic lurex. Trapped hackle fibres are then carefully picked out with a dubbing needle.
Wings: Blue dun hackle points tied sloping back over the body.
Hackle: Finish off with a bushy black cock hackle next to the eye of the hook.

CATERPILLARS

Caterpillars and other grubs fall into lakes quite frequently from trees and some of the largest trout will lie in wait for them. These creatures will often 'plop' into the water and it may sometimes help if the angler emulates this by using a slightly weighted pattern. Nevertheless, hairy caterpillars ('Hairy Mary' we called them as children) do float for a short while and may be imitated with 'dry-flies'. On smaller lake fisheries, it is often worth exploring the lightly fished and heavily wooded banks with a suitable caterpillar imitation, particularly during July, August and early September. Palmer-dressed caterpillar imitations may not be popular patterns, yet they have a long history and were used in the seventeenth-century by the like of Walton and Cotton.

Brown Caterpillar
Hook: Light-wire mayfly hook, sizes 8 – 12.
Silk: Brown.
Body: Dark brown seal's fur dubbed roughly and picked out with a needle. Rib with brown silk.
Hackle: Any brown, black or furnace cock hackle given two turns behind the eye and then ribbed along the body to the bend. The body hackle is kept in place by the brown silk rib.

Green Caterpillar
Exactly as above although the body is a dubbing of apple green seal's fur.

White Caterpillar
Exactly as above although the body is a dubbing of dirty-white seal's fur and the hackle is medium ginger cock.

COWDUNG FLY

Regardless of the importance of the natural insect, the artificial cowdung fly is a killing stillwater pattern and may be used throughout the season. The fly is particularly good at 'sedge time'.

Where farmlands border the lake, cowdung flies may occur in numbers since they are attracted by dung in which they lay their eggs. On breezy days, they may be blown on to the water in numbers and they may be important on cold days when few other flies are in evidence.

When newly hatched, the male cowdung fly is a bright tawny yellow although it may darken considerably: the female is an admixture of this colour with the addition of greenish brown and is generally the darker fly. Nevertheless, when fashioning an artificial, it seems unnecessary to create individual patterns for both sexes, since either are equally likely to be blown on to the water. My own cowdung pattern (Figure 21) is a development from a good old standard fly first published in 1836 by Alfred Ronalds. As with most of my terrestrials I prefer to include a palmer-dressing in order to suggest the 'buzz' of a struggling insect.

Figure 21: Artificial cowdung fly

Cowdung Fly
Hook: Size 12 or 14.
Silk: Brown.
Body: A mixture of yellow and brown seal's fur with just a pinch of dark olive. Rib the body with fine gold wire.
Hackle: Red-brown cock hackle dressed in palmer-style for three quarters of the body length and held in place by the gold wire. A further hackle may be added behind the eye of the hook.
Wing: Dark ginger hackle tips tied to lie flat over the body.

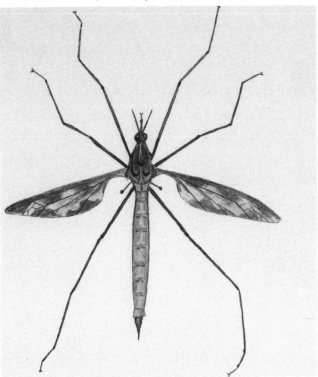

Figure 22: Daddy long-legs (*Tipula maxima*)

CRANE FLIES

The big crane flies (or daddy-longlegs) are among the most important of the stillwater dry-fly fisherman's flies and may well dominate his approach completely towards the end of the season when other flies are absent. The naturals are big flies and the fish which rise to them are also likely to be among the larger inhabitants of the lake. Since the artificial will also be large, it all adds up to the use of a strong leader point and particularly if you decide to employ the retrieve technique which often results in a smash take. Explosive rises will also be a frequent feature of using this pattern as a dapping fly when fishing from a boat. Fishing the 'daddy' from the bank can be just as productive either by merely drifting the fly or by retrieving it in a series of erratic little jerks. On occasions when the static fly proves disappointing, the moving artificial may well attract enough attention to multiply the angler's chances of success.

There are over 300 species of crane flies in Britain and the largest of them (*Tipula maxima*) (Figure 22) is the largest fly in the whole Diptera order. The Crane fly, with its slim body, inadequate wings and long gangling legs is easily recognised, and being a very poor flier, it often ends up on the water in considerable numbers. Crane flies may be in evidence throughout the trout season although they are particularly important to the fisherman in July, August and September when the larger specimens abound.

Crane flies are principally terrestrial creatures although some species are semi-aquatic, their larvae having adapted to life in lake margins where they feed on vegetable detritus and resemble the rat-tailed larvae of the drone flies. The large dirty-brown larvae of the terrestrial flies are very well known since they ruin many a lawn and prize cabbage patch.

One of the first crane fly artificials appeared in 1676; Charles Cotton's 'Harry-Long-Legs' being included in his addition to Izaak Walton's *Compleat Angler*:

> We have also this month [August], a Harry-Long-Legs; the body made of bear's dun and blue wool mixed, and a brown hackle feather over all.

This simple pattern will still catch fish although there are a number of good modern patterns which should be dressed on light-wire long-shank hooks.

Crane Fly (Fogg)
Hook: Size 8 or 10, long shank, light wire.
Silk: Brown.
Body: A dubbing of mole fur, blue dun seal's fur and brown seal's fur mixed in equal parts and ribbed with fine, dark copper wire. The body should be slender over all yet more bulbous at the thorax and towards the end of the abdomen.
Wings: Grizzle cock hackle tips tied in a 'spent' position.
Hackle: Two brown or dark ginger cock hackles wound from the eye to the end of the thorax.
Legs: Six pheasant tail fibres knotted twice.

Improved Daddy-longlegs (Fogg)
Hook: 10 long shank.
Silk: Brown.
Body: Tan coloured raffia. Cut a small strip of this material and rib along the shank to produce a slim body.
Legs: Knotted pheasant tail fibres as in other patterns. However, I now prefer them to splay out rather than trail backwards as Richard Walker recommends.

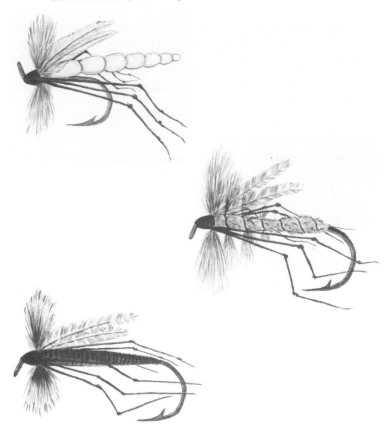

Figure 23: Daddy long-legs imitations
          (Top) Geoff Bucknall
          (Middle) Roger Fogg
          (Bottom) Richard Walker

Wings: Two small Cree hackle points tied 'spent', that is, protruding at right angles from the hook and only slightly raised from a level plane.
Hackle: Two red-brown cock hackles dressed quite bushily in front of the wings.

This Daddy-longlegs pattern produced two limit bags on the only two occasions I fished last October. These were two mild days when occasional rainbow trout were showing at the surface and were quite prepared to take a floating fly.

123

Richard Walker's Daddy-longlegs *(Fly Dressing Innovations)*
Hook: Size 10 bronzed round-bend long shank.
Silk: Brown.
Body: Swan secondary feather fibre dyed a muddy cork colour, tied in, twisted ropewise and wound over a whipped and varnished hook shank.
Wings: Cree cock hackle points tied 'spent'.
Legs: Six pheasant tail fibres knotted twice and allowed to slope backwards.
Hackle: As previous pattern.

Geoffrey Bucknall's Daddy-longlegs
This particular dressing, which employs a plastic mayfly body, is extremely buoyant, and is therefore the perfect pattern to choose when dapping with the artificial crane fly.
Hook: Normal shanked size 12.
Silk: Brown.
Body: Detached plastic mayfly body coloured a greyish-brown with waterproof Pantone pens.
Legs: Cock pheasant tail fibres knotted twice and tied in to slope backwards.
Wings: Brown cock hackle points tied 'spent'.
Hackle: Red cock.

When fishing large crane fly artificials, it is worth being aware of the possibilities of 'false' rises. Time after time, there will be a splash to your fly and no matter how you time your 'strike', you will miss the fish: it is very frustrating. What actually happens is that a trout simply attempts to drown the fly in a series of slashes so that it can devour it when it sinks. The very buoyant Bucknall pattern seems counter-productive at such times because the fish simply cannot sink it. The angler may succeed, however, if he adopts a rapid retrieve, thus, annoying the fish into taking positively. When using a less buoyant pattern, bide your time and let the fish play around until he has the fly under the water: he will register his take with a swirl.

In general, it is best to fish the daddy-longlegs either speculatively or simply cast into a general area of activity, rather than fishing to the 'ring of a rise'. Being such a large pattern it does not lend itself easily to the delicate presentation to individual fish. My greatest success with this pattern usually comes on windy, warm days in late August and September and if I am fishing from the bank, I begin with a long cast and allow the fly to drift with the waves. Then, if no takes are forthcoming, I adopt a cast and retrieve method which often proves successful. The retrieve should be in a series of twitches (rather than a rapid and continuous motion) and although this style of fishing may not be for the dry-fly purist, it is no less successful for that.

When dapping from a boat, the buoyant mayfly-bodied pattern is light enough to be tripped along the waves without being drowned and is light enough for the wind to occasionally lift it off the water completely. This is perfectly natural so that fish may well take just after the fly has left the surface and these are very dramatic. Although takes to the dapped crane fly are usually slash takes, on occasions, trout will take very gently indeed and you might simply think that the fly has been drowned by a wave.

DRONE FLIES

Drone flies are very important at times from an angling point of view. Strictly speaking, they are not terrestrial insects at all but are semi-aquatic, although some drones do lay their eggs in dung, trees, soil, or damp ground near to lakes. However, the drone flies most likely to interest the angler are those which spend most of their time over or near water. Drone flies are good fliers so that the insects which end up on the water are generally females of the semi-aquatic type caught during egg-laying, or spent males and females. The aquatic species lay their eggs directly on to the surface of lakes and reservoirs where the eggs hatch out into the well known rat-tailed maggot. This larva is dirty-white or grey in colour and has a unique telescopic breathing tube which it extends to the surface in order to inhale air. Generally, it is to be found only in shallow water.

The Syrphidae family (drone flies and hover flies) contains about 250 members, the largest being those of interest to the fly-fisherman. The drones closely resemble bees and wasps, and the most common semi-aquatic fly (*Eristalis tenax*) is similar to a wasp or to the male drone of the hive bee. Although it is commonly barred black and yellow, some flies are orange and black, whilst some specimens are dark brown all over.

When drone flies are present in large numbers, usually July and August, trout feed on them in a preoccupied manner so that reasonable artificials are essential to success. Fish the pattern either directly to a rising fish or simply cast it into an area of maximum activity and hope for the best. Once again, a slow and erratic retrieve is always worth trying particularly because it is necessary to attract attention in competition with hundreds of naturals. The moving artificial is by no means unnatural since it suggests the egg-laying female or, alternatively, any drone fly attempting to free itself from the surface of the water.

125

Figure 24: Drone fly

Drone Fly (Figure 24)
Hook: Size 10 or 12.
Silk: Red.
Body: Divided into abdomen and thorax, both tied over an underbody of cork or Plastazote. The abdomen is of seal's fur dubbed in alternate bands (either black and yellow or black and orange). The overall appearance of the abdomen should be fat cigar-shaped tapering towards the end of the hook and next to the thorax. The thorax is made up of black seal's fur dubbed roughly.
Wings: Blue dun cock hackle points slanting backwards over the body.
Hackle: Red game cock tied quite fully.
Head: Varnished red silk.

Although this dressing caters for the most commonly encountered drones, other specific insects may be of local importance and may, therefore, demand another pattern. In a family of over 250 flies, you just can't cater for all of them!

BLACK GNATS

By gnats, I am referring to members of the Bibionidae family and not *Culex pipiens* which is often called the 'common gnat'. Whilst *Culex pipiens* is an aquatic fly, the Bibionidae are terrestrial insects. The commonest gnat is *Bibio johannis* which has a stubby little body (which appears to be black, yet is dark brown) and transparent wings which are longer than the body and are held flat over it when at rest.

The legs of black gnats are long, black, and similar to those of chironomid midges. The female fly is the larger of the two and in some species the females can be distinguished from the males in that they have white tips to their wings.

These small black flies may be in evidence from April to September and sometimes appear in swarms. In a breeze, many of these flies will end up on the water where the trout will feed on them in a crazy and preoccupied manner. At such times, they are often very difficult to catch and the best bet is to cast to individual fish – casting as quickly as possible to the ring of a rise. With such a tiny fly, and so much competition from naturals, speculative casting is usually non-productive. A small black spider tied on a size 16 hook is a reasonable artificial as is the ubiquitous Knotted Midge. Halford included three imitations of the Black gnat in *Floating Flies and How to Dress Them* (1886) and although these have become standard patterns, my personal favourite is a fly designed by Cliff Henry.

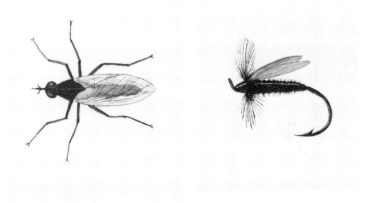

Figure 25: Black gnat (*bibio johannis*): natural and artificial

Cliff Henry's Black Gnat
Hook: Size 16.
Silk: Black.
Body: Black cock hackle, flue trimmed to within $\frac{1}{32}$ inch of the stalk.
Wings: Pale starling, tied sloping back.
Hackle: Black cock, short in the flue.

Particularly during warm and still weather, when the lake surface is glassy and calm, trout will rise in a very deceptive manner to natural black gnats. They will sip in the flies so gently at the surface that it appears as if nothing but minnows could possibly have acted so delicately. Generally, the take to the artificial fly will be a little more obvious, yet not necessarily so, and thus we have the problem of deciding whether or not our fly has been taken. This problem is compounded at distance by the fact that you cannot see such a dark and tiny fly. It is almost necessary to develop a sixth sense, otherwise you might well achieve a considerable number of rises but few, if any, fish.

GREENFLIES

Ludicrous it may seem, but I freely admit that, during summer months, I always carry a few imitations of this tiny aphid in my dry-fly box. More to the point, they catch trout too!

On most lakes and reservoirs you will find tree-fringed lengths of bank, or banks covered with other vegetation, likely to attract the greenfly, the gardener's 'friend'. Many of these tiny insects end up on the water and seem to be attracted by it. Some aphids can even use the surface tension to walk on and are quite capable of jumping free again. It follows, therefore, that they are eaten in numbers by trout and this often accounts for the infuriating situation when we witness rise after rise yet cannot detect any insect that the fish might be rising to. On calm days, particularly during the evening, when fish are feeding on an unseen creature, and you detect greenflies on the bankside vegetation, try the following artificial:

Greenfly
Hook: Size 20.
Silk: White.
Body: Construct a plump little body of lime green fluorescent floss.
Hackle: The tiniest of white cock hackles.

Fished on a very fine leader point I have caught a number of fish on this pattern and lost a few too! It is exciting fishing, but for those who do not like to fray their nerve edges, a larger pattern can be used. Greenflies often drift together into little clumps so that a trout rising to a clump of flies gets a reasonable mouthful in one go. The following pattern may be used when greenflies are around.

Greenfly, Clump,
Hook: Size 12 mayfly.
Silk: Green.

Body: A series of tiny plump bodies separated by hackles. The bodies themselves are fashioned out of lime green fluorescent floss.
Hackles: A series of the palest blue dun cock hackles. You may use larger hackles but trim close to the hook with a pair of scissors.

The advantage of this pattern over the tiny artificial is that it can be seen more easily (by both trout and angler) and enables the use of a stronger leader point. The greenfly pattern may seem something of an oddity but, believe me, trout *do* eat numbers of aphids so don't reject this pattern too readily.

GRASSHOPPERS

The suspicious and conservative British angler (myself included) has tended to reject the popular American 'hoppers' although American anglers seem to prize such artificials when seeking larger trout. Strangely, however, Courtney Williams did write the following, as long ago as 1949:

> When the natural grasshopper is prevalent in the meadow grass near river or lake, a good imitation will often account for fish and there is said to be nothing better for a really big trout. *Dictionary of Trout Flies.*

Figure 26: Common green grasshopper

I wonder. Although I have no experience of fishing the grasshopper, I recently tied a pattern which will be tried next season. Perhaps it will be a good artificial to use when stalking large trout on small lake fisheries. Here it is:

Grasshopper Muddler (Figure 27)
Hook: Size 8 or 10.
Silk: Brown.
Body: Medium olive green seal's fur or wool ribbed with oval gold tinsel.

Figure 27: Grasshopper Muddler

Wings: Two strips of mottled hen feather or turkey tail tied in sloping backwards.

Head and Legs: Fashion a small muddler head of deer's hair (about one third the length of the hook shank) and leave several hairs splayed out over the body.

If it doesn't work as a static fly, perhaps it may be retrieved like a surface muddler!

HAWTHORN FLIES AND HEATHER FLIES

For centuries, the hawthorn fly (*Bibio marci*) has filled the angler with excitement. When it appears, it does so in hordes and drives the trout crazy both on rivers and stillwaters alike. In the eighteenth century, Richard Bowlker wrote that the hawthorn 'comes about the beginning of May and continues about a fortnight, and is to be fished with after hot sunshine mornings; if winds and clouds appear, they then grow weak for loss of the sun and fall upon the waters in great quantities . . .'.

The name 'hawthorn fly' relates the appearance of the fly to that of hawthorn blossom whilst the Latin name, *Bibio marci*, is a little more precise in that it suggests that the fly emerges on St Mark's day, which is the 25th of April. Its exact time of appearance depends on the weather, and it only stays around for two or three weeks, yet when it does appear it is a very important fly for the stillwater dry-fly fisherman.

The distinctive hawthorn fly, with its slender and hairy abdomen, bulky thorax, dangling black legs, and inadequate looking wings, resembles something from the black arts (in America it is known as the 'black dance fly'). The hind pair of legs are much longer than the forward pairs and are prominent when it flies. Its flight is erratic and unsure, which explains the frequency with which it ends up on the

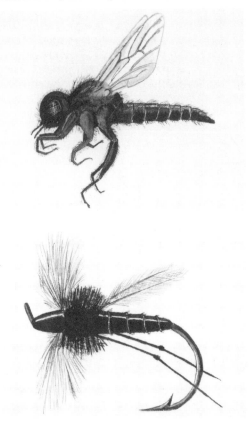

Figure 28: Hawthorn fly (*Bibio marci*): natural and artificial

water where its erratic struggles continue. There are many dressings of the hawthorn fly, the following being about the best:

Hawthorn Fly
Hook: Size 12.
Silk: Black.
Body: The abdomen is of black floss silk ribbed with the finest strand of black ostrich herl, trimmed short. The thorax is a ball of roughly dubbed black seal's fur or ostrich herl.
Hackle: Medium fibred black cock hackle.
Legs: Two knotted, dyed black pheasant tail fibres.
Wings: Two white or blue dun hackle points tied in to slope backwards.

The heather fly (*Bibio pomonae*) is a very close relative of the hawthorn fly and is similar in size and appearance although the upper parts of the legs are red-brown in colour. To imitate this fly, therefore, simply substitute a Coch-y-bondhu cock hackle for the black cock hackle used in the hawthorn fly dressing and use undyed pheasant tail fibres for the legs. The heather fly (as its name might suggest) inhabits hilly regions and generally occurs in August and early September. It is of local significance yet can be a very important angler's fly where it does occur.

MOTHS (*LEPIDOPTERA*)

On summer evenings aquatic and terrestrial moths abound by the waterside and are devoured by trout. I have a vivid memory of returning to my car late on a June evening and completely fishless. As I approached the car park two anglers stood chatting; one held two beautiful brown trout, both around the 5lb mark and both caught on a tiny moth pattern and this from a reservoir which generally yields its small brown trout very grudgingly. Few other fish had been caught on that particular evening and every fish caught, including the man's handsome brace, had fallen to floating flies. It was indeed that moment in time which confirmed my interest in the stillwater dry-fly and in the efficacy of moths.

Moths, many of which resemble sedge flies and appear along with them on summer evenings, come in a variety of sizes and colours. They appear in numbers at dusk when artificial patterns will kill well although takes are often discernible by sound rather than sight. Nevertheless, a white moth is worth trying since it is reasonably visible, particularly if fished close to the bank. At dusk, short casting is by no means a waste of time since trout come very close in and are only likely to move further out if spooked by a clumsy fisherman. In the evening, trout are less cautious and generally less selective: for this reason I prefer to use general moth patterns rather than imitations of specific creatures although there are a number of good imitations of particular moths. My usual moth short list consists of but three flies – the Brown Palmer, the Feather Duster and the White Moth – dressed in a variety of sizes they will imitate most moths.

The Brown Palmer, tied in large sizes, is a good imitation of the large brown moths which my locals call 'buzzards' (because of their annoying habit of buzzing around your head on summer evenings when you least expect an attack!), the Feather Duster is one of the best standard moth patterns, whilst the White Moth is best employed when visibility is important or when imitating any of the paler moths.

Brown Palmer
Hook: Size 14 – 18
Silk: Brown.
Body: Roughly dubbed brown seal's fur ribbed with fine gold wire.
Hackle: Two red-brown cock hackles are ribbed down the length of
the body and held in place by the gold wire. In addition, I include a
bushy hackle in front of the body in order to aid floatation. The front
hackle may even be cream or white (thus creating a bi-visible) which
makes the pattern easier to see in poor light.

Feather Duster
Hook: Size 14 – 18.
Silk: Grey.
Body: A mixture of grey and blue dun seal's fur.
Hackle: Blue dun tied bushily.

White Moth
Hook: Size 14 – 10.
Silk: White.
Body: White seal's fur ribbed with fluorescent white floss.
Hackle: Bushy white cock hackle.
Wings: White hen feathers tied in and cut to a roof-shape reminiscent
of sedge wings.

These patterns will suit most occasions and there is no need to go
moth-spotting with a book on Lepidoptera – simply decide what the
prevalent moths look like (if it is light enough to see them) and then
tie on the pattern which most resembles it.

SNAILS

By no stretch of the imagination can snails be called flies. However,
they often migrate to the surface where they float; trout eat them from
the surface and you can catch surface-feeding trout on floating
artificial snails. Thus, it follows that 'snail fishing' can be embraced
within the term dry-fly fishing.

During hot weather snails often leave the bottom or weedgrowth
and rise to the surface of the water where they float: presumably they
do so to gain a greater oxygen supply, since water becomes de-
oxygenated when the temperature rises. As they float at the surface,
snails become an easy prey for trout; they can gorge themselves
without expending a great deal of energy. At such times the stomachs
of trout are often distended with snails whilst their bellies positively
crunch to the touch. If trout are showing with consistent steady rises,

Figure 29: Snails: (Top left) Great pond snail shell (5cm long)
(Top right) Dwarf pond snail (1cm long)
(Centre) Artificial snail
(Bottom left) Wandering snail (2cm long)
(Bottom right) Great ramshorn snail (3cm long)

and snails are seen floating near the shore, then try a snail imitation
(if you haven't one with you, a Black and Peacock Spider will do at
a pinch).

There are a number of varieties of snail although the Bladder snails
are commonest and much appreciated by trout since they are bulkier
and 'juicier' than the Ramshorn snails. Cliff Henry developed an
excellent snail pattern:

Hook: Size 10 – 14 down-eyed wide gape.
Silk: Brown.
Body: Partially split a flat-topped, pear-shaped piece of cork, place
it over the hook shank, and then whip it in place with the silk. The

flat section should face the hook eye. Cover the cork with stripped peacock quill (or pheasant tail fibres) and the flat-topped section with bronze peacock herl to represent the pad of the snail.

To be honest, the cork body alone is quite adequate if it is coloured a dark brown with waterproof Pantone pens. Another idea is to fashion a snail shape out of clipped deer hair and then colour it appropriately with a Pantone pen. In this dressing, you need to cram the deer hair on to the hook, so that when it is clipped the artificial snail possesses a solid appearance.

Since snails float around for days the artificial is best fished statically and allowed to drift with the current. This pattern is not really suitable for casting delicately to individual fish and is best fished in a general area of feeding activity.

7

A variety of tactical approaches

THE EARLY SEASON DRY-FLY

I would be the last person on earth to claim that stillwater dry-fly fishing is regularly useful during the cold, raw spring days of March and early April. Nevertheless, it is worth considering as an odd kind of gambit when conventional sunk-line tactics either yield poor results or black and out-of-condition rainbows. The assumption that the dry-fly is useless during cold early season days is a reasonable one since there is unlikely to be any fly-life. There will be few or no rises unless such flies as Sepia Duns are in evidence, and since the method is never used anyway, it can't possibly be worth the consideration. Nevertheless, like most generalisations, this assumption is not entirely correct although I had agreed with it until accidental circumstances proved otherwise. (I sometimes feel that most of the profound discoveries of fly-fishing were bred of pure accident rather than logical deduction, insight or experimentation.)

A number of years ago, the new season was heralded with the usual cold and blustery weather which seems to make nonsense of those dead months of eager anticipation. The clouds, a dark leaden grey, moved quickly and hung low over the hilltops as if to shed the odd flurry of snow over the entire sombre scene. The waters of the reservoir were black and uninviting and an hour's tedium with lure and traditional loch patterns had produced only one tiny, fruitless tweak. Suddenly, there was a break in the clouds and streaks of watery sunshine shot through and glinted over the wave crests and troughs. Initially, this made me feel more optimistic although a further hour's toil revealed the folly of such optimism and ended with the cast breaking as a result of fouling some sunken obstacle. With cold and fumbling fingers, I tied on a new cast and laboriously attached a bushy Black and Peacock spider to the point. Normally, I would have soaked the fly in saliva in order to ensure a quick sinking rate and would have rubbed the leader with fuller's earth for the same reason: I didn't. To be quite honest, I was beginning to lose interest in the whole affair and this was one, last, half-hearted attempt to catch a fish before packing up. Had it not been for the fact that I had only seen one fish caught during the whole of the masochistic session, I am sure that I would also have lost faith in my ability to catch fish.

As I prepared to cast again, the sun brightened a little, and, though still rough, the height between wave crest and trough diminished. The line shot through the rod rings and being a slow sinker, began to bow round in an arc rather than sink. As it did so it towed the fly along the surface since it was not yet moist enough to sink. There was a huge splash and I struck instinctively, yet the reaction was fruitless because of the amount of slack line produced by the wind. Still, that fish had actually risen to the fly and spirits rose with it. It was worth continuing for a little longer and perhaps even worth using a floating line, greased cast and bona-fide dry-fly. Accordingly, I began to tackle up a second rod and as I did so, the sheer accident of the whole thing struck home. First of all, the use of the slow-sinker was initially a mistake since I had originally intended to use a fast sinker. Had I done so, even the unmoistened fly would have been pulled under quite quickly thus producing no rise. Secondly, when I had fumbled through my fly-box for the Black and Peacock, I had fondly imagined that I had selected a leaded pattern yet this was not the case. Perhaps, foolishly, I hadn't

Never take your eyes from a dry-fly! Doug Ashmore mends his line with the drift and concentrates intently.

137

added a little silver tag to my leaded patterns (as oft I had been told to do) in order to distinguish them from the unleaded patterns. Nevertheless, had I done so, then I am sure that no rise would have occurred and my morning would probably have remained fishless. It had all been fortuitous, or perhaps it was one of those pre-determined quirks of fate which so mysteriously haunt our lives from time to time.

The second rod was eventually tackled up and I cast a bushy Black Palmer out into the waves. As it floated round, the line was mended in order to avoid slack and my anticipation was rewarded with a second lusty rise, and this time, a hooked fish. The fish, a brown trout of 1¼lbs, was in reasonably good condition so I decided to keep it. Having dispatched it, I thrust a marrow spoon down its gullet, twisted it round, and drew it out again. Mainly, the spoon contained mushy grey digested matter although four caddis larvae (complete with cases) were distinct enough. Nothing within that fish's stomach contents even vaguely resembled an adult fly even though it had risen with conviction to my floating artificial.

That fish was my only fish of that arctic morning session and it might well have been easy to regard its capture as a mere freak, a one-off-job, had it not been for a second incident a couple of years later. On the particular reservoir which I fished with a companion, the stocking policy was limited, to say the least. Just before opening day, in went a mixed bag of brownies and rainbows and since spinning was allowed, most of them came out again within the first few days of the season.

We were fishing three weeks into the season. It was cold, and we hadn't even had so much as a slight offer from a fish between us. There was an inflow channel which flowed beneath a bridge into the reservoir and we tucked ourselves behind the wall of the bridge in order to keep a little warmer. I lit a cigarette and sighed thoughtfully. My companion, occasionally given to mad and irrational gestures, took a large orange abortion of a fly from his wallet and knotted it on to his cast. For some reason, he always claims that I dressed the 'fly' but I am sure that I didn't; at least, I hope that I didn't because it was positively obnoxious. The 'fly' was supposedly a lure, but, when flicked out into the flowing waters of the inflow channel, it bobbed along like an escaped fluorescent buoy. Obnoxious, odious and definitely unaesthetic it might have been, but would you believe it, it disappeared with a splash. A fish had actually risen to it.

Putting the two events together, it seemed obvious that as a last resort, a bushy dry-fly might often be worth trying during the early days of the season when other methods fail. So it has proved. The second episode illustrates that the design of the pattern doesn't matter, so long as it is buoyant enough to float in rough conditions, whilst bright colours may well help since they will at least enable the fish to see the fly. Recently, a pupil of mine presented me with a small collection of large and gaudy American dry-flies (his father had intended to place them in the band of his fishing hat but had presumably not dared to do so) and I look forward to giving them a try during early season conditions. Why not tie up a few bushy and gaudy Palmer flies and give them a try?

It is important to note that this section was written specifically with reference to early season conditions when fly-life is absent. There are obvious times when the dry-fly *should* be used early in the season if natural flies are emerging in numbers. Such times however, unless the weather is reasonably warm, are fairly uncommon.

BOAT OR BANK?

Apart from any considerations of relative effectiveness, there are some who prefer to fish from boats and some who prefer to fish from the bank. Under the right conditions either is capable of providing good sport with the dry-fly. Thus, to a certain extent it is a matter for personal choice, although the cost of boats on some waters may be thought to be prohibitive. Sometimes, your choice will be made at random, or based on some whim or other. At such times, it is amazing how the theory of Sod's Law becomes reality. You choose to fish from the bank and all the fish rise beyond casting range − it is too late to secure a boat because they are all out. You choose to fish from a boat and all the sport is had from the bank − having paid for the boat you decide to get your money's worth and stay in it without catching fish. In the latter case, the disappointment is usualy compounded by dropping a valuable piece of equipment over the side and watching in helpless grief as it sinks away into thirty feet of water. Or it may be rough, and you end up being sick!

Choice is often something of a negative factor. Given no options, for example when fishing a 'no-boating' and 'no wading' reservoir, all combatants suffer identical restrictions so that you can only be beaten by the fish. If the fish rise beyond your casting range, they will probably rise beyond everyone else's as well. Indeed, I am often ironically happiest under such circumstances because I enjoy walking and stalking around in search of a fish or two within range. Any fish caught, is a fish earned.

I think it is also true to say that on such reservoirs (commonly found in upland regions) fish tend to rise quite readily to the dry-fly. They are not scared from the surface by boats ploughing around everywhere nor by anglers splashing into the water and wading thoughtlessly. I am convinced that you can easily ruin a water's potential as a dry-fly fishery. By indiscriminate wading, insect life is destroyed in the shallows and even if fish are ready to rise, to terrestrials say, splashy wading will drive them away from the bank. They might well have continued to rise farther out in the reservoir, were it not for the fact that motor boats are zooming around everywhere and vulgar boatmen are catching proverbial 'crabs'. Other boat anglers, you will note, are clumping around in their boats and standing up to cast, thus sending depth charges of sound into the reservoir. Oh yes, fish will be caught, don't doubt it. They will be caught on lead core lines from the deeps and then some grinning hero will declare that he told everybody so: a lead core and a six-inch 'zoomer' will beat the dry-fly any day. If everybody were to treat a stillwater with the reverence of a chalk-stream, then the situation might be completely different. If bank anglers began to stalk and boat anglers to drift quietly or moor inconspicuously, then we might all be the happier for it.

Now, while the bile is flowing, I would like to get one more thing off my chest. Can I make a plea for courtesy towards bank anglers from those who lord it in boats. Admittedly, they have paid more for their fishing but that gives them no reason to spoil everyone else's.

A couple of years ago, I fished on a rather dour early October day at Rutland. After a couple of disappointing hours, fish began to show occasionally within casting range. I spent at least ten minutes stalking one particular fish and eventually prepared to cast to it. Just as the line levelled out behind me in the back cast, a boat ploughed speedily round the headland and swashed past me at a distance of no more than twenty feet. That was that! The two 'anglers' in the boat continued their joy ride around the bay and then shot off into the main arm of the reservoir. I will not put down in writing what I wished them, I will simply state that it was not a limit bag!

Unfortunately, fly-fishing has become so popular that crowded banks have become commonplace on reservoirs, particularly on opening days. This seems to have contributed to a kind of free-for-all syndrome which has completely destroyed the traditional ethics of the sport. Anglers now splash into the water only a couple of feet away from a resident angler and then proceed to cast right across him — at one time, it was courtesy to ask if you could fish within twenty or thirty yards of a fellow angler . . . I'm all right Jack . . . sod you!

Perhaps the price on certain waters has also contributed to the loss of a common code of reasonable behaviour. Anglers feel that they have to get a limit bag in order to get their money's worth and they will do anything to achieve it. They will even stick maggots and trout pellets on their hooks. At one little remove from this, they will manufacture imitation trout pellets in the firm belief that they are using artificial flies. Indeed, one famous angling magazine included artificial pellet-caught trout in its notable fish list as though it were a perfectly normal achievement. If the media accepts the unethical, then the unethical will become the norm. Still, enough of this, we were considering the matter of bank versus boat.

I must point out right now, that it is unlikely that I will eventually achieve a definite conclusion one way or the other. All it will be possible to do, will be to point out various circumstances which will suit either boat or bank best. Unfortunately, of course, it is often necessary to book boats in advance, which means that it is not simply a matter of judging conditions on any particular day. However, boats are often available 'on spec' and it is perhaps best not to book in advance and then impose Hobson's choice on yourself. If you get a boat when you need one, well and good; if not, then you have lost no money.

In general, boats should not be necessary on small lakes while they may well increase your options on larger expanses of water. Many of the very small lake fisheries shouldn't have boats on them at all because it should be possible to find enough fish feeding reasonably close to the bank. There will be trout out in the middle, no doubt, but you can't try to catch all the trout in the water at once anyway. On lakes of less than ten acres in extent, boats can easily disturb the fishing for everybody, even when the boat anglers are relatively careful — if they are clumsy, that can put an end to the sport for quite some time. One of the greatest pleasures on small fisheries is the stalking of large individual fish with nymph or dry-fly, boats can often spoil this. Stalking tactics are really only possible from the bank in any case, so that boat fishing results in the loss of this pleasure. The trouble is that anglers often clump around the banks without thinking and thus scare the fish close in. If you are going to use the dry-fly effectively, then you must not scare fish; you must learn to move very carefully, quietly and inconspicuously. You must creep around and look very carefully into the water for signs of fish. There are some lakes, however, which offer exceptions; lakes where boats *are* necessary. Normally, these will be tree-fringed lakes where bank fishing is often impossible from long stretches of bank. Such stretches will invariably hold large fish feeding on various tit-bits as they fall from the trees, and they will only be approached by boat. In a sense, you must still stalk your fish by approaching as quietly as your boat-handling skills permit.

On large reservoirs, though bank fishing with the dry-fly may be very good at times, one of the problems is locating trout. Although this may be achieved by walking around, a boat will offer a form of transport, if nothing else, and therefore save effective fishing time. A boat will also allow the angler to discover areas of surface activity well away from bank locations — hatches of Lake Olives perhaps — when areas near the bank are fruitless. A boat is also a good idea when the banks are crowded, for it is impossible to fish either nymph or dry-fly when you are sandwiched in between hosts of lure strippers. When calm lanes occur sufficiently far out from the bank to be out of casting range, then again, a boat will be necessary as the only way of reaching the fish. Trout often feed avidly in calm lanes and a drift along one will often provide dry-fly fishing of a very high order. In this case, a good drogue will be an essential item of equipment. At times, however, the boat may well be regarded simply as a casting platform and left securely at anchor — in this way it allows you to fish well beyond normal casting range. Boats are useful too on extremely calm evenings, either when trout are feeding well out or when they have been driven out by bankside disturbance; but they are only useful if they are allowed to drift very quietly and casting to rising fish is made as delicately as possible. Finally, when there is a good wind, a boat is useful if you decide to employ dapping tactics. It is possible to dap from the bank if you have a good breeze behind your shoulder, although the area you may cover will be rather restricted compared with dapping from a boat.

From the foregoing, it would seem to be a simple victory for the boat on larger waters, but nothing is ever quite that simple, is it? For example, on many late spring and summer evenings, fish will move close inshore and offer the bank dry-fly fisherman excellent sport, whereas the boat angler will fish over water which is relatively barren. Then again, when any 'hatch' involves species which emerge from shallow water (Pond Olives, for example) a boat offers no real advantage for the fish ought to be accessible from the bank. Similarly, when using the moving dry-fly as an imitation of adult flies skittering from the water to the land, the boat will add no advantages; in fact, quite the opposite. Whilst the bank angler's retrieved fly will travel in the same direction as the natural insect, the boat angler's retrieve will only pull the fly in the opposite direction. The argument now seems to be turning again, and becomes a matter of swings and roundabouts. Clearly, there are times for bank and times for boat. Now, I am back again with personal preference.

Whilst I readily appreciate the advantages often offered by a boat, I am not over-keen on boat fishing and much prefer fishing from the bank. Even on very popular, large reservoirs, it is possible to get away from the crowds and pursue fish. Indeed, in many ways, successful dry-fly fishing is quite a solitary affair. If you avoid human contact, since it often produces the kind of movements and noises likely to scare fish, you will normally be able to discover fish feeding quite close in – sometimes within a few feet of the bank, even during the daytime. To stalk such fish and rise them to a dry-fly is one of the greatest pleasures of stillwater angling and offers something which is almost as good as the holiness of the chalkstreams. The parallel is apt. To be a successful dry-fly fisherman on stillwaters, you must, to all intents and purposes, adopt the tactics and approaches of the river fisherman, and that kind of approach is most easily achieved from the bank rather than from a boat. For me, bank is best – but that is simply my own choice.

DRIFT FISHING AND 'WALKING-THE-FLY'

When there is a breeze and fish are only occasionally seen to be rising, it is often necessary to search the water and this is a more interesting tactic if you use a dry-fly rather than a wet-fly. This form of stillwater dry-fly fishing may be practised either from bank or boat and is not really dependent on an entomological approach. If you are searching around for a fish which is likely to take a dry-fly, then it makes sense to choose a general pattern which is likely to suggest several species of adult flies.

What type of fly suggests the kinds of naturals which would make it worthwhile for a fish to rise? A big fly! Thus, a larger palmer-dressed fly will be suitable since it will suggest a variety of insects, will float well under breezy conditions and, because of its size, is likely to account for the larger fish. In season, a large Daddy-longlegs is also an excellent general pattern for this style of fishing.

Searching the water means covering as much water with your fly as possible, and if this necessitates repeated casting, then it can become quite tiring. Fortunately, there is an easier approach which may be practised under the right conditions and it has the added advantage of creating little disturbance. The kind of disturbance often brought about by repeated casting (particularly when you become a little tired and careless).

From a boat, drift fishing with the dry-fly is an easy proposition so long as the boat can be checked sufficiently either by using a drogue or by a boatman. The object is to drift slowly along merely keeping pace with the drifting fly-line and fly. Casts of about fifteen yards or so are adequate and although longer casts have the advantage of distancing fish from any boat disturbance, they do present striking problems when a fish has risen to the fly. Traditional loch fly tactics with the wet-fly necessitate short casts in advance of the boat's drift, with a retrieve which dibbles the bob-fly on the surface. For such tactics a long rod is necessary, but this is not the case when drift fishing with a dry-fly.

The cast must be made at right angles to the drift of the waves and, as the fly floats along, the boat must be steadied and the fly-line mended in order to avoid slack line or the fly being skated along the surface as the line bows out in an arc. Repeated casts are not necessary and a fresh cast will only be made once the distance of the fly from the boat has been drastically reduced by constantly mending the line. Perhaps the main drawback to this method of fishing lies in the way in which an angler can be lulled into unawareness so that he glances around and inevitably misses the take when it occurs. Full concentration is demanded at all times. Naturally, the dapping method of fishing is a good alternative to the drift method, providing that there is a sufficient breeze and that you possess the right kind of tackle. (See the section on tackle for an outline of the dapping technique and later treatment in the present section.)

Even when there is little breeze, and the boat only drifts gently along (or hardly drifts at all), the 'static' method of fishing a dry-fly from a boat may pay dividends. Certainly, when it is time to eat your sandwiches, it is worth casting out a dry-fly and allowing it to remain there, rather than give up fishing altogether. However, it is best to keep a hand on the rod since trout have an uncanny habit of taking the fly when you least expect them.

From a bank, drift fishing with the dry-fly is rather more difficult and restricted although it is possible under the right conditions. If the right conditions exist, the method which I refer to as 'walking-the-fly', is perhaps more efficient than walking around casting here and there as you go (see Figure 30). For one thing, the repeated casting may well disturb fish whilst the 'walking-the-fly' method necessitates as little casting as possible. The necessary conditions for this method of drift fishing are as follows:

  i) A bank which is unfished by other anglers and thus allows you to explore on your own.
 ii) A bank which is reasonably straight so that you can walk along it with ease, and which may be reasonably fished without wading.
iii) A breeze blowing roughly parallel to the bank and preferably blowing from left to right (if you are a right-handed caster).

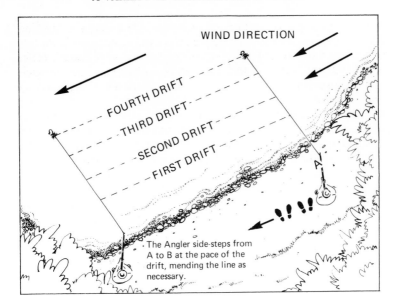

WIND DIRECTION

FOURTH DRIFT
THIRD DRIFT
SECOND DRIFT
FIRST DRIFT

A

The Angler side-steps from A to B at the pace of the drift, mending the line as necessary.

Figure 30: 'Walking the fly'

If these conditions exist, then this method will allow you to search a vast area with ease, and it can be a very deadly and interesting method of fishing. Perhaps it might be easiest to describe this technique by relating the events on the first occasion when I used it.

Before its sad demise as a fishery, I used to make regular visits to a small rectangular reservoir which held a number of average-sized brown trout and the odd fish in the 2lb class. The banks of the reservoir were of rough stone; they were steep and shelved away quickly into about ten feet of water. On one particular day, trout were showing spasmodically along one bank, yet chasing from point to point casting to the rise proved fruitless since the fish were obviously moving around quite quickly. Even if the fly landed in the ring of a rise a second or so after it had appeared, the trout had probably already moved a few yards away.

I had accounted for one small brownie by simply casting the fly out and leaving it, yet the problem with this method was that the breeze and waves soon carried the fly back towards the bank. It was not possible to simply cast out, stand still and keep the fly at the kind of distance demanded by the position of the rise forms. As a natural consequence, I eventually made my cast, and began to side-step slowly along the bank thus making it easy to keep pace with the drift of the fly and keep the line at a perfect right-angle to the bank. Once this had begun, I progressed quite naturally along the whole length of the bank (since I had it to myself) and collected two reasonable fish out of three rises to my fly.

On subsequent visits to that reservoir, when the wind blew along the bank, and even when no fish were showing, I used the same technique to good effect. Interestingly enough, it was partly because the reservoir was impossible to wade that I began to use the 'walking-the-fly' technique and learnt that wading was not essential.

Obviously, you cannot walk along with the drift of your fly when you are wading without creating a great deal of disturbance. 'Walking-the-fly' is a good technique when conditions allow it, and it stresses the need for the stillwater dry-fly fisherman to travel light and maintain maximum mobility. It is not the technique for the reservoir 'heron', intent on standing in the water, rooted to one spot.

In summary then, you may cover a great deal of water if you walk slowly along the bank at the pace of the drifting fly. It is essential that you face the fly directly, walk sideways; that you keep your eye on the fly and keep a straight line between the rod and the fly. Even when using this method a little mending of the line may be necessary, yet it may be done without hurry: indeed, you may gather all the slack line on to the reel so that when a fish is on, it may be played directly from the reel.

Having decided on the stretch of bank to be fished by this method, make a reasonably short first cast for the first drift, and then walk back to the initial position, extend the distance of the cast, and drift again. Several drifts of varying cast distances will thus allow you to make a systematic search of a great expanse of water and the chances of a fish seeing and taking your fly are very high indeed.

I must stress the fact that 'walking-the-fly' does require ideal conditions and reservoir banks. If the bank is not reasonably uniform and firm, you may easily end up in the water whilst concentrating on the fly rather than where you put your feet. If the bank undulates, then unintentional rod movement may easily disturb the drift of the fly. Make a careful study of the bank before you begin fishing and remember that you don't own it simply because you want to fish it all. If other anglers are around, or if they appear to the left, or to the right of you during a drift, then 'walking-the-fly' is not ethically permissible. Unfortunately, ethical considerations are rapidly diminishing on many stillwaters where aggressive self-assertion has replaced the old concept of the brotherhood of the angle.

MARGIN FISHING

Perhaps one of the strangest statements which we may make on stillwater fly-fishing is that 'wading and long casting makes wading and long casting necessary'.

At a first reading, the reader may well be excused for believing that this statement is either too obvious or, alternatively, nonsensical. Nevertheless, here we are presented with one of the greatest truths of stillwater fly-fishing. When a reservoir is a virgin water, the shallows are enriched with food forms (beetles, corixidae, caddis larvae, nymphs, chironomid larvae and pupae, snails, water lice, shrimps and so forth) and trout will, therefore, feed quite close into the bank if they are not disturbed. Contrary to popular belief, deeper water is *not* as rich in food forms. On waters where wading is either not possible, or not allowed, fish will be caught regularly quite close to the bank if the angler exercises the coarse fisherman's caution of quietness and camouflage. Naturally, if you clump around on the bank, then you can only expect to drive the fish further out and that is where you will have to seek them. However, indiscriminate wading and the desire to cast out as far as possible, remains the main cause of driving trout away from the bank and in this respect, the invention of the shooting head line is much to blame. Give a man a shooting head line and a powerful rod and he will, quite naturally, attempt to cast as far as he can (why else would be use such tackle?). As an added aid to distance, he will undoubtedly plough into the water and wade out as far as he is able. Oh yes, he will catch fish, but in so doing he will make it impossible for other anglers to exercise different methods and he will have contributed to the destruction of all aquatic life in the shallows. Once anglers plough up the bottom mud in any area, then the aquatic life will be destroyed, thus negating the possibility of fish feeding fruitfully in that area. Last year, I remember peering into the water in a bay on one lake only to see an intricate pattern of boot prints: the real aquatic life began beyond the limit of wading. I am not suggesting that anglers should not wade, rather that they should exercise a little more concern for the ecology that sustains their sport. Equally, it would be no bad thing for water authorities to designate a number of bank areas as 'no wading' areas, and I am sure that the result would pleasantly surprise many anglers. It would also reduce the need for powerful tackle and facilitate the constant use of less tiring equipment, thus enabling a more delicate and subtle approach.

As you may guess, on the averge stillwater, I am driven to accept that margin fishing with the dry-fly remains a minor tactic: not

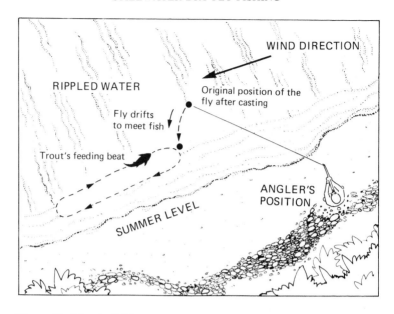

Figure 31: Margin fishing

because it doesn't work, but because the use of other techniques reduces its effectiveness. Notwithstanding this remark, there are still times when margin fishing with the dry-fly produces excellent results. On waters where wading is relatively rare, or on dam walls where it is impossible, fish may be caught on a margin-fished dry-fly from the end of May to the end of the season: whether or not fish are actually rising. However, they are most likely to be caught during early morning and evening sessions when the water is least disturbed and it is important that you cast a long line along the margins, thus exercising Charles Cotton's old dictum 'fine and far off'. A long leader is essential and the fly-line should be as light as you can manage: a double-tapered line *does* present a fly with greater delicacy and is, therefore, to be preferred. If you move quietly and keep a low profile (kneeling is often necessary) as you move along the bank, then sport may well be excellent. On occasions, you will also have the added incentive of being able to stalk individual rising fish. A breeze, particularly when it blows on to your bank at an angle of forty-five degrees, may well mean that fish will feed close in throughout the day since flies will be carried in towards the bank. Under such conditions, trout are least likely to be disturbed if you cast out beyond them and allow the wind to bring the fly in towards the bank. Using this method

148

I have even caught fish as close in as a foot from the bank so that it pays to allow the fly to drift right in before lifting it off the water.

As far as fly patterns are concerned, it makes sense to imitate whatever natural insects are in evidence although sparse emergences of flies will allow the use of general patterns. Most anglers will have their own favourite general dry-flies yet, in my opinion, there are two patterns which will beat all others: the Grey Duster and the Red Palmer. When conditions are relatively calm, these patterns are killing flies when dressed on size 14 hooks. Under breezier conditions, a large Red Palmer is preferable.

There is one particular time of the year when the margin fished dry-fly can beat all other techniques, even on reservoirs where wading is constantly practised, that is when drought conditions produce a low summer level. At such times, the well-waded muddy areas will be exposed above the waterline and the new margin shallows will contain a good store of underwater life. Such conditions are likeliest in July and August when the hot dog-days have probably driven the brigade of lure-strippers far away, for the lure will certainly come off second best at this stage in the season. As a result, the new margin water is relatively virginal and unwaded and will provide the imitative nymph and dry-fly fisherman with relatively good sport.

Even when the day is hot and still, fish will rise to the dry-fly fished near to the bank if you are prepared to take your time and stalk them. Often, it will necessitate quite an amount of time spent simply in observation as you plot the feeding paths of individual fish; then you must take your time, choosing the moment when the fly may be cast delicately just in front of the fish. However, should you land the cast heavily, or cause a disturbance on the bank, the fish will bolt, you can be sure of it. Ideally, there may be a slight breeze blowing at an angle to the bank and meeting a calm zone along the margins: if this is the case, then it is easy to cast out at an angle to the ripple and allow the fly to be carried into the marginal feeding zone. Insects will often collect where the rippled water meets the calm water and this is therefore the most lucrative region to explore. One further point of critical importance is that under sunny conditions the sun *must* lie before you, for, if it is at your back, the shadows produced by angler and rod will undoubtedly disturb the fish, particularly when casting. In this respect, it is often worthwhile standing well back from the water's edge so that some of your fly-line will actually fall on the margin mud. In such a manner, the angler will be able to disguise his whereabouts and put the maximum distance between himself and the fish, although he will of necessity need to clean his fly-line quite regularly. Mud and grit will collect on the line and will not only prevent it from floating well, but will also damage the surface plastic. Further, as a gritty fly-line shoots through the rings, it is likely to damage them, which in turn will damage any other line used with that rod.

When margin fishing, you must learn to read rise forms very carefully, and for two reasons. First of all, it is necessary to decide whether nymph or dry-fly will be most effective, and secondly, it is most interesting if you can distinguish between the rise forms produced by small fish, and those produced by specimens. Since margin fishing approaches the pleasure of stalking fish on rivers, it ought to be combined with a very selective approach. Indeed, this may mean that you ignore many feeding fish because they are obviously too small. This in turn may mean that a great amount of time is spent not actually fishing, but simply watching the water until a larger fish appears. Larger fish rise more infrequently, but they are worth waiting for and it is the patient angler who will catch them regularly on the dry-fly. In any case, if you go for the smaller fish, and hook them, they may well disturb the water which will result in the larger fish sheering off and not appearing again.

Margin fishing is often at its best when the water is dead calm — this is really a kind of perverse statement, for at such times, fish are maddeningly difficult to catch. Particularly on warm, still evenings, when the water is like a mirror and fish are rising everywhere, stillwater dry-fly fishing is extremely pleasurable. At such times, a tiny fly and light tackle are called for, coupled with an approach of incredible stealth. I remember one occasion at Ladybower when fish rose everywhere, sometimes only a couple of feet from the bank, yet they soon disappeared when you moved within twenty or so yards from them, no matter how cautiously. Ultimately, although I had only two rises and landed just one fish, I felt that I had really been fly-fishing because the excitement was always there and the adrenalin flowed. It was, perhaps, the angling equivalent of gambling, it was maddeningly frustrating and overwhelmingly exciting. Above all, it was an occasion when heavy tackle was totally unproductive, whilst very light tackle at least stood something of a chance. Stillwater dry-fly fishing is basically light tackle angling, and that means fly-fishing as an art, rather than a chore.

THE DRY-FLY AND NYMPH COMBINATION

On the whole, I do not favour the use of a team of flies, principally because the trailing flies can easily become snagged up once a fish has been hooked. Nevertheless, a team of flies does have its uses and particularly if the dry-fly is combined with either nymphs or pupal patterns. I often marvel at the lack of attention given to this kind of combination by stillwater anglers. Sometimes they will change frantically from a rod bearing a floating line, to one bearing a sinking line, or they will change their flies frequently, oblivious to the fact that a simple solution is readily available.

When a hatch is in progress, it is often possible to discern whether trout are taking floating flies or nymphs by 'reading' their rise forms, yet, on other occasions it is most difficult to tell. You may easily labour fruitlessly with a dry-fly when a nymph would be more successful, or vice versa. It is often the case that there is a rhythmic feeding pattern during a hatch: at the beginning, when adult flies are sparse, nymphs may be preferred; when the hatch increases in intensity, trout may then turn their attentions to the adult floating fly; finally, they may change back to the nymph again. As a result of this behaviour, it is sometimes difficult to decide what tactics to employ and particularly so when we consider that the rise form to a nymph just below the surface of the lake may be very similar to a bona fide dry-fly rise to either dun or spinner. The obvious solution is to use a dry-fly on the point or top dropper, combined with two nymphal or pupal patterns — this tactic will often allay the frustrations of those enigmatic evening rises. There is also an added advantage for those anglers who find difficulty in detecting a take to a nymph since the dry-fly will act rather like the coarse fisherman's float: even when a fish takes one of the nymphal patterns, the dry-fly will move in such a way that the take will be registered. When the dry-fly itself is taken you have absolutely no doubts: in either case, all you need to do is to watch the dry-fly.

Incidentally, I first used the combination tactic on a river in order to help detect takes to a little black beetle pattern which was always particularly successful. The pattern was fished in rapid glides and the takes were often imperceptible. Thus, I fished the beetle on the point and a large buoyant Red Palmer on the first dropper. The palmer certainly helped me to detect takes quickly enough to hook the fish and it had two added advantages. Firstly, it accounted for a number of fish in its own right and, secondly, it ensured that the beetle remained just below the surface and didn't sink too far. On stillwaters, the use of dry-fly will also help to stabilise nymphal patterns and make sure that they fish just below the surface film, but it will only do this if it is a very buoyant pattern and is annointed with a good floatant.

Dry-fly/nymph combinations may be fished statically, or allowed to drift, or retrieved very slowly: the method chosen will vary according to the species of insect to be imitated, or you may experiment if the initial method of fishing the team does not achieve success. On certain occasions, a very rapid retrieve is the only method which will achieve results even though this would seem to be quite unnatural when we consider the habits of real aquatic insects. Perhaps the reason for this is that the trout have so many natural creatures to choose from that they would be likely to ignore our imitations unless we can attract attention by making them move in an exaggerated manner. If a rapid retrieve is called for, then most dry-flies will become swamped and a better approach would be to use a Muddler on the point and nymphs, or pupae, on the droppers. The Muddler, of course, ought to be classed as a floating lure rather than a dry-fly, yet we may stretch a point a little in order to allow it into the confines of this book.

Although it is often well to experiment with the teams of flies to be used for this kind of fishing, the following combinations are as sound as any:

SEDGE FLY COMBINATION

A Red Palmer on the point; an Amber Sedge Pupa on the first dropper; a Green Sedge Pupa on the top dropper. By placing the dry-fly on the point, the pupae will fish quite close to the surface making this an ideal combination for using when sedge flies are actually emerging. During the daytime, the combination may be fished statically, on the drift if it is breezy, or with a very slow retrieve. In the evening, a slightly faster retrieve will often pay dividends.

The second sedge combination operates with a slow retrieve and presents an excellent imitation of three life-cycle stages simultaneously. Because the dry-fly is placed on the top dropper, the pupa on the point can be fished a little deeper than the pupae in the first combination. On the point I place an Amber or Green Sedge Pupa (occasionally I find a fluorescent orange pupa quite deadly), an Invicta on the first dropper (a superb imitation of a 'hatching' sedge) and the ubiquitous Red Palmer on the top dropper.

CHIRONOMID COMBINATION

Although anglers are in the habit of believing that trout only feed on midge pupae and never on adult flies, this is by no means true. By using an adult midge imitation on the point and by tying a couple of pupae directly to the cast, one of the deadliest stillwater combinations may be produced. The floating midge itself will account for a number of trout, whilst it will also ensure that the pupae fish right in the surface film, by supporting the leader. The technique to use here is to employ the very slowest of retrieves by inching the line steadily back to the angler. Each cast should take at least ten minutes to retrieve. Naturally, if you prefer to fish your pupae a little deeper, they may be attached to the cast with the conventional system of droppers. Although my adult midge imitation works well enough and does look realistic, a Grey Duster is certainly easier to tie and will still work well when fished in this manner.

EPHEMEROPTERA COMBINATION

There are many imitations of upwinged flies and nymphs so that combinations will either be made up of favourite flies or of imitations relevant to the dominant hatches at any given time. Nevertheless, whenever the stillwater olives are in evidence, the Greenwell's Glory combination cannot be bettered. On the point you may place a Greenwell nymph, although the old Greenwell's spider is an excellent nymphal imitation, a winged wet Greenwell on the first dropper as an imitation of a hatching fly, and a winged dry Greenwell's Glory on the top dropper. This presents a very light and mobile cast and the dry-fly will support the other two flies with ease if the dropper is well-greased and the fly well oiled. No retrieve is necessary although a slight draw on the line from time to time will raise the Greenwell spider and make it appear as an ascending mature nymph. The Greenwell spider may not look like a nymph when it is dry, but, once wet, it takes on a superb nymphal outline, whilst the body colour and hackle colour combine to produce the required olive shade.

Although the Sawyer Pheasant Tail nymph is an excellent imitation when fished in the correct manner, it is not suitable for a combination of flies since it is a little too heavy and impedes the floating abilities of the dry-fly.

When fishing combinations of flies in this manner, you always stand a chance of becoming snagged up once a fish has been hooked on one of the patterns. Further, netting a supposedly played out fish may become a problem. For example, if the fish has taken the point fly, you may easily get one of the dropper flies caught in the mesh before the fish has been netted. If this is the case, the battle is lost. If conditions allow, try to 'beach' a fish hooked when using a team of flies, it is much safer.

FISHING THE EMERGERS

There are times when trout will consistently refuse both conventional dry-flies and nymphs during a hatch, and at such times the angler encounters a great deal of frustration. In most cases, it will be found

153

that the fish are refusing dry-flies and nymphs because they are feeding on flies actually engaged in the process of 'hatching'. Once the nymph or pupa rises to the surface, it floats in the surface film, the nymphal/pupal integument splits and the adult insect struggles free. Trout are naturally attracted by the struggle of the creature and, if for any reason it takes some time to free itself from its nymphal case, the insect will offer an easy meal. Accordingly, an emerger pattern must be fished right in the surface film and the odd twitch imparted by the angler will attract the trout's attention by emulating the natural insect. Since we are neither fishing a nymph beneath the surface, nor a floating fly on the surface, we are practising a method which needs a new name. Perhaps the most appropriate name was coined by the American angler Vernon Hidy when he referred to 'Flymphs', although I believe the term 'Emergers' is adequately descriptive. Emergers on stillwaters may be from a number of different insect orders although chironomid midges, mayflies and sedges present the main possibilities for fishing emergers. Most of the following remarks on emergers will be based on chironomids (both because they are the most significant group of stillwater insects and because most of my research has centred on them) although the findings are equally true of the upwinged mayflies and sedges.

Emerger patterns are of greatest significance when a fly takes longer than usual to metamorphose from mature nymph (or pupa) to adult fly and although the emergence time may vary from species to species, the most important single factor is the weather.

In particularly cold weather, perhaps only chironomid midges will hatch out on stillwaters and then, only the smaller species are likely to be in evidence. I imagine that under such conditions it is difficult for the emergent fly to dry its wings adequately so that it will take some time to leave the water, whilst the emergence itself will be prolonged because the insect is rather sluggish under cold conditions. Thus, an emerger pattern fished right in the surface film will often outfish all other patterns at such times. Equally, rainfall may prevent a rapid drying of the adult's wings and under such circumstances many insects will fail completely to rid themselves of their pupal cases so that trout only need to swim around lazily in order to mop them up. Although it is often dangerous to generalise, there are two rise forms which I associate with fish feeding on emerging insects: a gentle 'kiss' rise under very calm conditions and a 'head-and-tail' rise when there is a slight breeze.

Because an insect's wings will dry quickly under warm conditions, warm weather hatches are normally more rapid yet, when the water is very calm, the hatch may be very slow indeed. Insects in general, and chironomids in particular, make use of the surface film tension in order to scramble free of their pupal shucks, and if the surface tension is reduced by scum, the process of emergence is made that much more difficult. Once a pupa reaches the surface, the shuck splits on top, from the thorax down the abdomen, and the legs of the adult fly appear first, followed by the head. Using the surface tension as a 'grip', the legs begin to pull the rest of the thorax, wings and abdomen out of the pupal case. Freeing the bulky thorax requires a great deal of effort and struggle and, when the tension of the surface film has been reduced by scum, many chironomids appear to die of exhaustion without ever freeing their abdominal segments. In a number of specimens which I have examined, the wings have also remained crumpled.

I also suspect that under hot and calm conditions, because the oxygen content of the water will be reduced, and since the pupa takes in an amount of oxygen before emergence in order to build up pressure within the pupal case to effect the split, the process of emergence will be further impeded.

From many years of watching emerging chironomids it seems that, in general, smaller flies emerge more quickly than larger insects. Thus, under conditions of calm water in hot weather, the larger flies may well take a great length of time to hatch thus offering optimum conditions for emerger fishing. This reminds me of a classic case when real success could only be achieved by actually imitating the very act of emergence.

It was late August, and in the heat of the afternoon the reservoir was perfectly calm, the surface appearing almost as thick as treacle. Lines of scum drifted gently and the only breaks in the surface film were products of a number of trout which rose persistently and within twenty yards of the bank. The subject of the fish's attentions was that beautiful and large chironomid known as the Large Red Midge, which, though emerging in fewer numbers than a hatch of Black Silverhorns was obviously preferred.

Despite the regular and accessible rises of fish, I tried many patterns of dry-flies which failed completely, although I did manage to tempt a couple of small brownies on a Red Palmer. Even so, the trout repeatedly rose short to the fly and the two fish which did find their way into the net had obviously taken the fly very tentatively, since it promptly fell from their mouths as soon as they were lifted on to the bank. There was nothing else to do but lay the rod aside and exercise a little close observation.

Midges were hatching in the deep, clear water only a short distance from the bank and patrolling trout showed a constant interest. Pupae were easily visible hanging motionless in the surface film, and adult midges rested and floated quietly as they dried and flexed their wings ready for flight. However, the trout appeared to ignore the insects in each of these stages and concentrated on flies which were engaged in the very act of struggling from their pupal shucks. The hatching process could be clearly seen, and as the fly emerged from its pupal case, its struggle elevated the thorax of the adult fly above the surface film while the redundant shuck, and the latter segments of the fly's abdomen, projected down into the water at a marked angle. This feature of emergence is often ignored yet I recall Skues having described the same kind of thing when writing about emerging ephemeropterans. Quite clearly, trout were attracted by the protracted struggle of emerging flies (which presented a very leisurely target) and would recognise them not only by movement, but also because of the angle of the insect and pupal case, which resulted in part of the fly being above the surface and part beneath it. In some way or other, the artificial needed to combine both the attributes of dry-fly and subsurface nymph.

A remarkable feature of this episode was the time taken for adult midges to free themselves completely. The metamorphosis from pupa to adult fly was extended in certain cases to as much as seventy seconds, while some flies failed to free themselves and died 'stillborn'.

To cut a long story short, as a result of my observation, I fashioned a special Emergent Red Midge which I put to use on the following day and which not only cocked at the angle of an emerging fly but also caught a number of fish. I wrote about the fly and my experiences in *Trout and Salmon* (February 1976) and although the pattern was in many respects very crude, and more acceptable patterns have since been developed, I have included the original dressing.

Since the occasion which I have just referred to, I have encountered a number of days and evenings when pupal imitations and dry-flies have been inadequate and when it was necessary to imitate chironomids in the act of 'hatching'.

Various imitations of emerging insects are illustrated in Figure 32.

EMERGER PATTERNS

THE EMERGENT RED MIDGE

This pattern, referred to previously, was my initial attempt to copy the angled profile of the hatching insect. Although it was dressed

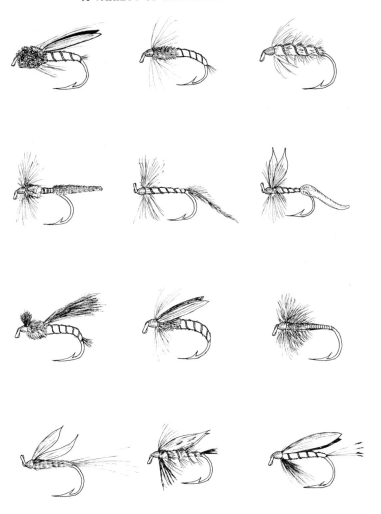

Figure 32: Various imitations of emerging insects
    1st Row . . . Small Muddler, Hackled Midge Pupa,
        Hen-Hackled Palmer
    2nd Row . . . Hatching Red Midge, Emerger with Feather
        Shuck, Emerger with Polythene Shuck
    3rd Row . . . Richard Walker's Hatching Midge, Orange
        Winged Emerger, The Flymph or Stewart
        Spider
    4th Row . . . No-Hackle Dun, Invicta, Traditional Loch
        Pattern

157

originally to represent the Large Red Midge, and used rich brown materials such as pheasant tail fibres, seal's fur and red cock hackle, other chironomids can be imitated by replacing the hackle and seal's fur with other appropriate colours and by using different colours of condor herl instead of the red-brown pheasant tail fibres. Later on, I will describe an improved version of this pattern.

The essential ingredient of the Emergent Red Midge was an extension to the hook shank using a length of thick nylon, over which layers of rich, brown pheasant tail fibres had been wound. The entire body extension was then soaked in varnish until it became hard and shiny. The weight of this imitation shuck resulted in that part of the pattern sinking below the surface, while the front half was held in the surface film by a sparsely dressed cock hackle and a dubbed thorax of seal's fur (which, being buoyant, aided floatation). This pattern is dressed in the following manner:

Hook: Up-eyed number 12. A hook with a longish shank is most suitable.
Shuck: Take a ¾ inch length of nylon line (15lbs) and crimp the end with pliers. The crimped end is then tied to the latter portion of the hook shank with brown tying silk and the binding is varnished. Varnish the nylon extension and wind the tying thread along the nylon (making sure that it is held horizontally and does not bend, resulting in an unnatural 'set'). Catch in three pheasant tail fibres and wind them along with the silk back along the nylon extension and half way along the hook shank. Tie in and snip off the excess. Soak the completed extension in several coats of varnish until it is hard and shiny.
Abdomen: Wind a few turns of stripped peacock herl in front of the shuck to represent the emerging abdomen of the adult fly.
Thorax: In front of the herl abdomen, dub a thorax of seal's fur.
Wings: Tied in front of the thorax and lying flat along the body. Cream, blue dun or pale ginger paired cock hackle points.
Hackle: Sparse red game cock.

Although this pattern worked well enough, it was a little crude and I was never very happy with the dark colour of the pupal shuck which seemed a little unrealistic.

CHIRONOMID EMERGER WITH FEATHER PUPAL CASE

This pattern is quite easy to tie and very effective. The previous pattern might be more realistic yet since the pupal shuck is quite hard, it is more likely to be rejected quickly by discerning trout. This pattern makes use of a shuck imitation which consists of two pale cream, ginger or blue dun cock hackle feathers tied in at the end of the hook shank. When wetted, these feathers look reasonably like the real thing although they don't always hang down into the water (suggestive of the correct angle of emergence). The standard tyings are as follows and are tied on hooks between size 16 and 10:

Black Emerger
Pupal shuck: Two blue dun cock hackle tips.
Abdomen: Extended only very slightly round the bend of the hook. Black condor or swan herl ribbed with narrow silver tinsel. The turns of tinsel should be quite close together.
Thorax: A dubbing of black seal's fur.
Hackle: Black cock, sparsely dressed. One turn of the hackle is quite sufficient.
Wings: Optional. Two tiny blue dun cock hackle tips.

Red-Brown Emerger
Dressed as above although pheasant tail fibres are used for the abdomen, claret seal's fur for the thorax and a red-brown cock hackle completes the pattern.

Olive Emerger
Dressed as above but with an abdomen of olive-green condor herl, a thorax of darker olive-brown seal's fur and an olive cock hackle.

Orange Silver Emerger
This pattern more closely represents the Orange Silver Midge. The hackle used is the same as that for the Red Emerger; the thorax is dark orange seal's fur and the abdomen grey heron herl ribbed with orange floss silk.

Although the above emergers were actually designed to represent various emerging chironomids, they are equally good when trout are feeding on emergent mayflies of various species. These emerger patterns should be fished statically or 'on the drift', although they become most effective when a slight twitch is imparted to them from time to time.

CHIRONOMID EMERGER WITH POLYTHENE PUPAL CASE

The dressing of this pattern is identical to that of the feather pupal case pattern, differing only in the material used in the construction of the pupal case itself. This is simply a tube of rolled polythene (the kind used in ordinary polythene bags, but as thin as possible) which is tied in slightly round the bend of the hook shank.

JOHN GODDARD'S SMALL HATCHING MIDGE

This is a good emerger pattern to use when drifting in a boat on calm evenings. In John Veniard's book *Reservoir and Lake Flies*, John Goddard describes one of the typical rise forms when trout are feeding on small emerging midges: '. . . the rise form is unmistakable as they [the trout] usually rise repeatedly in a circular pattern barely breaking the surface with their neb as they sip them down'. He developed the following pattern and declared that it should be fished 'with little or no movement on the point, or on the point and top dropper'.

Hook: Size 16.
Silk: Brown.
Body: Two turns of silver lurex round the bend of the hook followed by a main body of dark red, green or brown condor herl. The body is ribbed with narrow silver lurex.
Thorax: Buff condor herl.
Hackle: Small honey cock hackle tied in immediately behind the eye.

RICHARD WALKER'S HATCHING MIDGE

This pattern is simply a conventional midge pupa with a small bunch of black squirrel hair (natural grey or even orange will do) sloping backwards and tied in under the thorax. As a hatching midge it works quite well when retrieved slowly or in tiny twitches, just under the surface film. It should be fished on a very long leader. This fly also works very well when fished as a slow-sinking pupa from a boat; it may then be fished in a slow sink-and-draw manner.

Whilst this pattern is not strictly a dry-fly, it may be fished right in the surface film, which means that it comes pretty close to the concept of the dry-fly. Like the dry-fly itself, the emerger has often been neglected on stillwaters.

HACKLED PUPA

This pattern is simply a midge pupa with a hackle of the same colour as the body and thorax of the fly. It may be dressed with a hen hackle and fished in or just under the surface film, using a leader greased right up to the tip; or it may be dressed with a very sparse cock hackle which will allow the front end of the pattern to be held in the surface film. The hen-hackled pupa is intended for fishing with a very slow retrieve, whereas the cock-hackled pattern should be left to float or drift and merely given the tiniest of twitches from time to time in order to simulate the struggle of the mature fly as it attempts to escape the pupal shuck.

I dress the pattern in olive-green, pale green, brown, black and dark red according to the following prescription:

Hook: 10 – 16.
Hackle: Hen or cock hackle to match the body colour.
Body: Dressed well round the hook bend. Floss silk ribbed either with white hackle stalk or silver tinsel.
Thorax: Seal's fur, a darker shade than the body but of the same colour.

One of the advantages of this pattern, apart from the fact that it does catch fish, is that it is very simple to construct. One of its disadvantages is that it is often difficult to ensure that it cocks at the right angle in the water with hackle and thorax in the film and the rest underwater (when using the cock-hackled version that is).

A final note when using this kind of pattern is that it *must* be treated as a dry-fly rather than a nymph. Takes must be tightened on in a leisurely manner (for only small fish will take rapidly) or else the hook will be pulled out of the trout's mouth.

ORANGE-WINGED PUPA/EMERGER

A number of the chironomids possess orange tinted wings when they are emerging from their pupal cases and this coloration may well be an important recognition factor from a trout's point of view. The pupa itself may be dressed in any of the conventional styles and it is simply a matter of tying in short wings in front of the thorax, so that they protrude along each side of the thorax and at a slight upward inclination. The wings may be constructed of segments from a white hen or duck quill, dyed orange, or from two separate bunches of orange cock hackle fibres. Personally, I prefer to use orange raffeen which becomes quite mobile when thoroughly soaked and crumples like the newly emergent wings of the natural fly.

This pattern is best dressed with the addition of a very sparse hackle which may be of cock, if you wish the fly to fish in the surface film, or hen, if it is to be fished just beneath. The orange-winged pupa (which may be made with a variety of body colours) is most effective when retrieved very slowly on a very long, greased leader.

THE MUDDLER

The unusual thing about the Muddler Minnow is that this lure, constructed with a large head of trimmed deer's hair, is very buoyant and will float in the surface film. If you are skilled enough to tie the Muddler in *very* small sizes (for example, on short-shanked size 12 or 14 hooks), then you have one of the most effective emerger patterns at your disposal. By varying the body colour, and by colouring the clipped deer's hair head with Pantone pens, you can produce a variety of patterns to imitate most insects. The fly should be fished on a very long leader and retrieved very slowly along the surface. My dressing for the small Muddler is as follows:

Hook: Size 12 or 14 (short shank).
Body: Floss silk ribbed with fine gold wire.
Wing: (Tied in behind the deer's hair head) a small bunch of fur from a grey squirrel.
Head: Trimmed deer's hair either left in the natural colour or coloured with a Pantone pen to match the body colour, but a little darker in shade.

THE NO-HACKLE DUN

Recently, the 'No-hackle duns' have been firmly established as excellent flies as a result of a fine book, *Selective Trout* written by two Americans, Doug Swisher and Carl Richards. However, hackle-less flies are by no means innovations and were apparent in the first English work on fly-fishing, Dame Juliana Berners' *Treatise on Fishing with an Angle*, published in 1496.

The No-hackle duns have proved an excellent emerger pattern when fishing to ephemeroptera (mayfly) hatches because you can fish them statically right in the surface film. They are most effective when left unoiled, so that they become wet, and fished on greased leaders. Being so light in construction, they will only sink very slowly when wet, and with the drying process of false casting you can always keep them dry enough to float in the film, or just under it. Various colours may be used in the construction of the No-hackle emerger (so that you may imitate any upwinged flies) although in the following notes, I refer to the colours which in general I find most useful:

Hook: Size 10 – 16 (depending on species of fly).
Body: Seal's fur ribbed with fine gold wire. The body should have a plump thorax tapering down to the tail. The most common body colours are brown, olive (various shades), maroon and yellow.
Tails: Cockle hackle fibres to match the body colour. Tie in a bunch of fibres and splay them out into a fan.
Wings: Duck quill segments tied in split-winged style and inclined backwards at an angle of forty-five degrees.

'FLYMPHS' OR STEWART'S SPIDERS

The word 'Flymph' was coined by Vernon S. Hidy as the description of an aquatic insect's life between that of a nymph and adult fly. In *The Art of Tying the Wet Fly and Fishing the Flymph* (written in collaboration with James E. Leisenring) Hidy gave his definition of the pattern:

FLYMPH – A WINGLESS ARTIFICIAL FLY with a soft, translucent body of fur or wool which blends with the undercolor of the tying silk when wet, utilizing soft hackle fibres easily activated by the currents to give the effect of an insect alive in the water . . . for the trout to take just below or within a few inches of the surface film.

Naturally, Hidy was describing a fly for river fishing yet the Flymph is equally effective on stillwaters. Hidy developed his Flymphs from the flies of his mentor James E. Leisenring, who in turn had developed his wet-flies from the semi-palmered spiders of W. C. Stewart, a Scot, who published *The Practical Angler* in 1857.

Stewart fished the upstream wet-fly and the palmered style of hackling which he chose to adopt, when motivated by the current, produced a perfect impression of a struggling insect, particularly one which was about to hatch. G. E. M. Skues praised this style of fly-dressing and referred to the 'buzz' created by the palmered soft hackle. The current will impart much of the action to the hackle when fished in rivers, in stillwaters, and particularly on calm days, it is necessary to 'work' the fly by retrieving it in twitches and small draws, or employ the slowest of slow retrieves.

W. C. Stewart's spider patterns were hackled in palmer-style three-quarters of the way down the length of the body and all the Flymphs should be constructed in this manner. Our first three patterns are Stewart's most famous flies:

1st. *The Black Spider*. This is made of the small feather of the cock starling, dressed with brown silk, and is, upon the whole, the most killing imitation we know. We were first shown it by James Baillie, and have never been without one on our line ever since.
2nd. *The Red Spider* should be made of the small feather taken from the outside of the wing of the landrail, dressed with yellow silk, and is deserving of a very high rank, particularly in coloured water.
3rd. *The Dun Spider*. This should be made of the small soft dun or ash-coloured feather, taken from the outside of the wing of the dotterel. This bird is unfortunately very scarce; but a small feather may be taken from the inside of the wing of the starling, which will make an excellent substitute.

(I imagine that Stewart dressed the Dun Spider on yellow silk although he does not specify. It is important to note that the colours of the body silks used would be considerably darkened by a thorough application of wax.)

You may well develop several favourite Flymphs of your own but the following flies (my personal favourites) will be found to be as good as any:

Hare's Ear Flymph (Hare's Lug and Plover)
Hook: 10 – 16.
Silk: Brown.
Body: Spun Hare's Ear fur ribbed with fine gold tinsel. Pick out the hairs at the thorax.
Hackle: Golden Plover hackle tied in palmer style for three quarters the length of the body.

Pheasant Tail Flymph
Hook: 10 – 16.
Silk: Brown.
Body: Pheasant tail fibres ribbed with fine copper coloured wire.
Hackle: Coch-y-bondhu hen hackle dressed as before.

Olive Flymph
Hook: 10 – 16.
Silk: Olive.
Body: Olive condor herl or seal's fur (various shades) ribbed with gold wire.
Hackle: Hen hackle (to match the shade of the body) dressed as before.

Yellow Flymph
Hook: 10 – 16.
Silk: Yellow.
Body: Pale yellow seal's fur ribbed with fine gold wire.
Hackle: Ginger hen hackle dressed as before.

Blue Dun Flymph
Hook: 10 – 16.
Silk: Primrose.
Body: A mixture of grey seal's fur and blue rabbit fur ribbed with primrose tying silk.
Hackle: Blue dun hen dressed as before.

JAMES OGDEN'S INVICTA

Some sedge flies emerge with the pupa crawling ashore among the stones or reeds, or crawling up aquatic vegetation to the surface. However, other species of sedge do emerge in open water and provide excellent opportunities (generally during the evening) for fishing emergers.

One of the best emerger patterns for sedge flies is the Invicta retrieved very slowly just below the surface. The dressing is as follows:

Hook: Size 8 to 14.
Silk: Brown.
Body: Amber seal's fur ribbed with oval gold tinsel.
Tag: Red wool.
Body and Front hackle: Natural red hen or henny-cock.
Beard hackle: Barred blue jay feather fibres.
Wings: Hen pheasant centre tail.

Apart from the Invicta, the palmer flies included in the section on sedges may also be fished just under the surface film to represent the emerging fly. Unlike the floating patterns, they should be tied with hen hackles or henny-cock hackles rather than the normal cock hackles. Once again, they are fished in a very slow retrieve just under the surface film.

WHEN THE DRY-FLY SINKS

It was a warm but breezy day in June. The bank from which I fished was made up of shale and clay, and since the wind was blowing right on to it, the waves were churning against the bank and creating a yellowy slick along it. Fish rose and swirled in numbers close in and although I covered many fish with a dry Greenwell's Glory, only one fish had risen short to it. The fly needed constant drying and oiling to make it float and it was rapidly becoming waterlogged once again as I mended line to keep in touch with it. Suddenly it sank and the cast slowly dragged under; then the cast began to slip away quickly and I tightened into a good fish which bored away into the deeper water. Several other fish followed that first one into the bag yet were not taken on dry Greenwell, but, on a winged wet Greenwell. Strangely, when I spooned the first fish I had expected to see its maw crammed with nymphs or other aquatic fauna, yet most of the insects present were winged adult flies. Why hadn't the dry-fly worked? As it turned out, what was happening was that adult flies were being swamped by the rough water, and carried under by the undertow current against the bank, and thus the trout were taking fully-fledged adult flies under the water.

When the wind blows against the bank and neither dry-fly nor nymph works adequately, it may often be that the winged wet-fly will provide a more efficacious way of catching fish and a switch to a team of three small traditional loch flies will bring required results. Naturally, this is essentially a book about stillwater dry-fly fishing and traditional loch flies are wet-flies. However, the adult fly provides the necessary connection between the two so that I may be permitted to consider this minor tactical approach. For this reason, I feel justified in including a number of traditional wet-flies which will be found valuable on those occasions when both terrestrial and aquatic flies are swamped and drowned. Since it is likely that you will be fishing these flies into the wind, a short leader of around ten feet in length will prove to be most manageable. You may either fish the flies with a very slow retrieve or merely allow them to swing around; in the latter case, it will be necessary to draw in line as the flies drift in order to keep in touch with them. The use of a floating line will allow you to keep the flies fairly well up in the water whilst a very slow sinker will allow the same with the added advantage of stability. A line which will sink very slowly will still allow the flies to fish high yet it will drift less than a floating line. In this respect, I have found 'Meteor' sinking lines excellent for my purposes since they sink very slowly indeed. They are also of a very pale brown colour which makes them quite easy to see and this will enable you to detect takes without much difficulty. Having recently used the new neutral density lines under these conditions, I find them no different, nor better, than the line already referred to.

The following patterns will furnish the angler with all the flies he needs for this style of fishing:

Greenwell's Glory
Hook: 16 – 14.
Body: Well-waxed primrose tying silk ribbed with fine gold wire.
Hackle: Greenwell or coch-y-bondhu (hen).
Wings: Hen blackbird wing.

Woodcock Greenwell
As for the Greenwell's Glory but with a woodcock wing in place of the usual hen blackbird wing.

Teal and Red
Hook: 14 – 10.

166

Wing: Teal duck fibres.
Hackle: Red hen.
Tail: Golden pheasant tippets.
Body: Red seal's fur ribbed with oval gold tinsel.
In small sizes the Yellow, Green, Black and Red versions provide quite useful imitations of the appropriate colours of chironomid midges.

Teal and Yellow
Hook: 14 – 10.
Wing: Teal duck fibres.
Hackle: Yellow or ginger hen.
Tail: Golden pheasant tippets.
Body: Yellow seal's fur ribbed with oval gold tinsel.

Teal and Green
Hook: 14 – 10.
Wing: Teal duck fibres.
Hackle: Green hen.
Tail: Golden pheasant tippets.
Body: Green seal's fur ribbed with oval silver tinsel.

Teal and Black
Hook: 14 – 10.
Wing: Teal duck fibres.
Hackle: Black hen.
Tail: Golden pheasant tippets.
Body: Black seal's fur ribbed with oval silver tinsel.

Black and Blae
Hook: 16 – 12.
Body: Black seal's fur or floss silk ribbed with silver wire.
Hackle: Black hen.
Wings: Wild duck wing, medium starling or blae part of a jay's wing. (The above pattern with a change of body and hackle colour is excellent when chironomid midges are hatching. Other suggested colours are maroon, brown, green, olive and amber.)

Mallard and Claret
Hook: 14 – 10.
Wing: Bronze mallard duck.
Body: Claret wool or seal's fur ribbed with oval gold tinsel.
Hackle: Black hen, normally tied as a false beard hackle.
Tail: Golden pheasant tippets.

Red Quill
Hook: 12 – 16.
Tying Silk: Brown.
Tail: Red cock hackle fibres.
Body: Stripped peacock herl quill dyed red or coloured with Pantone pen.
Hackle: Red hen.
Wings: Starling.

Olive Quill
Hook: 12 – 16.
Tying Silk: Olive green.
Tail: Olive (dyed) cock hackle fibres.
Body: Stripped peacock herl quill dyed olive green or coloured with Pantone pen.
Hackle: Medium olive green hen.
Wings: Starling.

Ginger Quill
Hook: 12 – 16.
Tying Silk: Brown.
Tail: Ginger cock hackle fibres.
Body: Natural stripped peacock herl quill.
Hackle: Ginger hen.
Wings: Starling.
I believe this fly is a favoured imitation of chironomids on Eyebrook reservoir.

Dark Olive Quill
Hook: 12 – 16.
Tying Silk: Brown.
Tail: Brown cock hackle fibres.
Body: Natural stripped peacock herl quill.
Hackle: Dark olive-brown hen.
Wings: Hen blackbird.

Orange Quill
Hook: 12 – 16.
Tying silk: Orange.
Tail: Ginger cock hackle fibres.
Body: Stripped peacock herl quill dyed hot orange or coloured with Pantone pen.
Hackle: Hot orange hen.
Wings: Starling.
(The 'Quill' series may also be dressed with appropriately coloured seal's fur bodies ribbed tightly with stripped peacock quill.)

168

THE SURFACE LURE

By no stretch of the imagination can a lure be described as a 'dry-fly' and yet, when fished right at the surface, it may just about allow us to include it into the present book.

There are times when fish show themselves very near to the surface and are presumably feeding yet are extraordinarily difficult to tempt. They may, for example, be eating hosts of tiny daphnia. On such occasions, a surface fished lure will often provide the means of catching fish that otherwise might have escaped our infernal clutches. Nevertheless, I am no lover of lure fishing and will only use this technique as a last resort: thus, for me, it remains a minor tactic. Even then, I loathe the use of gaudy creations dressed on huge irons and prefer to use very small lures dressed on conventional size 10 and 8 short-shanked hooks. Fishing such lures on floating line and long leader, with a very slow retrieve, comes fairly near to nymph fishing in technique and, at times, may be quite pleasant.

The surface fished lure, and here I refer to lures which will actually float when left to drift, is often neglected even though it does kill well. Indeed, you only have to consider the recent success of American popping bugs and Falkus's use of floating lures for sea trout, to realise the possibilities. Since the surface lure is best fished on a floating line, and since the floating line creates line-wake, which may scare fish, the fly-line should be separated from the lure by a very long leader (as long as it is possible for you to cast with) and the leader itself must be rubbed with fuller's earth mixture to make it sink (where it will cause least disturbance).

Apart from using 'floating' lures out of sheer frustration, they may also be used when trout are feeding avidly on minnows, sticklebacks, or fry. At such times, trout will often work together, herding the tiny fish into tight shoals and then charge into the shoals in rushes. Though they may actually catch a number of fish during this process, they will also damage and stun a good number which will float to the surface where they will twitch and swim erratically. These fish will be mopped up at leisure by the trout and you may catch them by fishing a small floating lure. Cast into the area of general feeding activity, allow the lure to float for a little while and then twitch it erratically back in a slow retrieve. Sometimes the lure will be taken gently, at other times it will be taken with a real wallop which means that a strong leader point is essential.

Ironically, the lure sometimes produces poor results when trout are fry-feeding, and for some unaccountable reason, a bushy dry-fly cast into the feeding area will often gain better results. There is certainly a limit to logic in the pursuit of stillwater trout!

169

As far as surface lures themselves are concerned, any lure may be converted into a 'floater' if you use buoyant materials in its construction. A good idea is to wind a tight underbody of foam strip or Plastazote before constructing the lure over the top, but the lure itself must not be made of materials which absorb water readily. For example, chenille is useless in the construction of floating lures. Deer hair is, of course, very buoyant which thus makes the Muddler Minnow a classic floating lure. My personal preference is for two patterns only, although the present reader will undoubtedly be able to fashion plenty of his own design.

The Surface Muddler
My favoured dressing of this lure is as follows:

Hook: Size 8 short shank (or long shank if preferred).
Silk: Brown.
Body: Gold tinsel or mylar ribbed with oval gold tinsel or gold wire.
Wing: Grey squirrel hair or mottled turkey tail feather.
Head: Trimmed deer's hair. The head should be quite bulky and almost half the length of the hook shank. I like to leave some of the deer hairs uncut so that they trail back over the hook.
Tail: As wing.
(This is also a good fly to use in the evening when sedge flies are skittering about on the surface of the lake.)

The Surface Baby Doll
Hook: Size 8 or 10 short shank (or long shank if preferred).
Tying silk: White.
Underbody: Plastazote strip wound on tightly to produce a cigar shape.
Body: Fluffy white baby wool wound over the underbody.
Tail: Fluffed out white wool.
Back: Bright orange raffeen tied in at the head and tail.
(Make sure that you dampen the raffeen before use and stretch it over the back as you tie it in.)

BOB-FLY AND DAPPING TACTICS

These two techniques (already covered to some extent in Chapter 2) have a number of things in common; for one thing, since they both involve fishing flies at, or near the surface, they are allied to the use of the stillwater dry-fly. As far as England is concerned, each technique may be considered a minor tactic − but only because they are so rarely practised. On Irish loughs, dapping is an extremely common method, whilst on Scottish lochs, the use of a bob-fly on the top dropper is equally common and traditional − and both techniques provide a great deal of pleasure and success. Perhaps one of the most important factors which is common to both techniques is the use of specialised tackle, particularly in the form of a very long rod. (The reader would perhaps be advised to flip back to Chapter 2 for a resumé of the kind of equipment needed for this kind of fishing.)

Although dapping and bob-fly fishing are possible from the bank, they are obviously more effective when fishing from a boat. From a bank, these tactics are only fully effective under the optimum conditions, that is, a stiff breeze at your back and reasonably deep water within easy reach of you. Naturally, these conditions may easily exist when fishing from a dam wall so that such a location does present real possibilities of fishing 'on the dap' and with a bob-fly from the bank. However, fishing from a drifting boat remains the best way of achieving full success with the traditional techniques. These techniques are illustrated in Figure 33.

In order to effect a slow drift from a boat, a canvas drogue will be needed and although they are sometimes supplied with a boat, you may need to purchase your own for those waters where they are not provided. Good, functional drogues may be obtained from various tackle shops and mail order companies. The drogue itself is usually a conical cylinder of canvas with stiff hoops at each end and ropes from the wider end by which it is attached to the boat. The drogue fills out in the water and slows down the drift of the boat by acting rather like a parachute. If you attach the two ropes of the drogue to the side of the boat, then the boat will drift broadside to the wind and will allow an angler to fish comfortably from each end of the boat. When you have completed a drift, then you simply slip the drogue and row back again to begin another drift. Naturally, if you are fishing in Scotland or Ireland, then you may be lucky enough to obtain the services of a reputable boatman, which will mean that you may dispense with the use of the drogue.

Let us now look at bob-fly tactics. The bob-fly is a bushy fly tied to the top dropper of a cast of three, or even four wet-flies. With a short cast, and a long rod held high, the flies on the leader will fish at different depths with the point fly deepest and the bushy bob-fly itself 'dibbling' around at the surface and splashing in the wave crests. Fished in this manner, it is at its most seductive. Certainly, it is not a conventional dry-fly, and in a sense, it doesn't really float at all, since it works at the surface as a result of the steepness of the leader from point fly to rod, yet it still represents a surface tactic which may be considered a branch of stillwater dry-fly fishing.

THE DROGUE

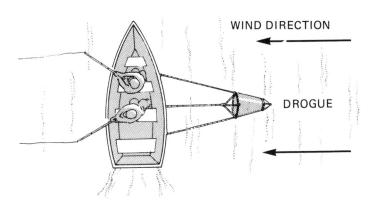

WIND DIRECTION

DROGUE

THE BOB—FLY TEAM

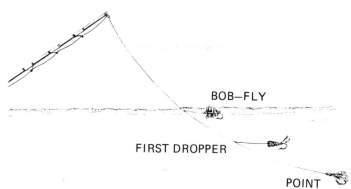

BOB—FLY

FIRST DROPPER

POINT

THE FEARSOME LOCH ORDIE
DAPPING FLY

Figure 33: Bob-fly and dapping tactics.

172

If we imagine that we are now in a drifting boat, then we can see what happens. Our rod is a long one, perhaps 10ft 6in or even 11 feet in length, and it is very light. It is not designed to cast a long line. Handling a line as light as size 5, and with the wind behind us, it flips out the line rather than casts it. Our cast is made up of three flies (on Loch Leven it would probably be four) — perhaps a Peter Ross on the point (size 14), a Mallard and Claret on the first dropper (size 10) and the top dropper, our bob-fly itself.

We might try a size 8 palmer-dressed Zulu, or indeed, any other palmer-dressed fly, since they suggest a real 'buzz' of movement when worked on the surface. We throw out a shortish line in front of the drift of the boat or a little to one side, and begin a gentle retrieve either in short draws with the left hand or with a 'figure-of-eight' retrieve. Perhaps we get a take shortly after the cast has been made, because in a good ripple we expect the fish to take well enough near to the surface; if not, well never mind, the best is yet to come. As we make the retrieve we are gradually raising the point of the rod and as the flies near the boat the rod tip is raised quite high. Not only will the lower flies now be rising in the water (and may thus be taken for ascending nymphs) but more importantly, the bob-fly will be dibbling around in the waves. Splash! Yes, that was a take to the bob-fly just as it reached the boat, but unfortunately we tightened too quickly and pulled the fly right out of the fish's mouth. Next time, if we get a take, a leisurely tightening will be called for because this will allow the fish to fully engulf the fly and then turn down again.

Once the rod has been raised high at the end of the retrieve, a gentle roll cast will unfurl out the line again for a new retrieve, and this will both lessen the chances of tangling the flies and lessen the chances of landing a hook in the lobes of our ears. We begin a new retrieve (only half conscious that our partner now has a fish on and we run the risk of tangling him) and just as the bob-fly bounces at the surface, there is a swirl, we tighten leisurely and a fish is on. . . . .

In truth, few techniques (other than perhaps the use of delicate dry-flies and nymphs) can surpass the pleasure of fishing the traditional wet-fly in this relaxed manner and it is to be recommended to all. The unexpected thrill of a swirl as the fly hits the surface during the retrieve is certainly exciting, yet the whole procedure has nothing of the dogged hard labour that may often result from a day's lure stripping.

Dapping too offers a very pleasurable traditional method of fishing from a drifting boat, although for dapping to be effective, a reasonably stiff breeze is really essential. As discussed previously in the section on tackle, a very light floss line is simply paid out into the wind when dapping, so that no casting is actually required. I have even seen people using little 'sails' of paper or material as an aid to this process, yet this kind of technique seems to lack a little delicacy.

For dapping, a long rod is necessary since it will not only aid the angler to pay out line into the wind, but will also ensure that the line is held clear of the water so that only the final point of the leader (attached to the floss blow-line) and the fly itself, touch the surface. A number of long modern carbon and glass rods (see the chapter on tackle) will be found 'adequate' although longer rods, 14 feet and upwards (even 20 feet rods were used in the old days) will be the only rods to fish 'perfectly'. As far as I remember, the last purpose-built dapping rod advertised commercially was made by Allcock's and, unfortunately, that noble firm has long since passed from the angling scene. However, if you can withstand the upturned noses of countless other anglers, you can always make use of a long and light match fishing rod coupled with a centre-pin reel (the old 'Rapidex', made by 'Youngs' and the 'Aerial', produced by 'Allcock's', were ideal).

The fly itself needs to be a very light and buoyant palmer-dressed floater and it ought to be dressed on a light-wire, long-shanked, mayfly hook. Any palmer fly will do although you have to go a long way to beat the traditional Loch Ordie pattern. Dapping is often at its best on warm and windy summer evenings when moths and sedges are around and the Loch Ordie imitates those natural flies excellently. The fly is simplicity itself to tie since it merely consists of winding several brown cock hackles in a bushy palmer manner from the eye to the bend of a long-shanked hook. The lack of body (actually the quill of the feathers does provide a kind of body) reduces weight from the pattern and not only ensures good floating properties, but also allows the pattern to blow freely in the wind. When dapping, you may well get many exciting and dramatic rises, yet the fish are often notoriously difficult to 'hit', so that many rises will come to nothing. For this reason, the traditional dressing of the 'Ordie' specifies the use of a small flying treble (about size 14) which is attached to the main hook with a short length of nylon, which in turn is whipped in at the head. In addition, the fly is often tied in the first place on a tandem hook so that the traditional dressing calls for up to five hook points! Certainly this will facilitate a greater percentage of hooked fish, yet it produces a certain crudity which the present reader may wish to forgo, taking his chance of hooking fish like a game of Russian roulette.

Apart from the Loch Ordie, other palmer-dressings may be used in dapping as well as patterns such as light mayfly designs, or Geoff Bucknall's Daddy-longlegs, which are more likely to suggest particular insects. However, in truth, it is the manner in which the flies are fished

174

that counts and the flies themselves are of secondary importance. With a stiff breeze, the fly may only rest on the surface for very short periods, being frequently borne off the water by the wind. A fish will rise and strike in the panic-stricken belief that its prey is escaping from the surface and it will have very little time to make a discerning study of the artificial. In addition, since dapping is only practised under windy conditions, the waves will prevent the fish from seeing a clear definition of the fly in any case, and it will simply be attracted by a fuzzy pattern in the surface film.

The longer the rod you are able to use, the longer the range you will be able to fish at, although fish will often be caught quite close to the boat, and at a short distance, hooking is always easier than it is at long range. Always begin by paying out only a little more line than the length of the rod and, with the wind at your back, you will be able to control the fly, make it flit along the surface, rest for a while, rise up from the water and fall down again. Rises are often sudden and dramatic, and full concentration is essential. Rapid splash takes are frequent because a trout believes that its prey is escaping and this may also mean that you have to tighten like lightning. On the other hand, rapid strikes may lose fish when a leisurely strike would be more effective. It is perhaps the erratic and unforeseeable nature of dapping which adds so greatly to its attraction as a technique.

Once you have to some degree mastered the art of dapping at short range, then you can extend the length of the line paid out with the wind and develop various interesting methods of presenting the fly. Be warned however, dapping flies are large flies and they often attract very large fish, so that your cast point ought to be quite strong and anything less than 6lbs breaking strain may well be suicidal. Indeed, should you use this tactic on a Scottish Loch, you never know what might take your fly, it might be a good sea trout — then again, it might even be a salmon!

Footnote: Since the fly will often blow off the water and against it again, dapping can provide an excellent way of imitating egg-laying female insects. Unfortunately, as yet, this technique has not been developed very far since dapping cannot be practised during a flat calm when egg-laying is often most significant. Further, when imitating egg-laying insects, we often choose to imitate small naturals whereas it takes a large fly to perfect dapping. Nevertheless, it seems worthwhile to experiment in an attempt to perfect a copy of an insect dipping against the water as it lays its eggs. At times, this very action stimulates trout to rise and the static artificial comes a very poor second.

8

A selection of flies

A GENERAL SELECTION: MY TOP TWENTY

There may be many readers who do not wish to tie, or buy, all the patterns listed in this book. Hopefully, I have convinced even the hardened lure or nymph man that the dry-fly is at least occasionally worth a try. Accordingly, there may be those who would wish an abbreviated list of flies which may be kept in reserve until the time is ripe. At first, I toyed with the idea of offering a 'desert-island-disc' selection of only ten patterns, but that seemed a little too limiting − a selection of twenty flies gave a little more scope and did not seem unnecessarily unwieldy. Here they are − my *Top Twenty*:

1 Blue Dun: An excellent general dry-fly which may be used throughout the season. It is a good pattern when trout are taking upwinged duns and in small sizes will catch fish preoccupied with tiny naturals.

2 Pheasant Tail: An excellent general pattern which may be used throughout the season. It will represent the early season Sepia Duns, the Claret Dun in May and June, the Olives and even the small brown stoneflies.

3 Greenwell's Glory: A good general pattern and imitation of the Olives; an excellent imitation of the Pond Olive and at its best from May to July.

4 Grey Wulf: Excellent pattern for the Mayfly hatches in May and June and a good fly in September when Daddy-longlegs are around.

5 Pheasant Tail Spinner: A good imitation of any upwinged spinners and excellent on evenings in late spring and summer.

6 Grey Duster: May be used throughout the season as a general pattern and particularly good for Midges, Caënis and any small flies.

7 Red Palmer: A good general pattern throughout the season, particularly in breezy weather. In spring and summer a good imitation of the sedges.

8 Ginger Palmer: An excellent general sedge pattern (at its best on summer evenings) and useful when moths are around.

9 Yellow Sally: A good imitation of the named fly from May to July and a fair imitation of the Yellow May Dun. It is also the kind of fly to try on dour days when nothing else seems likely to tempt the fish.

10 Black Midge: An excellent early season fly which will also catch fish throughout the season. In small sizes it is a useful fly when any tiny black flies are around.

11 Olive Midge: A good midge pattern throughout the season.

12 Red Midge: In various sizes this is an excellent fish-catcher from June to September when red and brown midges are around.

13 Orange Midge: It will catch fish under calm conditions throughout the season and is particularly good from April to June when the naturals appear in greatest numbers.

14 Bluebottle: At its best on warm and breezy summer days but will catch fish on cool days as well.

15 Daddy-longlegs: An excellent and killing fly when the naturals abound in July, August and September.

16 Drone Fly: The natural is commonest in July and August and an artificial is essential at such times. A good fly for Rutland. At a pinch, this pattern will also imitate bees and wasps.

17 Black Gnat or Knotted Midge: Either of these patterns will kill well throughout the season as imitations of midges, gnats, hawthorn flies and any other small black flies.

18 Hawthorn Fly: A must when the natural appears in April or May. On upland lakes the Heather fly may be imitated by this pattern in August and September.

19 Feather Duster: A good general pattern particularly when imitating moths. In large sizes this pattern will kill fish feeding on mayflies whilst tiny naturals may be imitated by the Feather Duster dressed on small hooks.

20 Snail: Once again, this pattern is a must when trout are preoccupied by the natural creature although it will produce rises at other times as well.

With the above selection of flies in your fly-box, you should manage to enjoy sport with the stillwater dry-fly on any lake or reservoir in Britain.

ADDITIONAL PATTERNS

Although I do not wish to confuse the reader by offering a vast array
of artificials, there are various dry-flies which will kill well on
stillwaters and are worthy of inclusion in this book.

Mole Fly
Hook: Size 14 – 16.
Silk: Dark olive.
Body: Dark olive floss silk ribbed with fine gold wire.
Hackle: Furnace cock tied bushy over the front half of the body.
Wings: Mottled hen pheasant tied in a forward position.

   This is a good imitation of the Olives but kills well on overcast days
in summer.

Coachman
Hook: Size 10 – 16.
Silk: Brown.
Body: Bronze peacock herl.
Hackle: Natural red cock hackle.
Wings: White duck wing quill.

   A good general dry-fly and very effective on summer evenings when
sedges are around. Unfortunately, once the herl body becomes wet,
the pattern ceases to float quite so well.

Traditional Cinnamon Sedge
Hook: Size 10 – 16.
Silk: Brown.
Body: Fibres from a cinnamon turkey tail ribbed with fine gold wire.
Body Hackle: Dark ginger cock held in place by the ribbing.
Front Hackle: Dark ginger cock tied quite bushy.
Wings: Brown hen wing quill tied 'rolled'.

   A good general sedge pattern, particularly when small cinnamon-
coloured sedge are in evidence which may well be during the daytime.

Gold Ribbed Hare's Ear
Hook: Size 14 – 16.
Silk: Primrose.
Body: Dark fur from the root of the hare's ear ribbed with fine gold
wire or primrose tying silk.
Hackle: Long strands of the body material picked out with a dubbing
needle.
Wings: Starling.
Tails: Three speckled fibres from a hen's wing quill.

   This famous fly is a particularly good fly on stillwaters when the surface is oily calm and Olives are finding it difficult to emerge quickly.

Blae and Black

Hook: Size 14 – 16.
Silk: Black.
Body: Black seal's fur ribbed with black tying silk.
Hackle: Black cock hackle.
Wings: Wild duck wing-feather or medium starling.
Tail: (Optional) A few golden pheasant tippet fibres or cock hackle fibres.

The Blae and Black is normally thought of as a wet-fly imitation of the black midge, or buzzer. It may, however, be successfully tied as a dry-fly capable of catching fish whenever small black flies are in evidence.

Zulu

Hook: Size 8 – 16.
Silk: Black.
Body: Black seal's fur ribbed with thin flat silver tinsel.
Body Hackle: Black cock held in place by the ribbing.
Front Hackle: Black cock tied bushy.
Tail: Red wool.

Although this is often regarded as a wet-fly it may be used as a dry-fly during choppy conditions: it is a good dapping fly. Above all, it excels as a fly to use when bob-fly fishing (which may be regarded as a cross-breed between wet-fly and dry-fly tactics).

John Storey

Hook: Size 14.
Silk: Crimson.
Body: Peacock herl ribbed with crimson tying silk.
Hackle: Natural red game cock.
Wings: Grey mallard flank feather fibres tied upright.
Tail: Fibres as per hackle.

This excellent Yorkshire pattern is regarded generally as a river fly yet it kills well on small lake fisheries on summer days and evenings.

Black Pennell

Hook: Size 8 – 12.
Silk: Black.
Body: Black floss silk ribbed with oval gold tinsel.
Hackle: Two black cock hackles tied bushy.
Tail: Golden pheasant tippets.

This is another pattern normally associated with wet-fly fishing although it is an excellent dapping fly in larger sizes.

John Henderson's Claret Dun
Hook: Size 14.
Silk: Mulberry.
Body: Dark claret seal's fur (I often mix in seal's fur dyed to an iron blue shade) ribbed with fine gold wire.
Hackle: Dark rusty dun cock.
Wings: (Optional) Starling.
Tail: A few fibres as per hackle.

John Goddard's Last Hope
Hook: Size 18.
Silk: Pale yellow.
Body: Two or three grey Norwegian goose or condor herls.
Hackle: A tiny dark honey dun cock hackle.
Tail: Fibres as per hackle.
   This pattern offers an excellent alternative to the Grey Duster as an imitation of the Caënis.

Orange Sedge
Hook: Size 12.
Silk: Orange.
Body: Pale buff coloured hare's ear ribbed with gold wire.
Hackle: Hot orange.
Wings: Partridge wing feather slip tied 'rolled'.
   I have no idea who originated this pattern although it, and dressings like it, do seem to account for a number of good fish. It is a particularly effective fly for evening fishing on small lakes.

Fuzzy-wuzzy
Hook: Size 12 long shank.
Silk: Orange.
Body: Ginger seal's fur ribbed with oval gold tinsel.
Hackle: Hackled 'fore' and 'aft' with two pairs of ginger cock hackles.
   This rather unlikely looking fly is a good floater and has an uncanny knack of catching large fish when nothing else will move them. It is not a pattern for the purist and is normally cast out surreptitiously when you are sure that nobody is watching!

Large Summer Dun
(C. F. Walker: *Lake Flies and their Imitation*)
Hook: Size 12.
Silk: Brown.
Body: Grey-brown condor herl stained to an olive shade in picric acid. Rib the body with fine gold tinsel.
Hackle: Dyed brown-olive cock hackle.

Wings: A bunch of grey fibres from near the tip of a mallard scapular feather.
Tail: Brown mallard fibres.

I neglected the Large Summer Dun (*Siphlonurus lacustris*) in the general section on upwinged flies because I regard it as of minor, or local, importance. Nevertheless, where it does occur (usually in Ireland and Scotland) the above pattern will not be found wanting.

Skues' Orange Quill

Hook: Size 14.
Silk: Orange.
Body: Stripped peacock or ostrich herl dyed hot orange.
Hackle: Natural bright red game cock.
Wings: Pale starling.
Tail: Fibres as per hackle.

Skues gained a great deal of fame and success with this fly when using it during BWO hatches or even when imitating the spinners. However, it is a good general dry-fly and worth using speculatively on small lake fisheries.

C. F. Walker's Sepia Dun

Hook: Size 12 or 14.
Silk: Brown.
Body: Grey-brown condor herl.
Hackle: Cock hackle dyed a dark sepia colour.
Wings: A bunch of feathers from a mallard scapular feather.
Tail: Very dark brown (almost black) cock spade hackle fibres.

An alternative to the patterns offered for this insect at earlier stages in the text.

J. R. Harris's Yellow Dun

(*An Angler's Entomology*)
Hook: Size 14.
Silk: Yellow.
Body: Bright orange floss ribbed with fine gold wire.
Hackle: Ginger cock.
Wings: A bunch of pale yellow cock hackle fibres, parted in a V-shape.
Tail: Ginger cock hackle fibres.

This is a good fly for the Yellow Evening Dun and the Yellow May Dun.

John Goddard's Nevamis Mayfly

Hook: Size 8 long-shank mayfly hook.
Silk: Yellow.
Body: Cream seal's fur ribbed with a honey dun cock hackle trimmed

181

very short. Rib with oval gold tinsel.
Hackle: Furnace cock.
Wings: Large pale blue dun cock hackle fibres parted in a V-shape.
Tail: Three pheasant tail fibres.

Whilst I am fully aware that there are many more dry-flies available to the stillwater angler, this selection should prove useful as a supplement to the flies presented elsewhere in the text. To some degree, Marryat's comment, 'It's not the fly, it's the driver,' must be accepted as a principle. A small selection of flies used correctly will always beat a vast assortment of artificials used incorrecly, or cast clumsily.

9

Stillwater dry-fly fishing for coarse fish

I don't believe that it is right to let a book on stillwater dry-fly fishing pass without a word being said on the capture of coarse fish. Most coarse fish may be caught by fly fishing tactics and indeed, I would go as far as to say that *all* coarse fish may be caught with fly-fishing tackle, the appropriate tactics and the appropriate 'flies'. Whether or not you class grayling as game or coarse fish, they are regularly caught on flies, whilst tiny dry-flies have accounted for many dace, and large bushy dry-flies have been traditionally effective in the pursuit of chub. Pike and perch regularly succumb to sunken lures, and attractors, and although they are normally caught accidentally by anglers fishing for trout, there are a number of modern anglers who have become fanatical winter pike fly-fishermen. However, fly-fishing for pike is by no means a recent development for H. Cholmondeley-Pennell (of the *Pennell* series of flies fame) included a Pike fly, which utilised complete peacock eye-feathers, in his *Book of the Pike* (1865). It is less likely that fly-fishing for perch will become anything of a cult and I am afraid that I have always regarded perch as something-of-a-nuisance fish − even large perch, which I caught during my coarse fishing days, never really did a great deal for me. The ultimate annoyance occurred a few years ago when fishing Cromwell Lake near Brighouse in Yorkshire (not to be confused with the Nottinghamshire lake of the same name). I only managed to account for one trout in a catch of forty-odd fish, the rest being perch. The ultimate irony was that in attempting to evade the perch-plague I switched exclusively to the dry-fly − and still caught the spined menace!

Other coarse fish which may be taken on the fly are roach, rudd and even bream (which I believe are sometimes caught by fly-fishing tactics on the Continent), although roach and rudd offer the greatest possibilities for the stillwater dry-fly fisherman. When you begin to think about it, there is absolutely no reason why coarse fish shouldn't be caught on imitative tactics since their staple diet actually differs very little from that of the trout − they *must* eat the only available food supply, although, admittedly, in over-fished coarse fisheries, maggots, bread and groundbait are heaved in in such quantities that the fish must believe them to be a natural food form.

Many years ago, when pursuing specimen roach in a reservoir (which incidentally contained a number of trout), I spooned a number of roach at intervals during the coarse fishing season in order to discover their staple diet and, therefore, enable myself to fish with 'natural' baits. As it turned out, the most popular food items were very little different from those eaten by the indigenous trout, that is: 'bloodworms' (the larvae of certain species of midges), chironomid pupae, caddis larvae (complete with cases), small mussels, snails, shrimps, ephemeropteran nymphs and, during the summer months, a number of adult floating flies. Initial experiments with natural baits such as bloodworms and caddis larvae, provided limited success, yet a number of these baits either proved difficult to hook or difficult to fish in a natural manner. A natural development from these early experiments was to think of using a fly rod and artificial patterns since I already went stillwater fly-fishing for trout. Indeed, in this very reservoir I had already taken a number of perch, rudd and roach when fishing soft-hackled wet-flies intended for the resident brownies, which were considerably outnumbered by their coarse fish brethren.

I was reasonable pleased with the roach which I eventually caught on artificial caddis, shrimp, snail and midge pupa patterns, and although I did not account for vast bags of fish (which wasn't my objective anyway) quality roach gave a good account of themselves on light fly-tackle and the fishing experience was altogether rewarding. The largest fish, a beautifully proportioned roach of 1¾lbs fell to a midge pupa fished a couple of feet beneath the surface.

My largest roach on fly-tackle was not caught on a dry-fly but it did emphasise the success of fly-fishing tactics and led to my use of floating flies on subsequent occasions. In all honesty, the dry-fly never accounted for fish in the specimen class and I suspect that the largest roach are essentially bottom feeders, but, nevertheless, the dry-fly did go on to account for roach up to ¾lb in weight and provided many pleasant fishing hours. In actual fact, I was pleasantly surprised by the size of roach which were caught on the dry-fly, for, although rudd are well known as surface feeders, it had originally appeared as if only the smallest roach would actually be prepared to feed at the surface.

During the summer months there are often chances to use a dry-fly in order to catch roach in canals, ponds, lakes and reservoirs. One of my local reservoirs is often dimpled all over on calm summer evenings by roach feeding mainly on midge pupae and, although they can certainly be caught on pupal imitations, they seem very ready to take small dry-flies as an alternative. The choice of fly does not seem as important as it does when fishing for trout, and whilst Grey Dusters, Greenwells, Knotted Midges and Black Spiders have all accounted for a number of fish, a smallish Red Palmer seems to have been the most consistently effective fly. Based on my assumption that the roach is a shy and sensitive fish, it seems as if flies no larger than those dressed on size 14 hooks are best and they should be presented on a light line (no heavier.than an AFTM 5 double-tapered floater) and with a long and fine leader. The point size of the leader need not be stronger than 2½lbs breaking strain and it ought to be at least twelve feet in length.

Since the roach is essentially a shoal fish, once you have located a number of them feeding near to the surface, it is only necessary to cast into the general feeding area. Delicate presentation of the fly and careful playing of the fish (which means getting him away from the rest of the shoal as quickly as possible) may well result in the capture of many fish, which provides a very pleasant evening's entertainment.

One of the greatest problems encountered by the angler who desires to catch roach on the dry-fly was made clear to me on one of the very first occasions when I tried this technique. Having moored for an evening meal on Salhouse Broad (in the days when boat traffic seemed considerably lighter than it is today on the Broads) I originally decided to have some fun by float fishing for roach with a light fly-rod. However, roach and bleak began to rise in numbers so I decided to try a small Knotted Midge which the fish rose to very readily. However, the rises to the fly were so rapid that I missed time and time again until I eventually succeeded in catching a number of small roach and one bleak. At least the experience provided a test for my reflexes and underlined the need for a very fast strike when dry-fly fishing for roach. On future occasions I enjoyed greater success on ponds, lakes and reservoirs, but it was notable that even larger fish could rise to the fly and reject it again with incredible speed. Of course, this will come as no surprise to most coarse fishermen who are accustomed to lightning bites and to the roach's ability to suck the contents of a caster, or chew a maggot to ribbons, without even registering any sign of a bite at all. Even if a roach does take your fly in a leisurely manner, it is well to strike quickly in order to lip-hook it so that it may be returned to the water without damage. The roach's teeth (known as Pharyngeal teeth) are in the throat so that if it desires to 'chew' an item of food, it does not do it in its mouth. It would be unfortunate to hook a fish in the throat if you intended to return it to the water, which should always be the case. Incidentally, this is one of the great virtues of fly-fishing for coarse fish, it teaches the angler to enjoy his sport without the desire to kill as many fish as possible.

185

Sadly, my favourite roach reservoir has now been filled in. Where an inlet channel created a rapid current between sand banks, plump roach used to congregate and would rise willingly to tiny dry-flies drifted over them. Suddenly, the fly would disappear with only the tiniest of rings, and, with luck, the hook would be set home with a flick of the wrist resulting in an impressive arching of the light 7ft 6in cane rod. On occasions, when the roach did not appear to be present, it was always possible to attract them by drifting casters along the current of the channel and into the reservoir. They would appear all of a sudden, swirling and splashing at the floating casters and could be caught easily with casters fished on fly-tackle and a greased leader. In a sense, this was itself almost like dry-fly fishing, but I would always switch to a dry-fly as soon as they had established their feeding station and they would rarely disappoint me.

Although grayling and dace can be caught with the dry-fly, they are river fish and rarely present in stillwaters. However, a few stillwaters do contain large shoals of sizable chub and a bushy dry-fly ought to enable the angler to catch them on fly. Personally, I have no experience of fishing for stillwater chub although I always intend to try the Welsh water, Lake Vyrnwy, where fly-fishermen do often catch good chub by accident when fishing for trout. That now leaves us with the rudd, a coarse fish which is closely related to the roach and certainly offers great possibilities of sport with the dry-fly.

Apart from details such as a dorsal fin located further back than that of a roach, and differences in the scale count along the lateral line, the main difference between roach and rudd is that the rudd's lower lip protrudes beyond its upper lip which thus makes it better equipped than the roach for surface feeding. The rudd does feed on the bottom, at mid-water, and among reedbeds, but it also feeds consistently near to the surface. Whilst large roach tend to feed rather exclusively on the bottom, even large rudd are disposed to feed at the surface, which thus suggests a fascinating challenge for the fly-fisherman. Rudd are beautiful fish and although the commonest colour pattern includes orange-red fins, bronze sides splashed with gold, and a silver belly, there are many variations of colour. Indeed, I once caught a rudd with bright red fins and golden-yellow flanks which for all the world looked like a refugee from an ornamental garden pond. Although rudd are present in some rivers, I regard them mainly as stillwater fish: they are present in larger reservoirs but often thrive in small lakes and even farm ponds (where unusually large specimens are sometimes encountered). Indeed, I know of many small farm ponds which contain large rudd and one such pond remains in my memory as one of the favourite haunts of childhood. If you discover a rudd pond near your home, and obtain permission to fish it, many a pleasant evening can be spent dry-fly fishing for a sporting fish which is by no means a substitute for the trout: it has a value of its own.

Traditionally, rudd have been attracted to feed near the surface by floating crusts wrapped in fine mesh and tethered to the bottom by a string and stone. They may be caught on light float fishing tackle, with a baited hook set no more than six inches under a tiny quill float: appropriate baits include maggot, breadcrust, bread paste and bread flake. On the other hand, you can always use a dry-fly. In warm weather, rudd quite naturally feed close to the surface of a lake or pond, where they will eat midge pupae, sedge pupae, nymphs and adult flies (both aquatic and terrestrial). A simple midge pupa pattern is excellent for rudd although they do seem to take a dry-fly at any time and are not as preoccupied with feeding just beneath the surface as trout often become. Obviously, rudd will accept imitations of whatever floating natural prevails at any given time, but they are not choosy about specific patterns, even if they are often very shy fish likely to be scared by clumsy presentation. Palmers of various shades (generally dressed on size 12 and 14 hooks) and particularly the gold-bodied Wickham, which is dressed in palmer-style, are excellent general patterns when fly-fishing for rudd. The line size should be as light as possible (size 6 being somewhat on the heavy side) and short and light rods are the most sporting where long casts are not essential. Although 2½lb breaking strain leader points will normally suffice, you may be lucky enough to make contact with fish in the 2lb and upwards class, which may well necessitate the use of stronger nylon. The presentation should be as delicate as possible, which really means keeping the fly-line as far away from the fly as you are able: use a leader which is as long as both the conditions and length of your rod will allow. Rudd fishing with a dry-fly is simply delightful and although trout fishing is my greatest love, I much prefer dry-fly fishing for rudd on some quiet and secluded farm pond to standing shoulder to shoulder with many other anglers, which is often the case on popular trout fisheries.

Rudd positively thrive in weed beds, and if you fish for them in a weeded pond, you may find that the largest specimens will rise consistently in the tiny pockets of water within the weedbeds themselves. This is certainly a challenging form of angling, for whilst it may be easy enough to land the fly within the pocket of water, once you have hooked a fish, you are in trouble. Under such circumstances, it is best to use nylon of at least 4lb breaking strain for your leader point, for you do not wish to be smashed by a good fish, which will only result in the poor fish swimming around with a hook in its mouth and trailing a couple of feet of nylon. Remember that although you may catch a number of smallish rudd, you may also hook fish over 2lbs and you may even hook one of those fish of a lifetime which pulls the scales down nearer to the 4lb mark. It is even possible that a record rudd might succumb to the stillwater dry-fly fished by an angler dedicated enough to devote many hours to such a venture.

Personally, my largest fly-caught rudd only weighed 1lb 2ozs, and in recent years my chances of fly-fishing for rudd have been limited by the 'march of progress'. At least three excellent little rudd ponds now lie beneath modern housing estates and are no more than a pleasant and distant memory. One little pond nestled in a field and was surrounded by gnarled and twisted oak trees. A stream fed the gin clear water of the pond which was richly vegetated with various pondweeds and lilies. Plovers nested in the fields around it; sand martins swooped low over the water, and a heron was a frequent visitor. Rabbits, their white tails bobbing up and down, played around you vigorously and in the distance, an old dog fox could often be observed slinking along a hedge.

The pond itself was full of life, from the thick slobber of frogspawn to the delicate antics of small corixidae; from the slow progress of snails to the quick swimming movements of pond olive nymphs; from the labour of caddis larvae to the aquabatics of newts. Amid this richly varied world, which fed the jam-jar science of local classrooms, perch, bullheads, loach, minnows, sticklebacks, roach and rudd fed themselves to plump perfection. On summer evenings, hatches of flies were positively thick, uncontaminated by agricultural pesticides which had not replaced the traditional method of manuring. Whilst the flies hatched, the rudd rose innocently to the artificial fly and would dive down again in shock and indignation when the hook went home. Each fish had to be pulled from its pocket of water and hustled over the weedbed to the waiting net and the resultant disturbance meant that the pond would not settle down again for at least ten minutes.

I saw a great deal of nature between casts, yet I rarely saw another angler. Perhaps it is a world seen partly through rose-tinted spectacles, yet it is a lazy-summer-dry-fly-world which may still be discovered in many little lakes and farm ponds remaining in this green and pleasant land of ours.

Stillwater coarse fish *can* be caught on the dry-fly, but, it seems to me, you must discover waters relatively secluded or private enough where you do not have to compete with the commercialised seduction of shop-bought baits. If you fish the dry-fly when others around you are hurling in maggots by the bank-balance-tipping-pint-full, not only will you be looked upon as some kind of freak, or an escapee from an asylum for the landed rich, you will also catch few fish. Fish are largely unsophisticated creatures and when offered the rich feeding of a host of maggots, they are unlikely to prefer the dry-fly because it is more appropriate to some mysterious code of piscatorial ethics.

Bibliography

FLY-DRESSING AND FLY PATTERNS
Fly Dresser's Guide John Veniard, A. and C. Black.
A Further Guide to Fly Dressing John Veniard, A. and C. Black.
Reservoir and Lake Flies John Veniard, A. and C. Black.
Fly Tying Techniques Jacqueline Wakeford, A. and C. Black.
Modern Fly Dressings for the Practical Angler Poul Jorgensen, Winchester Press.
Fly-Dressing David Collyer, David and Charles.
Fly-Dressing II David Collyer, David and Charles.
Fly-Dressing Innovations Richard Walker, A. and C. Black.
Two Hundred Popular Flies Tom Stewart, A. and C. Black.

STILLWATER ENTOMOLOGY

Trout Flies of Stillwater John Goddard, A. and C. Black.
An Angler's Entomology J. R. Harris, Collins.
Lake Flies and their Imitation C. F. Walker, Herbert Jenkins; Andre Deutsch (p'back).
Taff Price's Stillwater Flies Books 1, 2 and 3. A. and C. Black.
Stillwater Trout Flies Peter Lapsley, A. and C. Black.

FISHING TECHNIQUE

Loch Fishing R. C. Bridgett, Herbert Jenkins.
Fly-Fishing Tactics on Stillwater G. Bucknall, Frederick Muller.
Stillwater Fly Fishing T. C. Ivens, Andre Deutsch.
Lake and Loch Fishing Colonel Joscelyn Lane, Seeley Service & Co Ltd.
Fishing the Dry Fly Dermot Wilson, A. and C. Black.
Fishing for Lake Trout Conrad Voss Bark, Witherby.
A Modern Dry-Fly Code Vincent Marinaro, Crown.
Dry-Fly Fishing F. M. Halford, Barry Shurlock.
The Trout and the Fly J. Goddard and B. Clarke, A. and C. Black.
The Pursuit of Stillwater Trout Brian Clarke, A. and C. Black.
Fly Fishing for Coarse Fish W. J. Hayes, How to Catch Them Series, Barrie and Jenkins.
Stillwater Flies, how and when to fish them John Goddard & others, A. and C. Black.

Index

GENERAL INDEX

INDEX TO ARTIFICIAL FLIES

194